Ladybugs, Tiger Lilies and Wallflowers

ROBERT HENDRICKSON

PRENTICE HALL GENERAL REFERENCE
New York London Toronto Sydney Tokyo Singapore

For my little imp, Maegan

———————

PRENTICE HALL GENERAL REFERENCE
15 Columbus Circle
New York, New York, 10023

PRENTICE HALL and colophon are registered trademarks
of Simon & Schuster Inc.

Library of Congress Cataloging in Publication data
Hendrickson, Robert, 1933–
Ladybugs, tiger lilies and wallflowers / Robert Hendrickson.
p.   cm.
Includes bibliographical references and index.
ISBN 0-671-79910-X (pbk.)
1. Plant names, Popular. 2. Plants—Folklore. 3. Plants,
Cultivated—Nomenclature (Popular) 4. Plants, Cultivated—Folklore.
5. Gardening—Terminology. 6. English language—Etymology.
I. Title.
QK13.H39   1993
635'.014—dc20   93-18303

Designed by Rhea Braunstein

Manufactured in the United States of America

First Edition

ACKNOWLEDGMENTS

This book owes much in spirit, and even in substance, to my late grandfather, John Peter Hendrickson, a landscape architect educated at the University of Uppsala (where the great Linnaeus taught a century before), who created many estate gardens and could tell you, to exaggerate just a bit, the Latin names and botanical history of any plant on any continent. He would be happy to see this book dedicated to one of his scores of great-great grandchildren, all strong, healthy hybrids of an American soil.

Gardening has been a great love of mine all my life, and I could not possibly list here all the good people I am indebted to for teaching me what little I know of it. So I will confine myself to a blanket thank-you to everyone and make up for my sententiousness in my memoirs! I do, however, want to thank some of the many people who helped me more immediately with this treasury of garden lore. These include, to name but a few: as always, my wife, Marilyn; Karen Kafeiti; Lauren Walsh; Becky Hendrickson; Laura Hendrickson; Irene McShane and Ervin Lewis, all of whom suggested "green words" and stories or assisted in other ways. Many thanks also to my editor Gerry Helferich and to editors Traci Cothran and Maureen Clark, who did such a good job cultivating this garden of words.

I will be the gladdest thing under the sun!
I will touch a hundred flowers and not pick one.

—EDNA ST. VINCENT MILLAY,
"Afternoon on a Hill."

CONTENTS

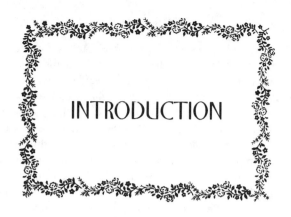

INTRODUCTION

An extraordinary number of English expressions have their roots in the gardens, fields, woods and jungles close by us or far away in space and time. These "green words" are hardly confined to the fascinating names of plants, flowers, fruits and vegetables—as any random harvest of these pages will show. Many such word origins are entirely unexpected. For example, who would suspect botanical roots for the words *aftermath, balk, book, Brazil, castanet, defalcation, farrago, grenade, imp, iodine, precocious, prevarication, propaganda, sardonic, sass, shibboleth, sycophant, tease, threshold, tribulation* and *zest*? Other green words such as *graft, hedge, hotbed* and *sub rosa* are more obvious, while expressions no one would have trouble identifying include "apple polisher" "bed of roses," "cool as a cucumber" and "don't let the grass grow under your feet." Then there are the fascinating names of plants such as "the blushing thigh of the aroused nymph" and etymological garden lore surrounding common plants as diverse as corn and roses. The list could, and does, go on for hundreds of pages in this romance of how plants got their names and how they gave their names to other things.

This *anthology* (which originally meant "a collection of flowers") is an attempt to gather the most important and interesting of such expressions, to write a big wordbook chock-full of garden and nature lore for constant reader and constant weeder alike, and to create a kind of gardener's almanac of botanical joys and curiosities as well as a reliable reference. Punning aside, it might be appropriate to call *Ladybugs, Tiger Lilies and Wallflowers* a "groundbreaking work," for it is the first book to treat many of these words and phrases, but I would rather call it an entertainment, whatever its scholastic merits, for the thousands of words and stories have brought me great pleasures of discovery over many years of gardening. The stories, I believe, will appeal to both experienced and inexperienced gardeners, as will some of the historical planting tips. I have tried to be as accurate as possible, to "lead no one down the garden path," checking several dependable sources for each entry, and have never eschewed legend or folklore, so often the underlying truth, simply labeling it as such when necessary. Neither have I rejected a tale as "forbidden fruit" merely because it might offend someone's prudish sensibilities. (Even the great Linnaeus could playfully describe the stamens and stigmas of the poppy as "twenty or thirty males in bed with a female," a description one of his critics called "loathsome harlotry.") About the only moral I've consciously kept in mind while "cultivating my own garden" here are words written by French entomologist Jean-Henri Fabre (1823–1915) while the bloody Great War was raging: "History records the battlefields on which we lose our lives, but it disdains to tell us of the cultivated fields on which we live; it can tell us the name of kings' bastards, but it cannot tell us the origin of wheat. Such is human folly." I've tried here, basically, to tell as well as I could something of the history of cultivated and uncultivated fields.

But all this "gilding (painting) the lily" must be "nipped in the bud"—there is so much planted in the bed of the book that I have no more space for the introduction! It's been "a long row to hoe." May your "random harvest" through these pages be a "bountiful harvest."

ROBERT HENDRICKSON
Peconic, New York

ACANTHUS. There are at least two charming stories, neither capable of being proved, about how the spiny or toothed leaves of the Mediterranean blue-flowered plant *Acanthus mollis* gave the name *acanthus* to the architectural ornament resembling these leaves that is used in the famous Corinthian capital or column. One tale has it that the Greek architect Callimachus placed a basket of flowers on his young daughter's grave, and an acanthus sprang up from it. This touched him so deeply that he invented and introduced a design based on the leaves. Another story, from an early-eighteenth-century book called *The Sentiment of Flowers*, tells it this way:

> *The architect Callimachus, passing near the tomb of a young maiden who had died a few days before the time appointed for her nuptials, moved by tenderness and pity, approached to scatter some flowers on her tomb. Another tribute to her memory had preceded his. Her nurse had collected the flowers which should have decked her on her wedding day; and, putting them with the marriage veil, in a little basket, had placed it near the grave upon a plant of acanthus, and then covered it with a tile. In the succeeding spring, the leaves of the acanthus grew around the basket: but, being stayed in their course by the projecting tile, they recoiled and surmounted its extremities. Callimachus, surprised by this rural decoration, which seemed the work of the Graces in tears, conceived the capital of the Corinthian column; a magnificent ornament still used and admired by the whole civilized world.*

ACONITE. Aconite (*Aconitum napellus*), a deadly poisonous plant, is also known as "wolfsbane" because it was once used to poison wolves, and "monkshood" because the plant somewhat resembles a monk's hood. The word *aconite* itself may derive from an ancient Greek word meaning "wolfsbane." Legend says the showy perennial herb is of the buttercup family and that it became poisonous from the foam that dropped from the mouth of Cerberus, the monstrous hound who guarded the gates of Hell, when Hercules dragged him up from the nether regions. Other authorities derive *aconite* from the Greek *akon*, "dart," claiming that it was once used as an arrow poison. It could just as likely come from the Greek *akoniti*, meaning "without work or labor," in reference to the plant poison's efficient killing power. (See *Poplar*.)

ACORN. *Acorn* is an ancient word deriving from the Old English *æcern*, meaning "fruit" or "berry." Its present form *acorn* is due in large part to folk etymology; people believed that the word *æcern* was made up of "oak" and "corn" because the fruit came from the oak and was a corn or seed of that tree. Thus *æcern* came to be pronounced and spelled "acorn."

ACRE. The Sumerian *agar* meant a watered field, a word the first farmers in Babylonia formed from their word *a* for water and applied to fertile watered land in their river valleys. *Agar*—related to the Sanskrit *ajras*, an open plain—came into Latin as *ager*, fertile field, and finally entered English as *acre* or *acras* in the tenth century. The word first meant any unoccupied land, but then came to mean the amount of land a yoke of oxen could plow from sunup to sundown. During the reign of Edward I, it was more fairly and accurately defined as a parcel of land 4 rods in width and 40 rods in length (a rod measures 16½ feet). The definition remains the same today except that the land does not have to be rectangular, that is, 4 × 40 rods. In case you want to measure your yard another way, in the United States and Great Britain an acre equals 43,560 square feet, or 1/64th of a square mile, or 4,047 square meters.

One old story says that Ben Jonson put down a landed aristocrat with "Where you have an acre of land, I have ten acres of wit," and that the gentleman retorted by calling him "Mr. Wiseacre." Acreage doesn't figure in this word, however. *Wiseacre* has lost its original meaning, having once been the Dutch *wijssegger*, "a wisesayer, soothsayer, or prophet," which is apparently an adaptation of the Old High German *wizzago*, meaning the same. By the time *wijssegger* passed into English as *wiseacre* in the late sixteenth century such soothsayers with their know-it-all airs were already regarded as pretentious fools.

ADAM-AND-EVE. This pretty North American woods orchid (*Aplectrum hyemale*) apparently takes its name from its two bulbous roots, which are joined together by a small filament about two inches long that suggested Adam and Eve, hand in hand, to some poetic soul. When the plant has three bulbous roots or corms joined together it is called "Adam-and-Eve-and-their-son." Adam-and-Eve is also known as "puttyroot," because the sticky substance in its corm is used for a cement. Other plants named Adam-and-Eve include the dogtooth violet, because its plant bears a large and a small flower at the same time, and the common "monkshood". It is said that when immersed in water one root or corm of the puttyroot sinks and the other floats—whether it is Adam or Eve who sinks is never told. Folklore also holds that Adam-and-Eve sewn together in a bag and carried on one's person protects the bearer from evil.

ADAM'S APPLE TREE. Few have heard of this interesting tree that thrives in subtropical gardens of the United States. The particular tree is popularly named for the biblical Adam, and the entire genus containing it was named by Linnaeus in honor of German botanist Dr. J. T. Tabernaemontanus (d. 1590), a celebrated Heidelberg botanist and physician who, despite the length of his patronym, also has species in two other plant genera commemorating him. Why the folkname Adam's apple tree? Clearly still another case of a claim on Eden. To quote from the *Encyclopædia of Gardening* (1838) by J. C. Loudon:

The inhabitants of Ceylon say that Paradise was placed in their country. . . . They also point out as the tree which bore the forbidden fruit, the Devi Ladner *or* Tabernaemontana alternifoxlia *[the species name has since been changed to* coronaria*]. . . . In confirmation of this tradition they refer to the beauty of the fruit, and the fine scent of the flowers, both of which are most tempting. The shape of the fruit gives the idea of a piece having been bitten off, and the inhabitants say it was excellent before Eve ate of it, though it is now poisonous.*

Tabernaemontana coronaria, a five-to-eight-foot-high tropical shrub with white fragrant flowers, has the following other names: "East Indian rosebay," "crape jasmine," and "Nero's crown," after the dissolute Roman emperor.

ADAM'S FLANNEL. This fanciful name for mullein (*Verbascum thapsus*) was coined by U.S. pioneers, who used its thick woolly leaves as a substitute for flannel in binding up sore throats. The strong-growing plant is so widely naturalized in North America that it is often considered a weed. Other names for it are "common mullein," "velvet plant," "candlewick" and "flannel-leaf."

ADAM'S NEEDLE. Adam and Eve sewed fig leaves together to cover their nakedness (Gen. 3:7). This led to the belief that they used a plant with needlelike spines as a needle. Most often the honor goes to the yucca (*Yucca filamentosa*) native to Mexico and Central America and widely grown in gardens all over the world.

ADAM'S PROFESSION. "There is no ancient gentlemen but gardeners, ditchers, and grave-makers; they hold up Adam's profession," Shakespeare wrote in *Hamlet*. The bard also said "And Adam was a gardener" in *King Henry VI, Part II*. Much later, Rudyard Kipling wrote: "Oh, Adam was a gardener, and God who made him sees / That half a proper gardener's work is done upon his knees." The phrase "Adam's profession" was proverbial for gardening long before both poets used it. No one has called it "Eve's profession," even though she picked the first apple. Thomas Jefferson, incidentally, wrote in a letter to a friend that he would rather follow Adam's profession and be "a common dirt gardener" than be president.

ADONIS FLOWER. The Greek goddess Aphrodite punished the king of Cyprus for his disrespect by having his daughter Myrrha fall in love with him. Discovering this, King Cinyras tried to kill Myrrha, but she was changed into a myrtle, from which the handsome youth Adonis was born. Aphrodite herself fell in love with Adonis, and when he was killed by a wild boar while hunting she caused a beautiful red flower to spring from his blood, which had been watered by her tears. Over the centuries, the anemone, the poppy and the rose have been said to be this Adonis Flower. John Gerard's famous *Herball* (1597) was the first source to mention the plant commonly called "pheasant's eye," of the family Ranunculaceae, being called the "Adonis." A species of butterfly is also so named.

An "Adonis garden" is any worthless or very perishable thing, or a momentary pleasure. Its source was the plots of earth in which quick-growing plants such as wheat, lettuce and fennel were planted during the Adonia, the ancient feast of Adonis celebrating his death and resurrection. Symbolic of the brief life of Adonis and grown around a statue of him, the plants were only tended for eight days, allowed to wither and then thrown into the sea along with little images of Adonis. The next year, of course, seeds were sown again and Adonis was resurrected, a ceremony symbolic of the course of vegetation.

AFRICAN VIOLET. (See *Saintpaulia.*)

AGAVE. (See *Century Plant.*)

AGERATUM. "The flower that never grows old" is the translation of this flower's name, from the Greek *a*, "not," and *geras*, "old age." Actually, the Greeks were probably referring to a different flower than our garden annual, the ageratum, but it seemed a good name to give this long-lasting, lavender-blue bedding plant, also known as the "everlasting flower."

AILANTHUS. (See *The Tree of Heaven.*)

ALLSPICE. Allspice, or pimento (*Pimenta officinalis*), is the dried, unripe berry of an aromatic 20- to 40-foot West Indian tree generally grown in Jamaica; it should not be confused with pimientos, the fruits of certain *Capsicum* garden peppers. Allspice has long been regarded and feared as an aphrodisiac. Pious Peter the Venerable forbade the monks under his charge at Cluny in 1132 to eat pimento because it was "provokative to lust." Allspice takes its name from the fact that the one berry smells and tastes something like cinnamon, nutmeg and cloves combined. It has a great many uses in cooking.

ALMOND. Almonds, which came out of China, are today the most popular of all nuts worldwide. They especially please the Japanese, who often have English signs reading ALMOND outside shops that would otherwise say BAKERY or CONFECTIONARY in their own language. But then this ancient nut (mentioned 73 times in the Old Testament) has been associated with beauty and virility for centuries. Rich in protein, amino acids, magnesium, iron, calcium and phosphorus, and a good source of vitamins B and E, the almond is also a harbinger of spring and the joyous expectancy of new life and love; in fact, the tree's pale pink blossoms appear about the time that the swallows return to Capistrano. The word *almond* has its roots in *amandola*, the medieval Latin word for the nut.

Jordan almonds come from Spain; they have no connection at all with the country named Jordan, as many people think. The term "Jordan almond" is simply a corruption of the French *jardin amande*, which translates as "garden almond."

ALYSSUM. The Greek word for "curing canine madness" is the chief component of this delicate perennial's name, for fable held that it cured both the rabies that came from the bite of a mad dog and allayed any rage that might afflict a person. First recorded in 1551, the word refers to plants of the Cruciferae family, especially the yellow-flowered British spring favorite commonly called "gold-dust" or "golden tuft." The much planted Sweet Alyssum or Sweet Alison is of the same family. Alyssum, a popular garden plant with its clusters of fragrant white or golden flowers, is also called "madwort" and was once known as "heal-dog." Another plant with a possible canine connection is the gladioluslike *antholyza*, which takes its name from the Greek for flower and rage, an allusion to the opening of its corolla, which resembles the mouth of an enraged dog or wild animal if you use a lot of imagination.

AMARANTH. The Greeks believed this flower never died and gave it the name *amarantos*, "everlasting." It is said to be a symbol of immortality because the flowers keep their deep blood-red color to the last. Milton wrote in *Paradise Lost*:

> *Immortal amarant, a flower which once*
> *In Paradise, fast by the Tree of Life,*
> *Began to bloom, but, soon for man's offence*
> *To heaven removed where first it grew, there grows*
> *And flowers aloft, shading the Fount of Life . . .*

The Greek *amaranton*, "unfading flower," is the ultimate source of *amaranth*, one species of which is called "love-lies-bleeding" after the deep red flower spikes and blood-red foliage, in some varieties. The flower is the source of the adjective *amaranthine*, something everlasting, unfading, especially referring to love.

AMARYLLIS. (See *Belladonna Lily*.)

ANDROMEDA. Linnaeus named this early blooming shrub with white blossoms for the mythological maiden Andromeda, daughter of the King of Ethiopia, who was chained to a rock as an offering to a sea monster, but was rescued by Perseus, the son of Zeus, who later married her. In order to keep the beautiful Andromeda, Perseus had to defeat another suitor who tried to carry off his bride. He did so by exposing his rival to the head of the Medusa, which changed him to stone.

ANEMONE. Also called the "windflower," the dainty anemone takes its name from the Greek words for "wind" and "habitation," the ancient Greeks having observed that it often grew in windy places. According to Greek legend, the anemone was born after the handsome Greek youth Adonis, beloved by Aphrodite, goddess of love and beauty, was killed in the forest on a wild boar hunt. Aphrodite was so grief-stricken that the gods took pity on her and allowed Adonis to spend each spring with her in the form of a flower, the anemone, which rose from his blood. (See *Adonis Flower*.)

ANGELICA. According to one story, the Archangel Raphael assured a pious hermit that this herb of the carrot family was a remedy against the terrible plague called the Black Death. This may account for its name, which comes from the Latin *herba angelica*, "the angelic root," or "root of the Holy Ghost," and was first recorded in English in 1570. A confection called "candied angelica" made from its roots in early times was widely used for medicines.

ANTHOLOGY. The word *anthology* is derived from the Greek word meaning "a collection of flowers"; the first recorded anthology, in fact, is the Greek *Garland of Meleager* (ca. 90 B.C.). Two of many historically famous ones include the *Anthologia Palatina*, popularly called the *Greek Anthology* (ca. 925), and Palgrave's *Golden Treasury* (1861), the most noted of English anthologies. Tens of thousands of anthologies have been compiled since the first.

API. The French gave this name to the old tasty apple variety that in English is called the "Red Lady." It is named after the legendary Roman gourmet Apicius, who is said to have produced it by grafting in his garden more than 2,000 years ago. (See *Apple*.)

APPLE. One of the oldest English words, *apple*, dates back to the Old Saxon *apl* or *appu*. The fruit probably figures in more expressions than any other fruit or vegetable, from the ancient Adam's apple to apple for a baseball, first recorded in the early 1920s.

Adam never ate an apple, at least not in the biblical account of his transgressions, which refers only to unspecified forbidden fruit on the tree in the Garden of Eden. The forbidden fruit of which the Lord said, "Ye shall not eat of the fruit which is in the midst of the garden, neither shall ye touch it, lest ye die" (Gen. 3:3), was probably an apricot or a pomegranate, and Muslims—intending no joke—believe it was a banana. Many fruits and vegetables have been called apples. Even in medieval times, pomegranates were "apples of Carthage"; tomatoes, "love apples" aphrodisiacs; dates, "finger apples"; and potatoes, "apples of the earth." In any case, tradition has it that Adam succumbed to Eve's wiles in the Garden of Eden and ate of an apple from which she took the first bite, that a piece stuck in his throat forming the lump we call the "Adam's apple," and that all of us, particularly males, inherited this mark of his "fall." Modern scientific physiology, as opposed to folk anatomy, explains this projection of the neck, most prominent in adolescents, as being anterior thyroid cartilage of the larynx. But pioneer anatomists honored the superstition in the mid-eighteenth century by calling it *pomum Adami* or "Adam's apple." They simply could find no other explanation for this evasive lump in the throat that even seemed to move up and down.

According to ancient tradition, each of the apples in the Garden of Eden changed in appearance and looked as if it had had a bite taken from it after Eve bit into the forbidden fruit. They became known as the "apples of Paradise." Another old legend says that apple trees grown near the Dead Sea "where the biblical Sodom and Gomorrah stood" bear beautiful fruit that turns to soot and ashes in the mouth. The gallnuts produced on apples by the insect *Cynips insana* are said to be the scientific fact behind the legend, but "apples of Sodom" still means anything disappointing, something that comes to nothing or worse.

Meaning that which one holds dearest, "You're the apple of my eye" also has its roots in the Bible (Deut. 32:10): The Lord kept Israel "as the apple of his eye." *Pupilla* (pupil) is the Latin word for the "apple" of the phrase, but English translators of the Bible used "apple" because this was the early word for the pupil of the eye, which was thought to be a solid apple-shaped body. Because injury to the eye's apple or pupil could result in blindness, and it therefore had to be cherished and protected, the "apple of one's eye" came to mean anything extremely precious. The literal translation of the Hebrew phrase, incidentally, is "as the little man in the eye," referring to one's own reflection in the pupil of another's eye.

Golden apples also figure in a number of expressions. In Scandinavian mythology "apples of perpetual youth" were golden apples in the care of Idhunn, daughter of old Svald the dwarf. By eating them the gods preserved their youth and sexual prowess.

The Hesperides, or "Daughters of Evening," in Greek mythology guarded a tree that yielded golden apples, a present given by Gaea, the personification of the Earth, to Hera, the goddess representative of women, when Hera married Zeus, the Greek's supreme God. Heracles (Hercules in Roman legend) later found his way to the garden of the Hesperides, slayed the dragon that guarded the entrance and carried off the golden apples, this feat one of the legendary Twelve Labors of Heracles. These "golden apples of the Hesperides" also figure in the story of Atalanta, a great hunter and runner, who refused to marry any man who couldn't beat her in a footrace. Any suitor who lost to her was put to death. Hippomenes challenged her, taking the advice of Aphrodite and carrying with him three golden apples of the Hesperides, which he dropped at strategic intervals during the race. Atalanta could not resist stopping to pick up each of the apples and thus lost the race and became his wife.

The legendary golden apple called "the apple of discord" was thrown on the table by the goddess Eris (Discord) at the wedding of Thetis and Peleus, to which all the Greek gods but Eris had been invited. The apple was said to be "for the most beautiful woman present," and Paris judged between Hera (Juno), Aphrodite (Venus) and Athene (Minerva), who offered him, respectively, bribes of power, sex and martial glory. He chose Aphrodite, and the vengeance of Hera and Athene supposedly led to the fall of Troy. The "apple of discord" still means the cause of a dispute, or something to be disputed.

The story of "William Tell's apple" invokes William Tell, the champion of Swiss independence when Switzerland was ruled by Austria. Tell refused to salute the imperial governor and was sentenced to shoot an apple from his son's head. After he did this, another arrow fell from his coat and the governor demanded to know what it had been intended for. "To shoot you with, had I failed in the task imposed upon me," Tell told him, and he was cast into prison, from which he was rescued and went on to lead his country to freedom. There are at least ten earlier versions of the tale involving other countries and heroes, the oldest found in the old Norse *Vilkinia Saga*.

The traditional picture of a student giving the teacher a bright, shiny apple is the source for the expression "apple-polisher" for a sycophant. This Americanism was first recorded in 1928, but is probably much older. Interestingly, the word *sycophant* has its origins in another fruit, figs.

Describing disguised flattery as *applesauce* dates to the early twentieth century and probably derives from "the boardinghouse trick of serving plenty of this cheap comestible when richer fare is scanty," according to a magazine of the time. The term also came to mean nonsense, lies and exaggerations. As a word for a sauce made from stewed, sweetened apples, it is an Americanism dating back at least to the mid-eighteenth century.

One old story has it that New England housewives were so meticulous and tidy when making their apple pies—carefully cutting thin slices of apples, methodically arranging them in rows inside the pie, making sure that the pinches joining the top and bottom crusts were perfectly even, etc.—that the expression "apple-pie order" arose for prim and precise orderliness. A variant on the yarn has an early American housewife baking seven pies each Monday and arranging them neatly on shelves, one for every day of the week in strict order. These are nice stories, but the term "apple-pie order" is probably British, dating back to at least the early seventeenth century and of uncertain origin.

A "wise apple" is a shrewd person. One theory holds that it has a completely different derivation than *wiseacre*, deriving from the *court pendu plat* apple, which, John F. Adams advises in *Guerrilla Gardening* (1983), "is commonly called 'the wise apple' in England because it blooms so late and misses the frost."

An "apple-knocker" is an abusive term for a stupid person, especially a rustic stupid person and is still used by city dwellers. It was first recorded in this sense in a 1939 *New Yorker* story: "I had a reform-school technique, whereas them other sailors was apple-knockers. They were so dumb they couldn't find their nose with both hands." Apple-knocker first meant a fruit picker, deriving from the mistaken urban belief that fruit is harvested by being knocked from trees with long sticks.

Finally, there's nothing new about calling New York City the "Big Apple"; the city, "full of opportunity, ripe for plucking," has been so named for about half a century. It may be that the "big apple," a dance craze of the swing era popular in New York, influenced the coinage. A better guess is that jazz musicians in 1910 first used it as a loose translation of the Spanish *manzana principal*, the "main apple orchard," in reference to New Orleans's main city block downtown where all the action was. (See *Adam's Apple Tree; Fig; Hercules' Club; Shaddock*.)

APRICOT. The Romans called this fruit *praecoquum*, meaning "early ripe." From there the word entered Arabic as *al-birqūq* and then Portuguese as *albricoque*, before it came into English as *abrecock*. By the eighteenth-century the shears of prudery had pruned the word from *abrecock* to *apricot*. One of the earliest fruits known to man, apricots are claimed by some to have been the forbidden fruit in the Garden of Eden. (See *Garden*.)

ARBORVITAE. The white cedar was named *arborvitae*, Latin for the "tree of life," by French explorers in Canada during the early seventeenth century. Champlain's men had observed that Indians drank a medicinal tea made from the bark and needles of the white cedar (*Thuja occidentalis*) and so named the tree because it saved lives.

ARIZONA STRAWBERRIES. American cowboys and lumberjacks used this term as a humorous synonym for beans, also employing the variations "Arkansas strawberries," "Mexican strawberries" and "prairie strawberries." Some fried beans *were* pink in color like strawberries. One Western wit noted that the only way these beans could be digested was for the consumer to break wild horses. (See *Beans.*)

ARROWROOT. The Arawak Indians of the Caribbean Islands called this plant (*Maranta arundinacea*) *aru-aru*, "meal of meals," because they highly valued its nutrition. It would have been more precise for English speakers to name the plant "aru-root" when they learned of it, but the plant was also a valuable medicine used to draw poison from wounds caused by poison arrows. Speakers thus associated "aru" with arrow and folk etymology added arrowroot to the dictionaries; the word was recorded as early as 1696.

ARTICHOKE. As poet Richard Armour observed, the artichoke is the one vegetable you have more of when you finish eating it, due to its compact leaves, which are scraped with the teeth and discarded. Often called the "globe" or "French artichoke," it is technically the flower bud of a thistle picked before it blooms. At one time it was seriously suggested that the plant was so named because an *arti*st had *choked* on the inedible "needles" covering its delicious base or "heart." Actually, the word *artichoke* has more prosaic and complicated origins. The Arabians called it *al-* (the) *khurshūf*, which became *alcarchofa* in Spanish. Northern Italians corrupted the Spanish version to *articiocco* and this entered French as *artichaut*, from which our *artichoke* evolved. It is true that the English *choke* in the word replacing the French *chaut* may have been influenced by the sensation one gets from eating the wrong part of the vegetable. (See *Jerusalem Artichoke.*)

ASPARAGUS. There is an old story that *asparagus* takes its name from the Greek *asparagos*, "as long as one's throat," because diners often swallowed the spears whole! But the meaning of the word *aspharagos* from which our asparagus derives is unclear and more likely meant "sprout" or "shoot" in Greek. The great chef Brillat-Savarin told of a giant asparagus stalk growing in an Episcopal bishop's garden, so immense that it became the talk of the town as it rose from the ground. Only when the bishop went out to cut the tempting stalk did he learn that it wasn't real but a perfect imitation made by a local canon, "who had carved a wooden asparagus . . . had stuck it by stealth into the bed, and lifted it a little every day to imitate the natural growth."

Some old-timers still call asparagus "grass," from the homely expression "sparrowgrass" commonly used as a name for the vegetable over the last three centuries. The Romans cultivated the vegetable as early as

200 B.C., growing some stalks at Ravenna that weighed a full three pounds and gathering stems in the Getulia plains of Africa that were actually twelve feet tall. The most flavorful "grass," however, is thin and tender and should be steamed or cooked in as little water and as rapidly as possible. Even the Romans knew this; their Emperor Augustus originated the saying "quicker than you can cook asparagus" for anything he wanted done within a few moments.

Asparagus has been regarded as a phallic symbol since earliest times, but this certainly isn't why perennial patches of it are called *beds,* which is just a common garden term. There is an interesting true story about blanched white asparagus, however. Reported a *New York Times* correspondent on a recent Bonn dinner party: "A certain guest complimented the elegant German hostess and said, 'This white asparagus is as beautiful as an undressed woman,' thereby probably becoming the first asparagus eater to have noted a resemblance between asparagus and the attributes of the *female* sex."

ASPIDISTRA. This old reliable foliage plant takes it's name from the Greek *aspis,* a small round shield, in reference to the shape of its stigma. It is often called the "cast-iron plant" because it withstands all kinds of ill-treatment. Widely used in bars, movie houses and other public places, it is also called the "beerplant," because the bartenders often water it with beer left on the bar at the end of the evening. An aspidistra growing in New South Wales, Australia, is 56 inches high, the tallest one of its kind in the world.

ASTER. This daisy is named from the Latin *aster,* "a star," in reference to the shape of its flower. However, when *aster* occurs at the end of other plant names, as in *Cotoneaster,* it doesn't have anything to do with this root but instead indicates inferiority. A little-used name for the common garden aster is the "starwort."

ATROPA. (See *Belladonna Lily.*)

AUBERGINE. Another word for the eggplant, deriving from the French *auberge,* a kind of peach, possibly because the first cultivated eggplants were about the size of a peach. Because of the aubergine's usual color, *aubergine* is also used as an adjective meaning "black" or "dark purple." (See *Eggplant.*)

AUBRIETA. Few great painters have a genus or species of plants named after them, not even French artist Claude Monet, whose paintings of his exquisite garden at Giverny are indisputable masterpieces. But one small genus of perennials honors Claude Aubriet (1651–1743), the venerable French natural history painter. Its only horticultural species is *Aubrieta deltoidea*, purple rock cress, which comes in many varieties and is often used for rock gardens and edgings. *Aubrieta* is pronounced "au-bree-sha."

AVOCADO. When Montezuma served the avocado or "alligator pear" to Cortés and his conquistadores, the Aztecs explained that their *ahuacatl* was so named from their word meaning "testicle," not only because the fruit resembled a testicle but because it supposedly excited sexual passion. The Aztecs even drew their guests pictures illustrating their story, but to the Spaniards *ahuacatl* sounded like avocado, their word for "advocate," and they named it so when they brought it back to Spain. In Europe the avocado became a great favorite, and France's Sun King called it *la bonne poire* because it seemed to get a rise out of his setting libido. Aphrodisiac or not, the fruit remains an important meat substitute in parts of the world today, a delicious dessert in others and is extensively grown in Florida, California and other areas by home gardeners. The most nutritious of fruits or vegetables, it contains 741 calories per edible pound. (For more plants named for their sexual resemblances see *Butterfly-pea*, *Jack-in-the-pulpit*, *Mandrake*, *Orchid*, *Papaya*, *Vanilla* and *Venus's-flytrap*.)

AZALEA. No one knows why the Greeks had the erroneous idea that this shrub required a dry, sandy soil and named it after *azaleos*, their word for "dry." For that matter, technically azaleas are not different from rhododendrons, but they are kept distinct from that genus by gardeners. Azaleas are, of course, among the handsomest and most widely planted shrubs, with hundreds of varieties. (See *Rhododendron*.)

BACHELOR'S BUTTONS. In his *Herball* John Gerard wrote, "The similitude these flowers have to the jagged cloth buttons anciently worne . . . gave occasion . . . to call them Bachelor's Buttons." But bachelor's buttons, a name applied now mainly to *Centaurea cyanus*, or the common cornflower, though also to the red campion, the upright crowfoot and the white ranunculus, may take their name from the old custom of bachelors carrying the flower in their pockets to determine how they stood with their sweethearts. If the flowers stayed fresh in the pocket, it was a good omen, if they shriveled up, "she loves me not." Other colorful names for the cornflower include "blue bonnet" and "ragged sailor." Farmers often call the blue flowers "bluebottles." To them it is a pervasive pernicious weed that strangles cornfields.

BAIT TREE. The quick-growing catalpa (*Catalpa bignonioides*) is called the "bait tree" because its branches provide homes to many caterpillars that can be used as fish bait. It is also known as the "Indian bean," "bean tree," "cigar tree" and "smoking bean tree" due to its long pods. *Catalpa* is a North American Indian name for the tree.

BANANA. *Banana* derives from the Arabic word *banana*, meaning "finger," and even today the individual fruits forming the familiar banana "hand" are called "fingers." The banana tree is really a giant herb with a rhizome instead of roots and its "trunk" is made up of large leaves, not wood. Linnaeus gave the fruit the scientific genus name *Musa,* comprising 18 species, in honor of Antonio Musa, who was the personal physician to the first emperor of Rome. *Musa sapientum,* the most common banana tree.species, takes its second name from the Latin word for "wise man," in reference to the Indian sages of old who reposed in its shade and ate of its fruit. Arabian slang and a score more languages make the fruit a synonym for the male sexual organ, as would be expected. "Where the banana grows man is sensual and cruel," Emerson wrote in his *Society and Solitude,* and the Koran says that the forbidden fruit in Paradise was a banana, not an apple. Banana oil, incidentally, is a synthetic so named because it *smells* like bananas— bananas produce no commercial oil. *Banana oil* is American slang for *hogwash, bunk, hokum, nonsense.*

Together with the plantain, a *Musa* species commonly called the "cooking banana," the fruit is a staple foodstuff throughout the world. The most common eating variety today is the Cavendish (*Musa cavendishi*), a dwarf plant less resistant to disease and wind damage that was discovered in southern China in 1829 and named either for its discoverer or developer.

BANDICOOT. A word like this is needed in a time noted for both green thumbs and slick fingers, when thefts of shrubs, flowers and vegetables right from the ground are occurring more frequently from public places and private residences. *Bandicoot* may not be exactly the right word, but it is the only such one I know of. *Bandicooting* is an Australian word for the practice of stealing just vegetables out of the ground and a bandicoot is a thief who does this. The word could have a wider application, covering all vegetative thefts. Human bandicoots, like the Australian marsupial they are named for, usually steal root vegetables, cutting them off and leaving their tops protruding from the ground to avoid suspicion for a longer time.

BANYAN TREE. Here is a tree named for merchants who sold their wares beneath it. This Indian tree, which spreads out by sprouting aerial extensions that grow into the ground to form new trunks, can cover an area large enough to shade thousands of people. Noticing this, Hindu merchants set up marketplaces underneath the trees, and the British later named the tree after the merchants, *banians,* who traded there. Being strictly religious, these Hindu merchants refused to eat meat of any kind. Visiting British sailors noticed this and "banyan days" came to mean the two days of the week when no meat was served in the British navy.

BAOBAB TREE. So thick is the baobab tree (*Adansonia digitata*)—up to 30 feet across—that several African tribes hollow it out so that families can live inside, much like the mesquite is used in Central America. The baobab is grown as a curiosity in the southernmost United States. Arabian legend holds that it has its peculiar shape because the devil plucked it out of the earth and replanted it with branches underground and roots in the air. The origin of the tree's name is obscure, but may have something to do with the legend.

BARBERRY. The barberry is an ornamental bush that is often planted for hedges in place of privet and valued for its flowers, its gorgeous fall foliage and the striking red berries that often hang on the bush all winter long. Few gardeners would believe that the common spiny barberry (*Berberis vulgaris*) provides fruit that can be eaten in a variety of ways. The English, in fact, once cultivated the handsome bush for its berries, and the Arabs before them grew barberries for their sherbets. The barberry may take its name from *berberys*, the Arabic name for a shell, possibly in reference to its leaves being hollow like shells. In any event, it is associated with the Berbers, who cultivated it on Africa's Barbary Coast. Some fifty species are widely grown in America.

BARTLETT PEAR. The yellow Bartlett pear, grown commercially mostly in Oregon and Washington where it is less susceptible to blight than in the East, represents 70 percent of the 713,000-ton U.S. pear crop and is certainly America's most commonly grown pear. It is a soft European-type fruit, in season from July to November, as opposed to earlier hard Asian varieties like the Seckel, which is named for the Philadelphia farmer who first grew it in America just after the Revolution. The Bartlett was not, in fact, developed by Enoch Bartlett (1779–1860), a merchant in Dorchester, Massachusetts, as is generally believed. Bartlett only promoted the fruit after Captain Thomas Brewer imported the trees from England and grew them on his Roxbury farm. The enterprising Yankee eventually purchased Brewer's farm and distributed the pears under his own name in the early 1800s. They had been long known in Europe as "Williams" or *William Bon Chretien* pears. Bartletts, by any name, are one of the most delicious of the more than 3,000 pear species, and pears have been one of humankind's favorite fruits from as early as 1000 B.C. (See *Pear*.)

BASIL. In olden times basil was thought to have great healing properties. It was also believed to have been used in making royal perfumes, and so the aromatic herb was named from the Greek *basilikon*, for "royal." In the Middle Ages basil was much feared, and the French physician Hilarius warned that even by smelling it a friend of his "had a scorpion breed in his brain." Boccaccio's *Decameron* tells the story of Isabella, who put her murdered lover's head in a pot, planted basil on top and watered it with her tears. Should you think that's strange cultivation, here's a planting tip that might make the neighbors think *you're* a bit odd: The ancient Greeks and Romans believed one had to curse when sowing basil to ensure its germination.

BAYBERRY. (See *Light on a Bush.*)

BAY LAUREL TREE. Because this tree (*Laurus nobilis*), the tree laurel of history, was sacred to the god Apollo it was thought to be immune to lightning. According to legend, Apollo fell in love with the beautiful Daphne, daughter of the river diety Peneos, who changed her into a bay laurel tree to protect her when she spurned the god's advances. Apollo vowed that thereafter he would always wear bay laurel leaves and that all who worshiped him should do the same. The legend inspired Tiberius and other Roman emperors to wear wreaths of bay laurel as an amulet during thunderstorms. Scientific observation, however, has proved that the bay laurel tree is no more immune to lightning than any other tree. Another ancient superstition holds that the withering of a bay tree is an omen of death. The historian Holinshed noted that in 1399 old bay trees throughout England withered and then inexplicably grew green again. Shakespeare made use of this note in *Richard II:* " 'Tis thought the king is dead. We'll not stay— / The bay-trees in our country are withered." (See *Laurels.*)

BEANS. Deriving from the Old English *bean,* and possibly akin to the Latin *faba* by a circuitous linguistic route, *bean* was long used to describe the seeds of many plants. "Common beans" (string beans, first recorded in 1759; lima beans; wax beans, etc.) are native to the Americas. Napoleon wouldn't eat string beans, afraid that he would choke on the strings, but today's varieties are virtually stringless and thus are often called "green beans." (As early as 1830, one observer noted: "We do not call it a string bean, because the pod is entirely stringless.") Yet "string bean" is still used for the vegetable, and Americanisms like "string bean" for a tall, thin person remain firmly in the language. "Bean pole," another Americanism for a lanky person, takes its name from the tall poles that support climbing bean plants.

Those who "know their beans" will know that "lentils" are the beans that made up the mess of pottage or soup that the Bible says Esau traded his brother for. Lentils take their name from the Latin word for this bean variety, which also gives us the word *lens,* because a double convex lens resembles a lentil bean in shape.

"Not worth a bean" is one of the oldest expressions in English, recorded as early as the thirteenth century and colloquial since at least 1400. Beans have little commercial value compared to other foods because they are so easy to grow and prolific, even the garden "hill of beans" in the American version of the English expression. The *hill* in "not worth a hill of beans" was a common term a century ago when the saying was born. It means not an actual hill but a group of bean plants planted close together in a circle. Because most people plant beans in straight rows now and the meaning of *hills* is unclear to many, the phrase used today is usually "not worth a row of beans."

The old saying "every bean has its black" means that everyone has his or her faults. It stems from the fact that many varieties of beans have black "eyes."

A fanciful story, widely printed, holds that members of Greek secret societies voted on the admission of new members by dropping beans into jars or helmets. White beans signified an affirmative vote and black beans a negative ballot. Occasionally, the story says, voters would accidentally knock over the jar or helmet, revealing the secret vote, "spilling the beans." However, this phrase is an American one that entered the language only around the beginning of this century. No one knows how it made its entrance, unless it was on the heels of some older unknown expression. That the phrase was born when a dish of covered baked beans was dropped at some Yankee gathering, spoiling the "surprise," seems as unlikely as the Greek version.

Boston, home of the bean eaters, home of the bean and the cod, may be behind the phrase "he [or she] doesn't know beans." William Walsh in his *Handbook of Literary Curiousities* (1892) says that this American expression originated as a sly dig at Boston's pretensions to culture, a hint that Bostonians knew that Boston-baked beans were good to eat, that they were made from small, white "pea beans" if Bostonians knew nothing else. It may also be that the American phrase is a negative rendering of the British saying "he knows how many beans make five"—that is, "he's no fool," "he's well informed"—an expression that probably originated in the days when children learned to count by using beans. But "he doesn't know beans," "he don't know from nothing," possibly has a much simpler origin than either of these theories. It probably refers to the fact that beans are little things of no great worth, as in the expression "not worth a row (or hill) of beans." *Bubkes* means "beans" in Yiddish and is used in such expressions as "I'm working for *bubkes* (or *bubkis*)": that is, "I'm working for beans, for next to nothing."

The phrase "full of beans" can mean "full of baloney," "full of soup" and worse, but usually means someone who is full of energy, high-spirited, lively—sometimes in a foolish or silly way. Some say it is a horsey expression, like "full of oats," going back to the days when horses were fed "horse beans" raised for fodder. The saying, however, is a British one from about 1870 and may derive from the earlier phrase "full of bread." The gas that beans inspire also has something to do with the expression; as the word *prunes* substituted in the phrase for *beans* some seventy years later would indicate, both beans and prunes have a laxative effect. In fact, beans were primarily regarded as an aphrodisiac by the ancients because the eructations they caused were thought to produce prodigious erections. But the United States Department of Agriculture (U.S.D.A.) has recently developed a "gasless variety," "a clean bean" seed guaranteed not to cause social distress at the dinner table or elsewhere. So bean eaters can now be as "full of beans" as ever and much less obnoxious, though maybe not as sexy. (See *Fava Bean*.)

BEAUTIFUL NUISANCE. A euphemistic Southern name for the kudzu vine, a scourge in the U.S. South, where it was introduced as a valuable forage crop and soil conditioner, but became a fast-growing weedy pest in Southern gardens. *Kudzu* is the Japanese name for this Asiatic plant (*Pueraria thunbergiana*) of the pea family. The kudzu has had more publicity but the most pernicious weed in the South, and in all America, is the purple nutsedge (*Cyperus rotundas*), which can grow 39 inches long and does far more damage.

BEE. "For aye as busy as bees been they," Chaucer wrote in *The Canterbury Tales* (1387), and this is the first recorded mention of the phrase. But bees must have been noticed busily pollinating plants since before civilization began, and no doubt the expression was used long before Chaucer's time. *Bee*, in fact, is a word found in all languages with Indo-European origins.

A humorous expression used by Southern farmers and gardeners is a "bumblebee crop." This is a name given to cotton or any crop stunted by drought, whence "the cotton's so low that the bees lie on their backs and suck the juice from the blooms."

BEECH. Smooth-skinned beech trees (*Fagus grandifolia*) have always been a favorite of lovers, who often carve names or initials inside a heart on their bark. The outer bark of the beech and slabs of its thin, inner bark were also the first writing materials used by Anglo-Saxon scribes. Saxons called the beech the *boc* and applied this name to bound writings made from slabs of beech, the word becoming *book* after many centuries of spelling changes. Numerous terms for things related to writing come from the names of raw plant material. *Folio*, now a book of the largest

size, is from the Latin word *folium,* "a tree leaf," which meant "a roll
of papyrus." *Volume* is from the Latin *volumen,* which meant "a roll
of papyrus manuscript"; and *code,* a system of laws, etc., is from the
Latin *codex,* "the trunk of a tree," from which wooden tablets were
made to write ancient codes upon.

BEERPLANT. (See *Aspidistra.*)

BEET. Beet comes to us from the Greek *beta,* for a similar plant. The
expression "red as a beet" probably has been used as long as man has
collected or grown the vegetable. Interestingly, the French *betterave,* "beet,"
once served as slang for the penis, an analogy not unknown in history,
despite the unlikely shape of the modern beet for such. (Catullus wrote
about a Roman matron who left her husband because the object of her desires
"dangled like a limp beet.") Beets do not make the blood richer, as one superstition holds, but they are a nutritious food so highly valued by the ancient
Greeks that they made small replicas of them in silver for jewelry. "Sugar
beets" have been used for making sugar since the early nineteenth century.

BEETLE. There are some 250,000 species of beetles; fortunately the
gardener comes in contact with relatively few of them. Beetles take their
name from the old English *bityl,* "biting," as anyone who has seen the
damage they do to plants can easily understand. Among the most harmful
ones are the "Colorado potato beetle," the "Japanese beetle," the
"Mexican bean beetle" and the "Asiatic beetle." (See *Confused Flower
Beetle; Ladybug.*)

BEGONIA. Michael Bégon (1638–1710) served as a minor navy official
at various French ports until a fortunate marriage led to his appointment
by Louis XIV as royal commissioner in Santo Domingo, though he
wasn't Santo Domingo's governor as is often claimed. Bégon primarily
concerned himself with protecting the natives from unscrupulous merchants and attending to their medical needs, but the amateur horticulturist
ordered a detailed study of the island's plant life and collected hundreds
of specimens in the process. Among these he found the begonia, now a
common house and garden plant, which he took back to France with
him and introduced to European botanists. The begonia wasn't named
for him until 67 years after his death, however, when it was first brought
to England.

Bégon is remembered for his patronage of science and his public spirit.
On the opening of his large private library to the public, for example,
friends advised him that he would surely lose numerous books. "I had

much rather lose my books," he replied, "than seem to distrust an honest man." The begonia he discovered is a valuable garden plant because it prefers the shade, where it flowers freely, is available in a large variety of colors and can be grown for its foliage as well as its beautiful blooms. The genus *Begonia* contains some 1,000 species.

BELLADONNA LILY. Belladonna means "beautiful lady" in Italian, and this flower (*Amaryllis belladonna*) was so named by Linnaeus either because its smooth pink and white petals resemble a pretty girl's skin, or because Italian women once used the red sap of the plant as a cosmetic. A beautiful shepherdess in the pastoral poems of Virgil and Theocritus gives the belladonna lily its scientific name *Amaryllis*.

The unrelated perennial herb *Atropa belladonna* is the fabled plant whose sap yields the important drugs atropine and belladonna. Its berries are extremely poisonous. This plant, also known as "deadly nightshade," is called belladonna because Italian ladies used a touch or two of its extract to brighten their eyes. It is called "atropa" after one of the Three Fates of Greek legend—Atropos, the beautiful dark-haired spirit whose "abhorred shears" cut short the thread of life, just as this deadly plant can do.

BELLYACHE ROOT. Bellyache root is a Southern plant (*Angelica lucida canadensis fortasse*) whose roots are used as a tonic for stomachaches. The *Angelica* genus itself is so named because of the reputed angelic virtue of many of its species as medicinal plants.

BELVEDERE. *Belvedere* is Italian for "fair or fine sight." Such summer houses commanding a fine view of the garden began to be built on English estates in the sixteenth century, when the word came into the language from Italy or France.

BERM. *Berm* is first recorded in 1854, in the sense of "the bank of a canal opposite the towing path." The word derives from the German *Berme*, "a path or strip of ground along a dike," and over the years has come to mean the side or shoulder of a road. Probably 999,999 gardeners out of a million don't know this, and don't care, but the berm can also be the space between the pile of dirt you excavate when digging a hole in the ground and the hole itself! (See *Snath*.)

BETEL NUT. The betel nut is a famous masticatory that people prize for the joy of a stimulating chew, even though it turns their teeth pitch-black. It comes from the areca or betel palm (*Areca catechu*); the tree's fruit, roughly the size of a hen's egg, contains the mottled gray seed or nut. The nuts are boiled, sliced and dried in the sun until they turn black or dark brown, when they are ready to be wrapped up in betel vine leaves and chewed. Native to Malaya and southern India, betel nuts are so widely used in Asian nations that it is estimated that one-tenth of all the people on earth indulge in betel chewing. The introduction of modern chewing gum has cut into this figure slightly, but the betel chewers aren't easily discouraged, not by the copious flow of brick-red saliva caused by chewing the betel nuts, which dyes the lips, mouth, and gums, nor by all those black teeth resulting from a betel nut habit. Betel is a true excitant and arouses a great craving in the addict. Legions of devotees—black-toothed, bloody-mouthed and bad-breathed—can still be seen throughout Asia chomping away and squirting scarlet juice all over walls.

BIBB LETTUCE. An amateur gardener named John B. Bibb developed Bibb lettuce in his backyard garden in Frankfort, Kentucky, around 1850, and the variety has been an American favorite ever since. Bibb is the most famous and best of what are called butterhead lettuces, having a tight, small head of a dark green color and a wonderful flavor. Because the variety is inclined to bolt in hot weather, a "summer Bibb" is now offered by nurserymen for the home garden. Several kinds of lettuce are named after their developers, including "blackseeded Simpson," a looseleaf variety. Bibb is not often found in stores, the most popular commercial sellers in the United States being iceberg lettuce, a heading variety, and looseleaf Boston lettuce. (See *Lettuce.*)

BIGNONIA. A widely distributed woody flowering vine, the bignonia is sometimes confused with the begonia, and the names of the man the two plants honor are often confused as well. The species are not related, and Abbé John Paul Bignon, court librarian to Louis XIV, did not discover the beautiful bignonia vine bearing his name. The bignonia was named by the French botanist Tournefort in about 1700 in honor of the abbé, who had never ventured from Europe. Bignon's name is also found in the plant family Bignoniaceae, comprising 100 genera and more than 750 species, as well as in the genus *Bignonia*, which contains the bignonia vine. The plant is popularly called the "trumpet flower" or "cross vine." (See *Begonia.*)

BILBERRIES. "Pinch the maids as blue as Billberry," Shakespeare wrote in *The Merry Wives of Windsor.* Bilberries, or "whortleberries," or "blaeberries," or "whinberries," as they are variously called, are of the same genus as the blueberry. The main differences between the two is that the bilberry (*Vaccinium myrtillus*) is a little plant no more than 18 inches tall that usually produces berries singly, not in clusters as blueberries do. "Nineteen bites to a bilberry," a centuries-old British expression, means to make a major production of an inconsequential act, just as it would be to take 19 bites of a berry no more than one-quarter inch in diameter.

BING CHERRY. Bing Cherries are the popular dark-red, nearly black, fruit of the Bigarreau or firm, crisp-fleshed cherry group. The tree was developed in 1875 by a Chinese man named Bing in Oregon, where more than a quarter of the country's sweet cherry crop is grown. Other cherry varieties named after their developers include the "Luelling," for the man who founded Oregon's cherry industry in 1847, the "Lambert" and the "Schmidt." Countless varieties honor famous people, such as the "Napoleon," the "Royal Anne," and the "Governor Wood," though none is named for George Washington. Surprisingly, sour cherries outnumber sweets two to one in the United States, probably because they are easier to grow and are more in demand for cooking and canning. Cherries were probably first cultivated in China more than 4,000 years ago. (See *Cherry*.)

BLACKBERRIES. In England blackberries, named for their color, of course, are the most common fruit growing in the wild and proverbially came to represent what is plentiful because they outyield all other bramble fruits: One plant can yield up to five gallons of berries. "Plentiful as blackberries" comes to us from Shakespeare, though what he actually wrote was "If reasons were as plenty as blackberries, I would give no man a reason upon compulsion, I" (*King Henry IV, Part I*). The English call a cold early May when blackberries are in bloom a "blackberry winter," and in America a "blackberry summer" is a period of fine weather in late September or early October.

The blackberry, a member of the rose family, has been valued since ancient times, when the Greeks enjoyed them and believed that they prevented gout. Blackberries, however, were cultivated commercially in the Americas before Europeans tried their hand at them.

A "blackberry winter" is a period of cool weather in spring, usually May or June, when the blackberries are in bloom. Robert Penn Warren wrote a highly regarded story entitled "Blackberry Winter," which is also the title Margaret Mead used for a memoir she published. "Dogwood winter" means the same thing.

"Blackberry baby" is a century-old American euphemism for an illegitimate child, suggesting that such children are secretly conceived in places like the distant woods where blackberries grow. (See *Boysenberry*.)

BLACK-EYED PEAS. So named for their black hilum, black-eyed peas (*Vigna sinensis*) are simply a variety of cowpeas that originated in India thousands of years ago (though the name "cowpea" originated in colonial America). George Washington grew these peas, which are actually botanically closer to the bean than pea family. They are best known when cooked Southern style: black-eyed peas fried with a bit of ham or pork fat. Black-eyed peas go by many names in the South, including "crowders," "black bean," "black-eyed bean," "black-eyed susan," "bung belly," "China bean," "cow bean," "cream pea" and even "chain-gang pea" because they are often fed to prisoners on chain gangs. (See *Pea*.)

BLIGHIA SAPIDA. Captain William Bligh, the captain of *Mutiny on the Bounty* fame, is remembered by the ackee fruit, which looks and tastes like scrambled eggs when properly prepared, but can be poisonous when over- or underripe. The ackee tree's botanical name is *Blighia sapida*, after the man who introduced it along to Europe with breadfruit. Bligh was called "Breadfruit Bligh" for his discovery of that fruit's virtues and was in fact bringing specimens of the breadfruit tree from Tahiti to the West Indies in 1789 when his mutinous crew foiled his plans. The lesson of the *Bounty* apparently taught him little or nothing, for his harsh methods and terrible temper aroused a second mutiny, the Rum Rebellion, while he served as governor of New South Wales. Bligh, a brave and able officer, retired from the navy as a vice admiral. He died in 1817 at the age of 63. (See *Breadfruit*.)

BLUEBERRY. The blueberry is, of course, named for the color of its berries. Blueberries have been a favorite food for centuries and are among the most widely distributed fruits. Early colonists gathered the "blues," "whortleberries" and "bilberries," and made good use of them as the Indians had done since prehistoric times. But more than any other fruit cultivated blueberries are children of the twentieth century. It was in the early 1900s that Elizabeth C. White of Whitesbog, New Jersey (one of several pioneer women fruit growers), offered local prizes for highbush blueberries bearing the largest fruits. Hearing of her work, U.S.D.A. plant breeder Dr. Frederick V. Coville began to work in cooperation with her, starting in 1909, and crossed many plants she or her contestants had selected from the wild in the Pine Barrens of New Jersey, an area with an acid, sandy, but fertile soil. By the time Coville died in 1937 there were 30 large-fruited, named highbush varieties where there had been none, and today there are myriad varieties that have been selected from hundreds of thousands of fruited hybrid seedlings. From its status as a lowly fruit often confused with the huckleberry (even though, unlike the bony-seeded huckleberry, its 50 to 75 seeds are small and barely noticeable when eaten), White and Coville had elevated the blueberry to a position where it became the basis for an entirely new agricultural industry. *Vaccinium corymbosum*, the highbush or swamp blueberry, had gone through a revolution rather than an evolution and became a mass-produced fruit in less than twenty-five years. (See *Bilberries; Rabbit-eye.*)

BLUEGRASS. Whether *Poa pratensis* or bluegrass was brought here from Europe or was here long before the first white settlers came is a matter of opinion among laymen if not scientists. The late John Ciardi discussed the question in *Good Words to You* (1987):

> *Various Kentucky historians . . . including Dr. Eslie Asbury, surgeon, raconteur, and well-known breeder of race horses, insist that the bluegrass was there when the first white settlers reached Kentucky. . . . I have driven across Kentucky many times, even on the Bluegrass Highway, without seeing any but green grass. A number of natives have assured me that I have seen only cropped pastures, and that the bluegrass of the bluegrass becomes visible only when the grass is allowed to go to seed, the seed covering having a distinctly blue cast. . . . Others have added that the bluegrass of bluegrass is visible only when the sun is low and a soft wind tosses the grass. . . . I choose to agree with Dr. Asbury, who attributes the blueness (in season) to the small blue flowers this grass bears. Even in season, they are not commonly visible because the grass is usually cropped.*

Another theory holds that bluegrass takes its name from a pest grass that settlers on the Atlantic coast so named because its leaves were distinctly bluish in color. When these settlers moved into what is now Kentucky they found this grass, of about the same size and shape as the bluegrass previously discovered, and gave it the same name, which we still use today. In any case, Kentucky is called the "Bluegrass State."

BLUSHING THIGH OF THE AROUSED NYMPH. The French gave this sensuous, poetic name (*La Cuisse de nymphe emu*) to a double pink alba rose developed in France in 1797. According to rosarian Stephen Scanniello (see *Yellow Rose of Texas*), the name was too daring for English gardeners who imported the lovely fragrant rose, so they bowdlerized it to "Great Maiden's Blush."

BODOCK. *Bodock* is another name for the Osage orange tree (*Maclura pomifera*). It is so called because the Indians used its wood for making bows, and the French thus called it the *bois d'arc* ("bowwood") tree, which became corrupted in English to *bodock*. It is called the "Osage orange" because it grew in Osage Indian country and has large, rough-skinned greenish fruits somewhat suggestive of an orange, though inedible. The spiny-branched tree is often used for hedges and called the "Osage thorn." It was first recorded in 1804 as the "Osage apple" by the Lewis and Clark expedition.

BOLL WEEVIL. *Weevil* comes from the Old English *wifel*, "beetle" and *boll*, first spelled "bowl," refers to the pod of the cotton plant, which the beetle attacks. In Enterprise, Alabama, there is a monument to the boll weevil that was erected at the turn of the century after the boll weevil so devastated the cotton crop in the area that farmers were forced to plant peanuts and as a result became more prosperous than they ever had been as cotton growers. Southern Democratic congressmen who supported many of President Ronald Reagan's policies in the 1980s were pejoratively called "boll weevils" by other Democrats. (See *Gull*.)

BONNET SQUASH. This common vegetable sponge (*Luffa cylindrica*) was so named in the American South because women made bonnets out of its fibrous matter. Wrote Joel Chandler Harris in *On the Plantation* (1892): "The girls made their hats of rye and wheat straw, and some very pretty bonnets were made of the fibrous substance that grew in the vegetable patch known as the bonnet squash." These inedible squashes are also called "dishcloth gourds" and "loofa." They are sold in tropical markets as sponges.

BOUGAINVILLAEA. The largest island in the Solomon group, two Pacific straits, and a brilliantly flowering South American vine are all named after the French navigator and adventurer Louis-Antoine de Bougainville (1729–1811). Bougainville commanded a French expedition around the world in 1766–69, discovering the Solomon Islands. Naturalists in his party named the woody climbing vine family Bougainvillaea in his honor; there are about a dozen known species. Bougainville helped popularize Rousseau's theories on the morality of man in his natural state, especially concerning sexual freedom. He fought for America during the Revolution and in his later years Napoleon I made him a senator, count of the empire and member of the Legion of Honor. The plant named after him is often cultivated in greenhouses, can be raised outside in the southern parts of the United States and is regarded as the handsomest of tropical vines.

BOYSENBERRY. Americans have always been pie makers without peer, thanks to abundant sugar resources, many native fruits and a willingness to experiment. The blackberry, long regarded as a nuisance and called a "bramble" or "brambleberry" in England, is a case in point. Many varieties of blackberries have been developed here, long before anyone paid attention to the genus *Rubus* in Europe. Among them is the boysenberry, a prolific, trailing variety that is a cross between the blackberry, raspberry and loganberry, another eponymous berry. The boysenberry, a dark wine-red fruit that tastes something like a raspberry, was developed by California botanist Rudolph Boysen in the 1930s. Single plants commonly produce two quarts of the large, ¾-inch round, 1½-inches-long fruit. (See *Blackberry*.)

BRAMLEY'S SEEDLING. Bramley's seedling is a delicious English apple, notable not only because it was discovered in his garden by a butcher named Bramley of Southwell, Nottinghamshire, but because it is a "sport" or mutation. Most mutations, or changes in genes, occur in seedlings, but the Bramley was the result of a bud mutation, a variation in which only part of a plant is affected. Thus the first Bramley, as well as the first Golden Delicious apple, and the first New Dawn rose, among others, developed on one branch of a plant that bore an entirely different race. The Boston fern, which originated in a shipment of ferns sent from Philadelphia to Boston in 1894, is another well-known mutation, but the most famous bud sport is the nectarine. The first nectarine, or smooth-skinned peach, occurred on a peach tree more than 2,000 years ago, and nectarines are still often found on peach trees, and vice versa, where there has been no cross-pollination. Sometimes one side of the fruit is a peach and the other a nectarine. No one knows what causes these random bud mutations, but they do occur.

BRAZILWOOD. The country of Brazil was named for the wood called brazilwood, not the other way around. Brazilwood is a red-colored wood used as a dye source that takes its name from the Spanish *brasa*, "red coal or ember." It was used in Europe centuries before what is now Brazil was discovered. Because so many similar dyewood trees were found there, Portuguese explorers named the country *terra de Brasil,* "land of red dyewood," which later became Brazil.

BREADFRUIT. Breadfruit (*Artocarpus incisus*), which grows wild on trees on South Pacific islands, was so named because English seamen who sampled the fruit in the seventeenth century believed its soft white pulp resembled fresh baked bread, although it tastes something like the sweet potato. (See *Blighia sapida.*)

BREVOORTIA IDA-MAIA. The "floral firecracker," as this plant is popularly called, shows how oddly things sometimes get their names. Ida May, the daughter of a nineteenth-century California stagecoach driver, had noticed the bulbous plant many times in her travels and pointed it out to Alphonso Wood, a naturalist interested in collecting botanical specimens. Wood gave the single plant, a member of the lily family, *Brevoortia Ida-Maia,* its prename in honor of his fellow American naturalist J. C. Brevoort, and its patronymic in gratitude to the observant little girl who had brought the scarlet-flowered perennial to his attention.

BRIER. The brier from which pipes are made has no connection with the thorny bush called the brier. Rather, pipes are made from the roots of the tree heath plant, which was called *bruyer* in Old English; this name corrupted to *brier* over the centuries. The tree heath (*Erica arborea*) is a small tree 10–20 feet high with long, fragrant flowers. It is popular in Southern Europe.

A "brierpatch child" or "brierpatch kid" is a term for an illegitimate child. This Americanism dates back at least a century. (See *Cabbage.*)

BRISTLECONE PINE. A specimen of bristlecone pine (*Pinus aristata*) growing in the White Mountains in California is the oldest living tree on earth. Named *Methuselah*, it is at least 6,217 years old and might be more than 8,000 years of age. Methuselah still produces seedlings, and its exact location is never given by dendrochronologists to prevent vandalism. The slow-growing bristlecone pine species is common in the southwestern United States, where it is also called the "hickory pine," "Jack pine," "cattail pine" and "foxtail pine," the last two names alluding to the tufts at the end of its twigs.

BROCCOLI. Roman farmers, who must have been more poetic than their contemporary counterparts, are said to have called broccoli "the five green fingers of Jupiter." The word has a more prosaic derivation, however, coming from the Latin *bracchium,* "a strong arm or branch," in reference to its shape. According to Pliny the Elder, Drusus, the eldest son of Emperor Tiberius, ate so much broccoli that his urine turned bright green! Today, broccoli is said to contain cancer-fighting properties.

BROOM. The small wild broom shrub's Latin name is *Planta genista* and from this plant the English royal dynasty the Plantagenets took their name, because the founder of the dynasty, Geoffrey of Anjou (father of Henry II), customarily wore a sprig of its yellow blossoms in his hat.

British housewives in early times used the *besom*, "a handful of twigs with the leaves attached," to sweep their homes. Because these "besoms" were often made of twigs from the wild broom shrub they came to be called brooms by about the year 1,000. "Besom," however, remained the name for a sweeping implement well into the nineteenth century. Brooms were often placed across the door of a house to ward off witches, for even though witches were believed to ride on brooms, it was thought that before she could open a door, a witch had to count every straw in a broom placed across it.

BROWN AS A BERRY. The expression "brown as a berry" was first used by Chaucer in 1386: "His palfrey [small saddle horse] was as broun as is a berye." Though most berries aren't brown, the reference is possibly to brown berries like those of the juniper or cedar. (See *Blackberry; Strawberry.*)

BROWN-EYED PEAS. These are black-eyed peas with a brown rather than black spot where they were attached to the pod. They also go by the name "brown-eyed crowder peas." Regardless, they always taste just like black-eyed peas. (See *Black-eyed Peas.*)

BRUSSELS SPROUTS. A member of the cabbage family, Brussels sprouts are named for Brussels, Belgium, the vicinity in which they were first developed. A relatively "new" vegetable, the tall stems with many small individual heads have apparently been around for only four or five centuries.

BUBBY BUSH. The strawberry shrub (*Calycanthus floridus* or *glaucus*) is possibly named the "bubby bush" because its blossoms resemble a woman's breasts, sometimes called "bubbies." However, according to Thomas Anburey in his *Travels Through the Interior Parts of America* (1791), the word derives "from a custom that the [American] women have of putting this flower down their bosums . . . till it has lost all its grateful perfume." The plant is also called the "bubby," "bubby blossom," "bubby flower," "bubby shrub" and "sweet bubbies."

BUCKEYE. American pioneers in what is now Ohio so named this horse-chestnut tree because its dark-brown nut resembles the eye of a buck deer "when the shell first cracks and exposes it to sight." A useful tree whose long, soft wood shavings were decorations for ladies' hats and whose very roots were made into a soap, the buckeye (*Aesculus glabra*) eventually gave its name to all natives of the "Buckeye State." The nuts or buckeye beans of the tree were carried as good-luck charms and thought to ward off piles, rheumatism and chills, among other maladies.

BURBANK POTATO. There has been muted controversy over whether the plant breeder Luther Burbank (1849–1926) was a "plant wizard" or something of a failure. Burbank was born in Lancaster, Massachusetts, and there developed the Burbank potato, his most important achievement, while just a boy experimenting with seeds in his mother's garden. At 26 he moved to Santa Rosa, California, using the $150 he made from the sale of his potato to pay for the journey. It was in Santa Rosa, his "chosen spot of the earth," that he bred almost all the varieties of fruit, vegetables and ornamentals for which he became famous. These included at least 66 new tree fruits, 12 new bush fruits, 7 tree nuts and 9 vegetables, of which a number, notably the Burbank plum, bear his name. He once grew half a million strawberry plants to obtain one prize plant. However, according to Dr. W. L. Howard (University of California Agricultural Experiment Station Bulletin, 1945), only a few of the several hundred varieties developed by Burbank have stood the test of time.

The patient Burbank was not the first American plant breeder—Thomas Jefferson, George Washington Carver, and Charles Hovey, originator of the Hovey strawberry, came long before him. Burbank was strongly influenced by Darwin's *The Variation of Animals and Plants Under Domestication*. His credo can be summed up in his statement "I shall be contented if, because of me, there shall be better fruits and fairer flowers." Burbank did have a sense of humor, unlike some of his critics. The renowned horticulturist was working in his experimental garden one day when approached by an obnoxious neighbor:

> *"Well, what on earth are you working on now?"* the man asked.
> *"I'm trying to cross an eggplant and milkweed,"* Burbank replied.
> *"What in heaven do you expect to get from that?"* asked the neighbor.
> *"Custard pie,"* said Burbank calmly.

The city of Burbank, California, was named for the famous plant breeder.

BUTTERCUP. Centuries ago English dairy farmers believed that if their cows ate the little yellow flowers that commonly grew in the meadows, the butter they yielded would be colored the same rich yellow. Experience seemed to prove that this was true and so the flowers were named buttercups. Actually, the field buttercup (*Ranunculus acris*) did improve the quality of Bossey's output, because the flower grows only on good pasture, which thus provides good feed. The flower's scientific genus name, *Ranunculus,* is Latin for "a little frog," in allusion to the meadow habit of the wildflower.

BUTTERFLY-PEA. A woody perennial vine of the pea family, the butterfly-pea (*Clitoria mariana*) has pale blue flowers that appear as if upside down, the standard (the upper, broad and usually erect petal of a pea flower) much larger than the rest of the flowers. It takes its popular name from its imagined resemblance to a butterfly. One gardening guide says "the origin of [the genus name] *clitoria* is unprintable"; fortunately, it is not too difficult to figure out. (See *Avocado; Pea.*)

CABBAGE. Ask for a head of cabbage and you are repeating yourself, for *cabbage* means "head," the name of the vegetable deriving from the old French *caboce*, "swollen head." *Caboce* itself is made up of the Old French *boce*, "a swelling," the *ca* in the word very likely suggested by the Latin *caput*, meaning "head." Cabbage, probably the most ancient of vegetables, has been cultivated for more than 4,000 years. In Greek mythology it is said to have sprung from sweat on the head of Jupiter. The Greeks also believed that eating it cured baldness.

Describing a fool as a "cabbage head" dates back to the late seventeenth century and is best explained by the old music-hall lyrics: "I ought to call him a cabbage head, / He is so very green . . ." "Cabbages and kings," which means "odds and ends," "anything and everything," an expression O. Henry used as the title for his first book of stories, is from Lewis Carroll's *Through the Looking Glass*:

> *"The time has come," the Walrus said,*
> *"To talk of many things:*
> *Of shoes and ships—and sealing wax—*
> *Of cabbages—and kings—*
> *And why the sea is boiling hot—*
> *And whether pigs have wings."*

Abraham Lincoln waxed eloquent with the help of the lowly cabbage in his second campaign speech against Stephen Douglas: "In my poor, lean, lank face nobody has ever seen that any cabbages were sprouting out. . . . They have seen in his [Douglas's] round, jolly, fruitful face, postoffices, land-offices, marshalships and cabinet appointments, chargeships, and foreign missions, bursting and sprouting out in wonderful exuberance, ready to be laid hold of by their greedy hands."

Since I've gone on about cabbages at an alarming rate, I might as well add that the much maligned marshland skunk cabbage (*Symplocarpus foetidus*) bears little relation or resemblance to the cabbage (*Brassica capitata*). The plant takes its name from its fetid smell and its leaves' supposed resemblance to cabbage leaves. Actually, the skunk cabbage's large, nearly round leaves are far more handsome, and its sheath-like spathe is beautifully colored. But the plant's foul smell has caused it to be called "pole-cat weed" as well as skunk cabbage. (See *Rafflesia.*)

It's also interesting to note that a "cabbage patch" is a nineteenth-century southern expression for a place of very little importance, as in "We lived in that cabbage patch town down the road." The expression has become well known recently with the introduction of the dolls called Cabbage Patch Kids™.

Another southern expression concerning cabbage is "that's how the cow ate the cabbage," a phrase used to indicate the speaker is "laying it on the line," "telling it like it is," "getting down to the brass tacks"—with the connotation of telling someone what he or she needs to know but probably doesn't want to hear. According to Little Rock attorney Alston Jennings, who submitted this expression to Richard Allen's February 2, 1991, "Our Towns" column in the *Arkansas Gazette,* the expression has its roots in a story about an elephant that escaped from the zoo and wandered into a woman's cabbage patch. The woman observed the elephant pulling up her cabbages with its trunk and eating them. She called the police to report that there was a cow in her cabbage patch pulling up cabbages with its *tail*. When the surprised police officer inquired as to what the cow was doing with the cabbages, the woman replied, "You wouldn't believe me if I told you." A good story, regardless.

To end our capacious cabbage entry on a note of mystery, no one knows just why the ancient Greeks used "Rhodesian cabbage!" as a strong curse. Cabbage from Rhodes was valued as a hangover cure, but that seems to have nothing to do with its use as a swear word. It remains a minor historical mystery.

CACAO TREE. The drink called "cocoa" is made from the cocoa beans of the South American cacao tree, *cocoa* being simply a variant spelling of *cacao*. Chocolate is also made from the beans, taking its name from the Nahuatl (Aztec) word *xocoatl,* "food made from the cacao." For many years the cacao tree was confused with the coco tree because a printing error in Samuel Johnson's great dictionary (1755) listed the two trees together under the *cocoa* entry. (See *Coconut.*)

CACTUS. (See *Carnegiea gigantea*.)

CAESAR'S MUSHROOM. *Amanita caesaria* or Caesar's mushroom, honoring Julius Caesar, happens to be one species of the deadly *Amanita* genus that is edible, but more than a few "experts" have been poisoned thinking that they had distinguished this delicacy from its deadly relatives. Every summer brings a score of deaths from mushroom poisoning. Hippocrates referred to cases of mushroom poisoning, and Horace warned the ancients to beware of all fungi, no matter how appetizing the appearance. One of the first recorded cases of mushroom poisoning occurred in the family of the Greek poet Euripides, who lost his wife, two sons and a daughter when they partook of a deadly *Amanita* species. Pope Clement VII, the Emperor Jovian, Emperor Charles VI, Czar Alexander I, the wife of Czar Alexis and the Emperor Claudius (his niece and wife Agrippina poisoned his boleti) are among historical figures who lost their lives in the same way. Many species of *Amanita* are lethal even when eaten in minuscule amounts, and *Amanita verna*, the destroying angel, is easily confused with several edible species. (See *Mushroom.*)

TO CALL A SPADE A SPADE. To be straightforward and call things by their right names, to avoid euphemisms or beating around the bush. The words are from the garden, not from the game of poker. So old is this expression that it wasn't original with Plutarch, who used it back in the first century when writing about Philip of Macedon, Alexander the Great's father. The saying has been credited to the Greek comic poet Menander, who described the life of ancient Athens so faithfully that he inspired a critic to exclaim "O Menander and Life, which of you imitated the other!" If this is so, to "call a spade a spade" goes back to at least 300 B.C., and the faithful Menander could have been quoting a much older Greek proverb. The expression was introduced into English by Protestant reformer John Knox, who translated it from the Latin of Erasmus as: "I have learned to call wickedness by its own terms: A fig, a fig, and a spade a spade." Erasmus had taken the phrase from Lucian, a Greek writer of the second century and translated it as "to call a fig a fig and a boat a boat," which is possible because the Greek words for boat and garden spade are very similar.

CALVARY CLOVER. Legend holds that the common trefoil Calvary clover (*Medicago echinus*) sprang up in the footsteps of Pontius Pilate when he went to Christ's cross at Calvary or Golgotha. Each of the plant's three leaves has a carmine spot in the center, the leaves roughly form a cross in the daytime, and in flowering season the plant bears a little yellow flower resembling a crown of thorns.

CAMELLIA. One of the most beautiful of flowering plants, the evergreen camellia is named for George Joseph Kamel (1661–1706), a Moravian Jesuit missionary and amateur botanist who wrote extensive accounts of the shrub, which he found in the Philippine Islands in the late seventeenth century. Kamel, who called himself Camellus, the Latinized form of his name, operated a pharmacy for the poor in Manila, planting an herb garden to supply it. He published reports of the plants he grew and observed in the Royal Society of London's *Philosophical Transactions*. Some authorities say that Kamel sent the first specimens of the shiny-leaved camellia back to Europe. In any event, he was the first to describe the shrub, a relative of the tea plant. The great Swedish botanist Linnaeus read his accounts in *Transactions* and named the plant camellia after him. Camellias are used extensively as garden shrubs in southern areas of the United States and England. Their waxlike, long-lasting flowers are white, red or pink.

Marie Duplessis, a beautiful French courtesan and the lover of French author Alexandre Dumas fils, had a great love for camellias. She died of tuberculosis when only 23 years old, and Dumas immortalized her in his novel *La Dame aux camélias,* in which Marguerite, the heroine based on Marie, wore white camellias 25 days of each month and for five days wore red camellias.

CANOE BIRCH. The birchbark canoes of American Indian fame were made from the birch species *Betula papyrifera,* which is the most widespread birch in the world. This canoe birch is also called "white birch," "silver birch" and "paper birch" and is very common in eastern North America.

CANTALOUPE. The melon called a cantaloupe in the United States is not a cantaloupe. The cantaloupe, a variety of muskmelon, is named for Cantalupo, the Pope's country seat near Rome, where the melon was first bred in Italy from an Armenian variety. True cantaloupes are only grown in Europe. The "cantaloupe" grown in the United States is really the netted or nutmeg muskmelon, which originated in Persia (Iran). Muskmelons were introduced to America by Columbus, who brought seeds to Hispaniola on his second voyage, and many delicious varieties are grown here today, but not the cantaloupe. Other varieties of muskmelons include the honeydew, Persian, casaba, and banana melons.

CANTERBURY BELLS. Pilgrims to Canterbury in Chaucer's time thought that the bellflowers (*Campanula medium*) they saw along the road resembled the little bells on their horses and called the flowers

"Canterbury bells." *Campanula,* the plant's genus name, is itself the Latin word for "bell."

CARNATION. The word *carnation,* meaning "fleshlike," was first the name of a fleshlike color developed by artists in the fifteenth century, derived from the Latin *carnis,* "flesh." Soon a gillyflower of this color was developed and took the same name for its pinkish color. The carnation (*Dianthus caryophyllus*) has retained its name even though it is available in many other shades; in fact, it is also popularly called a "pink." Carnations with two or three stripes of contrasting colors in the petals are called "bizarres," while those with only one color are called "flakes."

A carnation played a part in the attempted rescue of Marie-Antoinette from the guillotine on August 28, 1793. On that day the royalist noble Chevalier de Rougeville visited her in her cell and left a carnation in which a tiny note was hidden telling the French queen of a plan to save her. The plot failed, and Marie was executed when her guard refused to go along with a bribe attempt, but the "affair of the carnation" lives on in history.

CARNEGIEA GIGANTEA. The largest cactus in the world, *Carnegiea gigantea,* or the saguaro, takes its botanical name from one of the world's richest philanthropists, Andrew Carnegie (1835–1919). A *Carnegiea* specimen found near Gila Bend, Arizona, in 1988 had candelabralike branches rising to 57 feet, 11¾ inches. Full-grown saguaro may weigh six tons and be 250 years old. The species had been named for Carnegie a half-century earlier in gratitude for his help in financing Tucson's former Desert Laboratory.

Carnegie, whose family immigrated to America from Scotland when he was a youth, rose from rags to riches, starting as a bobbin boy in a cotton factory at $1.20 a week and becoming a multimillionaire with his Carnegie Steel Company, which was merged with the United States Steel Corporation in 1901 after he retired to live on his estate in Scotland. Carnegie believed that it was a disgrace to die rich, and he became one of the greatest individual philanthropists in history, his benefactions totaling about $350 million.

CAROLINA RICE. Some sources say that the first rice successfully grown in Carolina was introduced into Charleston in 1694 by a Dutch brig out of Madagascar, while others hold that Yankee shipmaster Captain John Thurber presented a packet of Madagascar rice to one of the early settlers upon pulling into Charleston harbor late in the 1680s. According to the latter story, the settler planted the rice rather than dining on it, and after it sprouted, he gave seed to his friends, who in turn raised rice on their fertile land. Charleston and the Carolina Low Country soon became the "Rice Coast." Rice fortunes built Charleston and marked the beginning of a plantocracy considered by many to be the New World aristocracy. In any case, the Madagascar rice raised there was being called "Carolina rice" or "golden rice" by 1787. (See *Piedmont rice; Wild rice.*)

CARROT. The word *carrot* comes from the Latin *carota* for the vegetable, which in turn is derived from the Greek *karōton*. Carrots probably originated in Afghanistan. The ancient Greeks extolled them as "love medicine" and called them *philtron,* also using them as a stomach tonic. When carrots were first brought to England, women liked to use the plant's ferns as hair decorations, but no one much cared for them as food until about the thirteenth century. They were brought to America on the first European voyages of exploration.

CASTILLA ELASTICA. This tree species, commonly called the *ule* or "Mexican rubber tree," is not by any means the most important source of rubber today. It is an historical curiosity, having yielded the heavy black rubber balls Columbus was amazed to see natives playing with on his second voyage to South America—the first recorded observation of rubber by a European. The tree *Castilla elastica* is a species of the *Castilla* genus, of the mulberry family, and is named for Spanish botanist Juan Castillo y Lopez. Like Columbus, later explorers were astounded by the resilient balls made from the tree's vegetable gum, remarking that they rebounded so much that they "seemed alive," but rubber wasn't brought into commercial use in Europe until three centuries after its discovery. The tree *Hevea brasiliensis,* yielding high-grade Para, is by far the most important rubber source today. *Castilla elastica,* however, still yields a good-quality Caucho rubber, and the large tree is particularly valuable when Para rubber is high-priced.

CATAWBA GRAPES. A light-reddish variety of grape grown in the eastern United States, the Catawba grape was developed by John Adlum in his vineyard near Georgetown in 1829; its dominant parent was the wild northern fox grape. It was named three years later for the Catawba Indians of the Carolinas, or for the Catawba River, which takes its name from the Indian tribe. The Catawba, long a traditional favorite, contains some vinifera blood and is one of the best grapes for domestic white wines. By 1860, nine-tenths of all grapes grown east of the Rockies were

Catawbas, but they were thereafter replaced by the Concord, perfected in 1850, as the leading American variety. (See *Grape.*)

CATERPILLAR. A caterpillar is a *chatepelose,* a "hairy cat," in Old French, and it is from this word that we originally got our word for the "wyrm among fruite," as the Old English called the creature. But the meaning and spelling of caterpillar were strengthened and changed by two Old English words. "To pill" meant "to strip or plunder," as in "pillage," which came to be associated with the little worm stripping the bark off trees, and a glutton was a "cater," which the creature most certainly is. Thus the caterpillar became a "greedy pillager" as well as a "hairy cat," both good descriptions of its mien and manner.

CATTLEYA. This most popular of florist's orchids has nothing to do with cattle, having been named for William Cattley (d. 1832), English amateur botanist and botany patron. The *Cattleya* genus includes some 40 species, though more than 300 hybridized forms are known. *Cattleya labiata,* with its 200 or so named varieties, is the most commonly cultivated orchid in America—the showy, magenta-purple-lipped, yellow-throated "florist's orchid"—although the enormous orchid family contains perhaps 500 genera and 15,000 species. The Cattleyea fly and the Cattley guava, a subtropical fruit, also commemorate the English plant lover. (See *Orchid.*)

CAULIFLOWER. Cultivated for some 2,000 years, cauliflower takes its name from the Latin *caulis,* "cabbage," and *floris,* "flower." Its delicate flavor led Mark Twain to call it "cabbage with a college education." It is a relative youngster, however, when compared to cabbage, which has been grown for more than 4,000 years.

Too many blows to the ear produce the condition known in boxing circles and generally since about 1900 as "cauliflower ear." Such an abused ear, deformed and swollen, does resemble a head of cauliflower.

CELERY. Celery is the *selinon* mentioned by Homer in the *The Odyssey,* but the word comes to us directly from the French *céleri,* a derivation of the Greek word for the vegetable. Celery has been cultivated for centuries and its wild form, *smallage,* has been gathered in its native Mediterranean home for thousands of years. The Greeks held bitter smallage in high esteem and awarded stalks of it to winners of athletic contests.

CENTURY PLANT. *Agave americana,* common to the American West and widely cultivated, is called the "century plant" because it is thought to take a century to bloom and to die shortly after it does. The name is a misnomer, for, depending on the variety, century plants take from 10 to 50 years to bloom. The plant is also called the "American aloe."

The alcoholic drink pulque is made from the *Agave atrovirens* species, and tequila and mescal are made from *Agave tequilana.* Pulque, the national drink of Mexico, is traditionally drunk while one snacks on "nutty-flavored" maguey worms, which are the larvae of a butterfly that bores into the maguey or agave plant that is the source of the drink. Named for Agave, daughter of the legendary Cadmus, who introduced the Greek alphabet, the *Agave* genus includes many other plants. Introduced to Europe from America in the sixteenth century, the century plant is often used for fences. It is regarded as a religious charm by pilgrims to Mecca, who hang a leaf of it over their doors to ward off evil spirits and indicate that they have made a pilgrimage.

CHAIN-GANG PEA. (See *Black-eyed Peas.*)

CHERRY. In English *cherries* first meant *one* cherry, the word deriving from the French *cerise* (which came from the Latin *cerasus*) for the fruit. *Cerise* became *cherries* in English, but the *s* in *cherries* was dropped, because it made the singular word sound like a plural, and the result was *cherrie* or *cherry.* In times past "cherry fairs" were held in cherry orchards where the fruit was sold, and often developed into boisterous but happy celebrations, which led to the phrase "life is a cherry fair." The word *cherry* has, of course, been much used as a simile in love poetry, from the Chinese poet Po Chü-i's "mouth like a red cherry" to Robert Herrick's "cherry ripe" and after.

Attempts have been made to link the expression "life is just a bowl of cherries" with a much older one, "life is but a cherry fair." However, the older phrase, from the early sixteenth century, means life is all too short and fleeting, as short as the annual English cherry fairs where cherries were sold each spring. Evanescence is not the spirit of "life is just a bowl of cherries," which means "life is joyous, wonderful" and seems to have originally been the title of a popular song of the late nineteenth century. (See *Bing Cherry.*)

CHESTNUT. No one is sure about the antecedents of *chestnut.* The word may derive from the name of Castana in Asia Minor, a city near which chestnuts grew, or from the Armenian *kaskene,* meaning, "chestnut." The traditional U.S. chestnut tree, under which the village smithy labored, has been wiped out by blight, but we still harvest a chestnut crop from disease-resistant Chinese chestnut tree varieties.

The first castanets were made of ivory or very hard wood, but the Spanish dancers who invented this musical instrument saw their resemblance to two chestnuts and named them *castanets* after the Spanish word *castaña* for that nut. (See *Nut*.)

CHICAGO FIRE. The only plant named after a great fire, this midwestern bush (*Kochia scoparia*) with bright red foliage takes its unusual name from the Chicago fire of 1871, which raged for three days and took several hundred lives. It is also called "firebush," "burning bush," "summer cypress" and "Kochia bush," after the German botanist W. D. J. Koch for whom the brilliant Eurasian genus is named. The Chinese make brushes from the bushy plant, which is grown as an ornamental here.

CHICKENWEED. This name is given to common ragwort, a bane of gardeners, because its seed used to be mixed with chicken feed as a remedy for various maladies of chickens. Other plants named after chickens include the "chicken grape" of the South, valued for its fragrance, the common "hen and chicks" and "chicken on the wing" (the fringed polygala), so called because of the shape of its flower.

CHICKPEA. *Chickpea* came into English in the sixteenth century from the French *pois chiche* for the vegetable and was originally called the *chiche pea,* until people began to confuse the word *chiche* with *chick.* *Cicer arietinum* is also known as the "chick bean." The word has nothing to do with the "chick" of *chicken,* as is often claimed.

CHILDREN'S DEATH. The terrible common name of this plant (*Cicuta maculata*) reflects the fact that children have died after mistaking its root for an edible carrot and eating it. It is also called "children's bane," "musquash root," "beaver poison," "spotted cowbane" and, most frequently, "water hemlock." A member of the carrot family with feathery leaves, its roots contain a deadly alkaloid. It thrives on pond edges and in bogs.

CHILI PEPPER. The pungent pods of *Capsicum annuum longum* and several other species are named after the Nahuatl *chilli,* meaning the same. *Chilli,* in turn, derives from a Nahuatl word meaning "sharp" or "pointed," because it is so pungent or biting to the tongue. Both "hot" and "sweet" varieties of garden peppers belong to the *Capsicum* genus native to tropical America. They are no relation to the condiment pepper, which is made from the berries of a climbing shrub of the *Piper* genus. Hottest of the hot peppers is the *habanero* variety, which is said to cause slight, temporary deafness—so you don't hear your screams when you eat them, some people believe.

Cayenne is an English word contributed by the Tupi language of Brazil. It derives from the Tupi *quiynha,* meaning "capsicum," or "pepper." *Quiynha* is derived from the name of the French Guiana seaport (now called Cayenne) where the seeds and pods of the dried red peppers are ground to make the hot, biting condiment.

CHOKE'EM. A colorful popular name in the western United States for dodder, a plant of the genus *Cuscuta,* because of its parasitic effect on host plants: It literally chokes or smothers them to death. Few plants can match dodder's colorful derogatory names. The sprawling, yellow, threadlike plants are also called "beggarweed," "devil's guts," "hairybird," "hellweed," "robber vine," "strangle-weed," "tangle-gut," "love-in-a-tangle" and "witch shoelaces."

CHOKE PEAR. The choke pear, whose name also became the synonym for "a severe reproof" in the sixteenth century, has to be among the most perverse instruments of torture man has invented. Named after the indigestible pear called a *choke pear,* it was "of iron, shaped like a pear" and originally "used in Holland" by robbers. According to an early source:

> *This iron pear they forced into the mouths of persons from whom they intended to extort money; and of turning a key, certain interior springs thrust forth a number of points, in all directions, which so enlarged it, that it could not be taken from the mouth: and the iron, being case-hardened, could not be filed; the only methods of getting rid of it were either by cutting the mouth, or advertising a reward for the key. These pears were also called "pears of agony."*

Figuratively, a choke pear is merely something hard to swallow. The fruit is so named because of its rough astringent taste, which could make a person choke. Later the term was applied to anything that stopped someone from speaking, such as biting sarcasm or an unanswerable argument. The wild black cherry is sometimes called the "chokecherry" for similar reasons, and there is a berry called the "chokeberry."

CHRYSANTHEMUM. These fall flowers are of many colors today, but when the ancient Greeks grew them they were mostly gold-colored; hence their name *chrysanthemum* from the Greek *chrysos anthemon,* gold flowers.

In the city of Himeji in Japan locals consider the chrysanthemum unlucky and refuse to grow the flower or display it. This stems from a legend about a servant girl named Chrysanthemum Blossom (O-Kiku) who threw herself into a well and drowned upon discovering that one of ten golden plates it was her duty to safeguard had disappeared. According to the story, Chrysanthemum Blossom returned every night to the castle where she lived to count the plates, screaming each time she reached the count of nine. So persistent were her visits and so fiendish her screams that the inhabitants of the castle were forced to desert it. In most of Japan, of course, the chrysanthemum is much prized and a symbol of the nation. The largest fireworks in the world, more than 2,000 feet in diameter, are made in Japan and explode into the shape of a chrysanthemum. The chrysanthemum's botanical name has recently been changed to *Dendranthema x grandiflora.* But people will still be calling the flowers "mums" for years to come.

CIMARRON. This big-horned sheep ultimately takes its name from a plant. The Latin *cyma,* meaning the spring shoots of any plant, yielded the Spanish *cima,* mountain peak or summit. This became the Spanish *cimaron,* meaning any wild, unruly solitary creature, probably because such animals roamed the mountains. In American English, however, *cimarron* is mainly used for the big horn or mountain sheep (*Ovis canadensis*), the word first recorded in 1840. In *Western Words* (1944), Ramon Adams points out that Mexicans and some Americans in the West use *cimarron* "for an animal, horse, bovine, or even human, which, deserted by all its friends, runs alone and has little to do with the rest of its kind. Literally, it signifies one who flees from civilization and becomes a fugitive or wild person."

CINCHONA. In about 1640 the Condesa de Ana de Chinchón, wife of the Conde de Chinchón (ca. 1590–1647), Spanish viceroy of Peru, was stricken with a persistent tropical fever. After European doctors failed to restore her health, she was cured by the powdered bark of a native evergreen tree that Peruvian Indians brought to her. The Condesa and her husband collected the dried bark, which contains quinine, and sent it back to Spain. There the miracle bark was at first called "Countess bark" or "Peruvian bark," but when Linnaeus named the genus of trees and shrubs yielding it in the Condesa's honor, he misspelled her name. What should have been the "Chinchona tree" became known to history as "Cinchona tree." Today the native South American cinchona is widely grown throughout the world, notably in Java and India. The quinine extracted from its bark derives from *quinaquina,* its Peruvian Indian name.

CINNAMON. Cinnamon was called *rínnamon* by the Greeks, who adapted the word from an earlier Semitic one. The bark of the tropical cinnamon tree (*Cinnamomum zeylamium*) yields cinnamon, which has been used as a spice for thousands of years. Most of it comes from Malaya and Indonesia, and the Arabs, seeking to keep their monopoly on trading it, concocted some incredible tales about its harvesting. The Greek historian Herodotus repeated this story:

> *What they say is that the dry sticks . . . are brought by large birds which carry them to their nests, made of mud, on mountain precipices which no man can climb, and that the method the Arabians have invented for getting hold of them is to cut up the bodies of dead oxen, or donkeys, or other animals, into very large joints which they carry to the spot in question and leave on the ground near the nests. They then retire to a safe distance and the birds fly down and carry off the joints of meat to their nests, which, not being strong enough to bear the weight, break, and fall to the ground. Then the men come along and pick up the cinnamon, which is . . . exported to other countries.*

CLEMATIS. The clematis is a woody twining vine, which led the Greeks to name it *klematis* from their word *klema* or "vine-branch." The species *Clematis virginiana* is popularly called "old man's beard" because its seed pods have feathery appendages. The clematis genus contains some of the most beautiful of climbing plants and there are thousands of varieties available.

CLARKIA. Captain William Clark (1770–1838) is best known for his leadership with Meriwether Lewis of the Lewis and Clark expedition to find an overland route to the Pacific; their party was the first to cross the continent within the limits of the United States. But the army officer and veteran Indian fighter had an avid interest in natural history, and described many plants in his journals of the 1804–1806 expedition. The showy *Clarkia* genus, native to California, was named in his honor. These hardy annual flowers, available in several showy colors, have been popular for many years in American gardens. Clark, the youngest brother of the famous frontier military leader George Rogers Clark, was appointed superintendent of Indian affairs when his expedition returned.

Clark's partner, Captain Meriwether Lewis, has *Lewisia,* a genus of 12 species of low-growing perennial flowers widely grown in the rock garden, named in his honor. Lewis, who had been Thomas Jefferson's secretary, was appointed governor of the Louisiana Territory after the expedition. He died suddenly in 1809, only 35 years old, possibly murdered, his death shrouded by a mystery still unsolved.

CLOVER. Rather than the other way around, as one might expect, the clover of the *Trifolium* genus takes its name from the suit of clubs at cards, which was *claver* in Old English. The four-leaf clover has, of course, long been a symbol of luck, having one more leaf than clovers usually do (this tradition was first recorded in about 1840), but there have been several authenticated cases of people finding 14-leaf clovers. Someone who is "in clover" is well nourished, rich and happy. This American metaphor, first recorded in 1847, has its source in the protein-rich clover species used here for fattening cattle.

COCONUT. Safe in its buoyant, waterproof pod, the coconut sailed the high seas from southern Asia in prehistoric times and was propagated and cultivated throughout tropical regions. But it wasn't given its name until the late fifteenth century, when Portuguese explorers came upon it in the Indian Ocean islands and fancied that the little indentations at the base of the nut looked like eyes. Thinking that these three "eyes" gave the nut the look of a smiling face, they named it the *coconut, coco* being the Portuguese word for a "grinning face." But the nut deserves a better appellation, having been "the fruit of life" for ages and providing people with food, drink, oil, medicines, fuel and even bowls, not to mention the many uses of the 60–100-foot tree it grows on.

In India, coconut palm leaves were long used for disposable dishes to satisfy dietary laws specifying that every earthenware dish be broken after one use; in fact, tables were often made of the interlaced leaves of the coconut palm, and these, too, disposed of after one meal—at least by those rich enough to have such tables made every day. Copra, important to the plot of many a South Sea tale, is the dried meat of coconuts that oil is pressed from, and *coconut* itself is slang for a "head," which takes the word back to its origins. In the United States the coconut tree is successfully grown only in the warmest parts of Florida.

COFFEE. Coffee was introduced to England from Turkey, where it was called *qahwa,* pronounced *kahve,* a word that apparently first meant some kind of wine and derived from a verb meaning "to have no appetite." The word came to England, perhaps from the Italian *caffè,* in about

1600. At first coffee's reputation wasn't good, one early English traveler warning that it "intoxicated the brain." It has had widely varying reviews since. The brew is made from the roasted seeds (coffee beans) of certain coffee trees of the *Coffea* genus.

"Seed-tick coffee" is used to describe any of several coffee substitutes (rye, okra seed, parched wheat, sweet potato, etc.) common in the United States during the Civil War and other bad times. Noted the *Century Magazine* in September 1888:

> *With seed-tick coffee and ordinary brown sugar costing fabulous sums and almost impossible to obtain, it is small matter of wonder that the unsatisfied appetite of the rebel sharpshooter often impelled him to call a parlay with the Yankee across the line.*

COLLARDS. Although they are associated with Southern cooking in the United States, collards, which take their name from the Anglo-Saxon *coleworts,* "cabbage plants," probably originated in Asia Minor. One of the most primitive members of the cabbage family, the ancient Greeks grew them, and the Romans brought them to England.

COLUMBINE. In medieval times people thought the inverted white flower on this plant bore a resemblance to five doves or pigeons clustered together, and it was given the name *columbine* from the Latin *columba,* "dove." There are 60 known species of the genus *Aquilegia* comprising columbines. The flowers' horned nectaries were symbols of cuckoldry during medieval times. The Catholic church frowned upon the use of the plant in religious artwork, and women were hesitant to plant them in their gardens. The same applied, however, to any horned flower.

COME TO A HEAD. When we wait for something to come to a head— wait for it to come to maturity—we are doing what gardeners have long done in waiting for cabbage leaves to come together and form a head. The expression is an old one from the garden, probably dating back at least two or three centuries. (See *Cabbage.*)

COMPASS PLANT.

> *Look at this vigorous plant that lifts its head*
> *   from the meadow,*
> *See how its leaves are turned to the north, as true*
> *   as the magnet;*

This is the compass flower, that the finger of God
    had planted
Here in the houseless wild, to direct the traveler's
    journey
Over the sea-like, pathless, limitless waste of
    the desert.
                LONGFELLOW, *Evangeline* (1847)

A huge coarse-stemmed plant 6–8 feet tall with flowers like the common sunflower, the compass plant (*Silphium laciniatum*) was much valued by pioneers on the great western plains, because its leaves show polarity, always pointing north and south. For this reason it was called not only the "compass plant" but "polar plant" and "pilotweed" as well.

COMPTONIA. Henry Compton, Bishop of London, was a collector of rare and exotic plants. The prelate, an antipapal leader during the Revolution of 1688, had many admirers in England, even after his death in 1713 at the ripe old age of 81. One of these was the great naturalist Sir Joseph Banks, who traveled to Newfoundland and Labrador in 1766 to collect native plants and accompanied Captain Cook on his first voyage two years later for the same purpose. Banks expressed his admiration for the plant-loving divine by naming the comptonia bush (*Comptonia peregrina*) after him. The comptonia is a single shrub, sometimes called "sweet bush" or "sweet fern." Native to eastern North America, it is highly aromatic, with fernlike leaves and green, rather inconspicuous flowers.

CONFUSED FLOWER BEETLE. This little fellow is so named not because he is frequently confused, but because scientists often have trouble identifying him. The confused flower beetle (*Tribolium confusum*) it seems, looks remarkably like the red flower beetle (*Tribolium castaneum*). (See *Beetle*.)

CONJUER JOHN. "Solomon's seal," a member of the lily family, was dubbed "Conjuer John" because the plant was considered a powerful charm in conjuring. It is also called "Big John the Conjuer" and "Big John the Conqueror." In the southern United States it has been used to induce spells in voodoo ceremonies.

CONKER. This name for the horse chestnut is used mainly in England, but the English game called "conkers" is sometimes played by children in the United States. In the game, a horse chestnut is hollowed out with a penknife and is knotted to one end of a length of string. The children then swing their strings, trying to break each other's conkers. The game may have first been called "conqueror," which corrupted to *conker*, which in turn gave its name to the horse chestnut used in the game. It could, however, derive from the French *conque*, a "shell," for the game was originally played with small shells instead of horse chestnuts.

COREOPSIS. No one calls it the "bedbug plant," but this beautiful long-blooming member of the daisy family has seeds that look like little bedbugs, which inspired gardeners of old to name it coreopsis from the Greek *koris*, "bug," and *opsis*, "appearance."

CORINTHIAN COLUMN. (See *Acanthus.*)

CORN. When in Keats's "Ode to a Nightingale" a homesick Ruth stands "in tears amid the alien corn" (the phrase is Keats's own and not from the King James Bible), she is standing in a field of wheat or rye, any grain but New World corn. The English have always used the word *corn* to describe all grains used for food and never specifically for the grain that built the Mayan and Incan empires. Corn derives from the Old Teutonic *kurnom*, which is akin to *granum*, the Latin word for grain. *Kurnom* eventually became the Old Saxon *korn* and then *corn* in Old English. The semantic confusion arose when English settlers in America named corn on the cob "Indian corn" soon after Squanto brought ears to the starving Puritan colony in Massachusetts, and then dropped the cumbrous qualifying adjective *Indian* over the years.

The British call our "corn" *maize*, a word that derives from the Spanish *maíz*, which has its origins in *mahiz*, a Caribbean Indian tribe's name for the plant. But while "corn" is the most valuable food plant native to the New World and has a fascinating history and manifold uses (employed in more than 600 products, it may even have been used as a binding for this book), it is still little-known in Europe. This is perhaps because most corn loses some 90 percent of its sugar content an hour after harvesting and can't survive a transatlantic voyage without losing practically all its taste, though today there are new varieties that hold their sugar much longer.

Corny, for something old-fashioned, unsophisticated and unsubtle, what is often called "tacky" in today's slang, has its origin in America's Corn Belt. Comedians playing unsophisticated "corn-fed" audiences in the Midwest gave them the "corn-fed humor" they wanted, so much so that corn came to be known as "what farmers feed pigs and comedians feed farmers.'' Soon corn-fed humor became simply "corny jokes," the phrase possibly helped along by the Italian word *carne* "cheap meat," being applied to the "cheap jokes" the comedians told. *Corny* eventually was used to describe anything old-fashioned, full of clichés or mawkishly sentimental.

Most people are familiar with how Squanto taught American settlers to grow corn, but few are aware that for 40 days after corn planting, all the dogs in the Plymouth Colony hopped around with one forepaw tied to the neck so that they could not dig up the fish fertilizer planted between the hills of corn. Even fewer know that the Aztecs had a law permitting starving people or hungry travelers to pick corn from the first four rows of corn bordering any road. There has been no similar law in all of America since then.

Corn that is raised as feed for livestock is called "field corn," even though all corn is, of course, grown in fields. Before the nineteenth century, when sweet corn was developed, what is now called field corn served as both fodder for animals and human consumption (when the ears were picked young and tender). As the late John Ciardi pointed out, "fodder corn" would be a less absurd name for field corn, but neither language nor great writing is always a matter of logic.

An ear of corn wrapped in its husk can be thought of as content and cozy in its little house, for the word *husk* is simply a shortening of the Dutch *huisken,* meaning "little house." The name was first applied to the shells of various nuts and finally to corn when it was discovered in America.

The expression *shucks* may derive from worthless "shucks" or husks of corn, but the interjection, used to express mild disgust or regret, first recorded in 1847, is thought by some to be simply a euphemism for "shit," as its oldest quotation in the *Dictionary of Americanisms* would seem to indicate: "And Mr. Bagley was there [to shoot] any gentleman who might say 'shucks.' "

"Corn pone" is a famous Southern cornmeal cake or bread, defined by *Bartlett* in 1859 as "a superior type of corn bread, made with milk and eggs and cooked in a pan." It is often called "corn bread." "Corn pone" can also be a derogatory term for someone or something rural and unsophisticated: "That's a corn pone accent."

"Corn coffee" is a substitute coffee made from parched corn and other ingredients. In 1844, a traveler in the South wrote: "The supper consisted of coffee made of burnt acorns and maize. . . . He advised us to drink some of this corn coffee." The traveler didn't like it very much.

"Hominy" is not a vegetable, as many people believe, but the inner part of corn (maize) that has been soaked to remove the hull. The word derives from the Algonquin Indian *rockahominy* for the dish.

In a "cornhusking bee" or "husking bee," the terms used in America since at least 1693, neighbors got together to help husk corn. A young man who found an ear of red corn got a kiss from the girl of his choice, a custom the Iroquois had originated, though an Iroquois youth got more than a kiss in the Indian fertility rite. There were also "apple bees" in the early days of America. The *bee* in the terms may refer to busy, laboring bees in a hive, but more probably it derives from the Yorkshire dialect, where the word *bean* meant a "day," similar gatherings having been held on special days in Yorkshire.

A *cracker* is a poor white person, especially one from Georgia (the "Cracker State") so-called, perhaps, from the use of cracked corn. Originally the term was *corncracker*, someone who cracks corn to make grits or cornmeal. In the eighteenth century *cracker* meant "liar," but after the Civil War, when many people in the South became too poor to buy cornmeal and had to make their own from corn, *cracker* came to mean a poor white, usually one living in Georgia or Florida. The term is generally offensive, and is now regarded as a racial epithet; its use is a violation under the Florida Hate Crimes Act. Many people, however, are proud to call themselves "Georgia Crackers" or "Florida Crackers," just as long as they're the ones doing the calling.

"Corn in Egypt" is an expression that has come to mean anything that can be purchased relatively cheaply in abundance. The Bible is the origin of the expression (Gen. 42:2): "And he said, Behold, I have heard that there is corn in Egypt; get you down hither, and buy us from thence; that we may live, and not die."

Perhaps only racial, religious and national slurs have killed as many as the word *shibboleth*. *Shibboleth* has been extended to signify a catchphrase, especially one used so often that it has lost its effectiveness. But it still means a "password," which was its original biblical meaning. The word, deriving from the Hebrew *shibboleth*, for "ear of corn," is first recorded in Judges 12:1-16, where the Gileadites used it to pick out the sons of Ephraim from the members of other tribes. Jephthah's men slew 42,000 Ephraimites, who couldn't pronounce the *sh* in the password *shibboleth* and had to say "sibboleth."

To "acknowledge the corn" is to agree that one has lost an argument, or to "cop a plea." This old expression is of unknown origin, but one story traces it to an early-nineteenth-century farmer who was arrested and charged with stealing four horses and the corn (grain) to feed them. "I acknowledge [admit to] the corn," the wily farmer declared.

CORNELIAN CHERRY. The berries of several dogwood species are edible, but those of the Cornelian cherry (*Cornus mas*) have the longest history as a food. Called "cornet plums" in England, this tree's scarlet berries were once used to make preserves, tarts and drinks, and were even packed in brine to be used like olives. In addition, the Cornelian cherry has exceedingly hard wood that gives more heat than most fire-woods, and is said to have been used to build the Trojan horse. Its bark yields the red dye used for the traditional Turkish fez, and the berries of a dwarf form of it (*Cornus sericea*) were believed by the Scottish Highlanders to create appetite, inspiring them to name the plant *Lus-a-chraois*, Gaelic for "plant of gluttony." Like all species of dogwood, the Cornelian cherry's bark is rich in tannin and has been used medicinally (just as the bark of the flowering dogwood, *Cornus florida*, was used as a substitute for quinine). Virgil in the *Aeneid* tells how Aeneas, landing in Thrace, pulls up several cornel cherry bushes and finds their roots dripping blood. Groans came from the hole and a voice cries out that his murdered kinsman Polydorus is buried there. Aeneas then performs funeral rites so that the spirit of Polydorus can rest in peace. (See *Dogwood tree*.)

COTTONWOOD BLOSSOM. In the Old West, an outlaw hanged from the limb of any tree was called a "cottonwood blossom" after the cottonwood tree (*Populus balsamifera*) common in the West, which was often used as a gallows tree. This use of the cottonwood led to the saying "to have the cottonwood on one," meaning to have the advantage over someone. Among the most unusual American desserts of pioneer days was "cottonwood ice cream," a sweet, pulpy white mass scraped in the spring from the inner bark of the cottonwood.

COWSLIP. Surprisingly enough the *slip* in this word is an old term for *dung*, thus the pretty wildflower might be called the *cowdung* or worse. Having nothing at all to do with a "cow's lip," it takes its name from the cow dung in the pastures where it thrives.

CRACKERBERRY. No, this berry doesn't taste like or resemble a cracker. *Crackerberry* is simply another name for the common huckleberry (*Gaylussacia baccata*) also called "crackers" and "black snaps," because its seeds crack or snap so between biting teeth.

CRANBERRY. This berry grows wild in the marshland favored by cranes, which leads some experts to trace it to the Low German word *kraanbere*. However, since the word is recorded in America as early as

1647—a time when it is unlikely that Low German terms would have had much currency here—it could be that Americans coined the word independently, noting themselves that the berry grew where cranes lived. (See *Geranium*.)

CREOSOTE BUSH. The evergreen creosote bush (*Larrea tridentata*), which is so named because it has a strong odor of creosote (a distillation of wood tar), is now regarded as the world's oldest living plant. A specimen found in 1985 in the Mojave desert is believed to be 11,700 years old, making it far older than the previous record-holder, a 6,217-year-old bristlecone pine.

CROCUS. The showy solitary flower known as the crocus, one of the first flowers of spring, takes its name from the Greek word for *saffron*. The stamens of *Crocus sativus*, the autumn crocus, one of the 80 or so species of crocus, have indeed been used to make saffron since prehistoric times. It takes some 225,000 hand-picked stamens to produce just one pound of saffron, making it one of the world's costliest spices.

A "crocus sack," or gunnysack, a sack made of coarse material like burlap, is so named because crocus, or saffron, was first shipped in sacks made of this material. Hall of Fame sportscaster Red Barber (1907–1992) sometimes used the Southern American expression "tied up in a crocus sack" for a game that was sewed up, a sure win for one team. (See *Saffron*.)

CROP. A crop was originally the top or head of a plant; these were gathered during the harvest, of course, and came to be the general name for what was collected, the crop.

CROW. The crow has long been regarded as *the* worst feathered pest feeding on crops. We've heard of sheep-herds (shepherds) and cow-herds, but "crow-herds"? Crow-herds, it seems, were boys or old men equipped with makeshift bows and employed to keep crows off planted fields. They were apparently first called "crow-keepers," a term mentioned in Shakespeare's *King Lear:* "That fellow handles his bow like a crow-keeper . . ." A crow-keeper could also be called a "scarecrow," a word first recorded as applying to humans hired to scare off crows (1553) and applied to a straw dummy dressed like a man about a half-century later.

CROWDERS. (See *Black-eyed Peas*.)

CUCUMBER. It took scientists with thermometers until 1970 to find out what has been folk knowledge for centuries—that cucumbers are indeed cool, so much so that the inside of a field cucumber on a warm day registers about 20 degrees cooler than the outside air. The belief is ancient, but was first put on paper by Francis Beaumont and John Fletcher in their play *Cupid's Revenge* (1610), when they referred to certain women "as cold as cucumbers." The metaphor describes anyone self-possessed and unemotional. *Cucumber,* which derives from the Latin *cucumir,* was considered "bookish" and commonly pronounced *cowcumber* in England in the early nineteenth century, the way Sara Gump said it in Dickens's *Martin Chuzzlewit.* Roman Emperor Tiberius is said to have enjoyed the fruits so much that he ordered them served to him every day, even though they had to be grown in greenhouses out of season.

Cucumbers, of course, give us pickles, and a pickle is the last thing anyone would expect to be named after a man. Yet more than one source claims that the word *pickle* derives from the name of William Beukel or Beukelz, a fourteenth-century Dutchman who supposedly pickled the first fish, inventing the process by which we shrink and sour our cucumbers. This pickled herring theory may be a red herring, however. All the major dictionaries follow the *Oxford English Dictionary*'s lead in tracing *pickle* to the medieval Dutch word *pekel,* whose origin is ultimately unknown.

The "Kirby pickle" familiar to gardeners is a name applied generally to all pickling cucumbers and definitely is named in honor of a man. It bears the name of the developer of a once-popular pickling cucumber called the *Kirby*—Norvel E. Kirby of Philadelphia's I. N. Simon & Son seed company, now out of business. Simon introduced Kirby's development in 1920 and it remained popular until the mid-1930s, when more disease-resistant types replaced it. Its name remained, however, as a designation for all pickling cucumbers.

CURARE. This well-known deadly poison, with which South American natives sometime tip their arrows, takes its name from *wrari* of the Brazilian Tupi Indians. In Tupi it translates as the poetically apt "he to whom it comes always falls." The blackish poison is made from the tropical plants of the genus *Strychnos,* especially *Strychnos toxifera,* and from the root of *pareira,* a tropical vine (*Chondodendron tomentosum*). Curare, which is also used as a common name for these plants, has medical uses as well.

CURRANTS. Currants may taste nothing like them, but they take their name indirectly from grapes. In the early fourteenth century the chief place of export for the small seedless raisins made from grapes was Corinth, Greece. As Corinth was pronounced *Corauntz* in Anglo-French at the time, these dried raisins were called "raisins of Corauntz." Later, the tart berries of the genus *Ribes* were given the same appellation because their plant clusters looked like the dried grapes or raisins of Corauntz. *Corauntz* was eventually corrupted to *currants* and this became the tasty fruit's name.

Wrote early-seventeenth-century poet Richard Hughes:

> *Puddings should be*
> *Full of currants for me:*
> *Boiled in a pail*
> *Tied in the tail*
> *Of an old bleached shirt:*
> *So hot that they hurt.*

The most famous dish made from red and white currants has to be the seedless currant jelly once laboriously made by professional "seeders," who used goose feathers to delicately pick out the currant seeds without damaging the berries. The jelly used to be a gourmet delicacy made only in Bar-le-Duc, France, on the banks of the Meuse. Ever since 1559, when Mary Stuart, later Mary Queen of Scots, was given a jar of the rare jelly, it was presented to every visiting chief of state. But a decade ago its last manufacturer went out of business, and the gastronomical rarity is no more.

CUSH-CUSH. This South American relative of the yam is also called the "yampee." *Dioscorea trifida*, which grows in the wild, is valued for its edible orange-colored tubers, but no one knows how it got the unusual name *cush-cush*.

CUT AND DRIED. The allusion is not to ready-cut timber, as some say, but to the cut and dried herbs that were sold in the herbalists' shops of seventeenth-century England. Herbs used as remedies were more effective cut and dried than they were fresh picked, and herbalists stocked great quantities of them. The phrase came to mean "far from fresh, hackneyed," its first recorded use in this sense being in a 1710 letter to a preacher whose sermon was described as *cut and dry'd*. By the time Swift used the phrase for hackneyed literary style in his poem "Betty the Grizette" (1730), it was already fairly hackneyed itself:

> *Sets of phrases, cut and dry,*
> *Ever more thy tongue supply.*

CYCLAMEN. Here is a flowering plant *Cyclamen indicium* named for the shape of its bulbous roots, *cyclamen* deriving from the Greek *kyklos,* "circle." "Sowbread," the plant's common name, refers to the fact that its fleshy roots were once fed to pigs. Cyclamen is a very popular florists' plant, and its handsome flowers come in many colors today.

CYMLING. A stupid person is called a "cymling head" after the small, round variety of melon or squash called the "cymling" (*Cucurbita pepo melopepo*). In the South the melon is often called a "simling" which better shows its origins—its name derives from its shape resembling the fruitcake called a simnel cake. Other names for the cymling are the "scallop squash" and the "pattycake squash."

CYPRESS. An old legend tells of Cyparissus, a young friend of Apollo who died of grief because he killed Apollo's favorite stag and was transformed by the god into a cypress tree. Once cut the cypress never grows again, which probably led to its being dedicated to Pluto, the king of the infernal regions in Roman mythology. For this reason the beautiful *Cupressus funebris* was often planted in cemeteries along the Mediterranean, and its wood was used to make coffins. The Romans placed a branch of cypress in front of their houses when a friend died, and the Turks customarily plant a cypress on the graves of loved ones. Cypress wood can last for hundreds of years. According to one story, the cypress gates of St. Peter's Church in Rome lasted from the time of Constantine to that of Pope Eugene III, more than 1,100 years, with no decay.

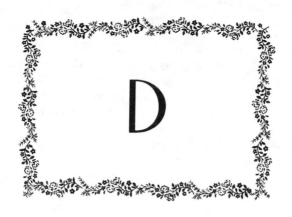

DAFFODIL. No one knows for certain why people in the fifteenth century began to call the flower *asphodel,* which carpeted Elysium, *affodill.* But the apparent mispronunciation stuck and eventually *affodill* was corrupted further to *daffodil,* which remains the flower's name today. The best explanation, according to the *Oxford English Dictionary,* is that the change was "due to childish or playful distortions, as in *Ted* for *Edward* or *tante* for *aunt* . . ." "Daffodil," "narcissus" and "jonquil," though there are differences among them, are often used interchangeably for "daffodil." The "dainty daffodil," the "lamp of beauty," is perhaps English lyric poetry's favorite flower (next to roses and rosebuds) from Herrick's "Fair daffodils, we weep to see / You haste away so soon," to Wordsworth's host "of golden daffodils; / Beside the lake, beneath the trees, / Fluttering and dancing in the breeze . . . / Continuous as the stars that shine . . . / Tossing their heads in sprightly dance . . ." (See *Jonquil; Narcissus.*)

DAHLIA. More than 14,000 named varieties of dahlias have been cultivated and crossed from a single plant discovered in Mexico in 1789. Sent to Spain in that year, the specimen was named there by the head of Madrid's Botanic Garden, Professor Cavanilles. Cavanilles named the plant for fellow professor Anders Dahl (1751–1789), a Swedish botanist and pupil of Linnaeus, who died at about the time the flower was discovered. The first single-flowered dahlia bore little resemblance to the giant, colorful double-flowered species so important in gardens today. There was, incidentally, a time in the nineteenth century when dahlia roots were touted as an excellent substitute for potatoes. They were easy to grow and resistant to blight, said their advocates, but unfortunately no one seemed to like the way they tasted.

DAISY. *Daisy* still sounds like the Old English word for the flower, "day's eye' or "eye of the day." *Bellis perennis* was so named in allusion to its appearance and because it closes its ray in the evening to conceal the flower's yellow disk, and opens it again in the morning. "Fresh as a daisy" is first recorded in Captain Frederick Marryat's *Peter Simple* (1833), but there is no telling if he coined the popular phrase. The daisy takes its scientific name *Bellis* from a Roman legend about Belides, one of the Dryads. Vortumnus, the god of orchards, beheld and admired Belides dancing in the fields and pursued her. Wishing to escape him, she was changed into the little flower called *bellis* by the Romans.

"Up-see-daisy," a variation on the earlier *up-a-daisy,* is a playful term said when lifting a small child up into the air, often by the arms. The "daisy" could refer to the little child, pretty or delicate as a flower plucked from the earth, although the *Oxford English Dictionary* prosaically suggests that the word is patterned on "lack-a-daisy" and "lack-a-day." In any case, the term is first recorded in Jonathan Swift's *Journal to Stella* (1721): "Come stand away, let me rise . . . So-up-a-dazy." Other variations include "oop-a-daisy," "up-see-day," "up-see-daddy" and "up-a-deedies."

DAMASK ROSE. Brought to England as a present for Henry VIII by his physician in about 1540, the famous damask rose is named for the Syrian city of Damascus. Long used in making attar of roses, *Rosa damascena* was then only pink in color, which led poets to write of fair ladies with damask complexions. (See *Rose.*)

DANDELION. "Lion's-tooth"—referring to the plant's indented leaf— was the old English name for this flower, but apparently some language snob gave it the French name *dent de lion* in the sixteenth century. Since the French *dent de* was pronounced *dan de,* the word soon became *dandelion.* In modern French the dandelion is called the *pissenlit,* or "wet-the-bed," from the belief that eating dandelion greens at dinner results in nocturnal bedwetting.

"If you can't beat 'em eat 'em" is a phrase that has been applied over the years to the gardener's perennial battle against weeds, most recently by Dr. James Duke, a botanist at the U.S. Department of Agriculture. Dr. Duke, quoted in Anne Raver's gardening column in the *New York Times,* made the remark specifically in reference to dandelions, which make a dandy salad and wine, among other comestibles. But the words have been applied to garden insects as well. The best example is a little book by English farmer V. M. Holt entitled *Why Not Eat Insects* (1885). "The insects eat up every blessed green thing that do grow and us farmers starve,'' Holt reasoned. ''Well, eat *them* and grow fat.'' He then proceeded to give a series of appropriate recipes, including ''Fried soles with woodlouse sauce,'' ''curried cockchafers,'' ''fricasse of chicken with chrysalids,'' ''boiled neck of mutton with wireworm sauce,'' ''cauliflowers garnished with caterpillars,'' and ''moths on toast.'' Nutritionists today say that insects could be a useful protein supplement to the human diet. Locusts, for example, are said to be about 75 percent protein and 20 percent fat, as well as being rich in some vitamins.

DARLINGTONIA. When an insect enters the pitcher-shaped leaves of the curious California pitcher plant, *Darlingtonia*, it is trapped by down-pointing hairs, which allow it to crawl in but not out. It then drowns in liquid from the leaves, and according to some scientists, is ultimately eaten or digested by the plant. It is not a particularly appetizing thing to have named after one, but the single species' scientific name honors William Darlington (1782–1863), an American botanist who wrote several biographies of famous botanists and authored *American Weeds and Useful Plants* (1859). The naming was done by a fellow botanist John Torrey, and there is no record of bad feelings between the two men. *Darlingtonia* is sometimes sold as *Chrysamphora californica* and is not the only insectivorous plant. Others include the famous Venus's-flytrap, bladderwort, sundew, butterwort, and pitcher plants, which belong to the genus *Sarracenia* but all vary in the ways they capture their prey. (See *Venus's-flytrap*.)

DATE. Date palms from the Mediterranean area were introduced to America by Spanish missionaries in the early 1700s. The fruit of this palm takes its name from the Latin *dactylus,* ''finger,'' as people in ancient times believed it resembled the human finger. The date has been called ''the candy that grows on trees'' because about half its weight is sugar. Thousands of acres of date trees grow in California's Coachella Valley. Their large bunches of fruit are wrapped in heavy paper to protect them from insects and moisture, and helicopters periodically hover over the groves to fan away dampness. A merely ''average'' date palm produces about 100 pounds of fruit a year. In times past, dates were cheaper than grain in some regions, and the tree was said to have 360 uses, ranging from fermented drinks made from its sap to the ''cabbage'' consisting of the new foliage sprouting from its crown. (See *Phoenix Tree.*)

DEADLY NIGHTSHADE. (See *Belladonna Lily.*)

DEADMAN'S VINE. Deadman's vine, also called *ayahuasco*, was used by Columbian Indians in religious rituals. A sip of the brew they made from this vine sends one into a deathlike coma. The woody vine is scientifically named *Banisteriopsis caapi* and today its bark is the source of the hallucinogenic alkaloid harmine.

DECIDUOUS. Trees that keep their leaves all year long are called "evergreen"; those that lose their leaves in fall are called "deciduous." *Evergreen* is, of course, self-explanatory; *deciduous* derives from the Latin *deciduus*, "falling down."

DELPHINIUM. We grow all sorts of wondrous things in our gardens. Even the friendly dolphin can find a home out of water there, at least in the form of the perennial delphinium, which the Greeks named "little dolphin" (*delfinium*) because they thought the flower's nectary looked like the marine mammal. There are about 200 species of delphiniums, all of which have a poisonous juice in their foliage. (See *Larkspur*.)

DEVIL'S WALKING STICK. (See *Hercules' Club*.)

DEWBERRY. Dewberries, which are trailing blackberries, are cultivated today by gardeners in many parts of the world. In Europe the dewberry can be traced back to the sixteenth century, when Shakespeare praised it. Its name, in fact, may be a corruption of "dove berry," which it has been called for centuries in Germany, but it has long been associated with "dew" in English use.

DIEFFENBACHIA. (See *Mother-in-law Plant*.)

DIOSCOREA. While many genera and species of flowers and fruits are named for people, the yam is the only major vegetable (excluding vegetable varieties) to take even its scientific name from a real person. The yam's botanical name is *Dioscorea batatas*. The genus, containing many species, was named by Linnaeus for Pedanius Dioscorides, a first-century Greek physician and an early father of botany. A surgeon in Nero's Roman army, Dioscorides gathered information about 600 medicinal plants and other remedies of the period, which he recorded in his *De materia medica*, translated in 1934 as the *Greek Herbal of Dioscorides*. Dioscorides' work remained the standard for centuries, and he is considered to be the first man to establish medical botany as an applied science.

The yam is often incorrectly called a sweet potato, to which it is no relation despite the similarity in taste. The vine, with tubers two to three feet below the ground, is primarily grown in the southern United States. The sweet potato (*Ipomoea batatas*) is a member of the morning glory family. A sweet potato in the South is also called a "dooley," probably after someone who developed a superior variety.

DOG GRASS. Said to be eaten by dogs when they have lost their appetite, "dog grass" is another name for the very troublesome weedy "quack grass," "witch grass" or "couch grass" (*Agropyron repens*). The plant acts as an emetic and purgative, illustrating the fact that even the most pernicious garden plants have their uses.

DOG ROSE. The wild, hardy dog rose (*Rosa canina,* called *cynorrodon* by Pliny) is said to have been so named because the Romans thought eating the flower cured the rabid bites of wild dogs. But then the Romans also believed that shortening a dog's tail was a preventative for rabies, and the Greeks thought dogs could cure many diseases by licking patients. Today the dog rose is more realistically valued for the high vitamin C content of its "hips." (See *Rose.*)

DOGWOOD TREE. This common tree has a mysterious name. John C. Loudon wrote in *The Hardy Trees and Shrubs of Britain* (1838) that the beautiful tree "is called Dogwood because a decoction of its leaves was used to wash dogs, to free them from vermin." This may be true, but no evidence has been found to support the theory. The popular ornamental (*Cornus florida*) was in early times called the "dogger tree," the "dogge berie tree," the "hounder tree" and the "hounde berie tree" as well as the dogwood, so it surely has some connection with dogs. Another possibility is that it was named the "dogberry tree" because its dark-purple berries resembled the berries of another, unknown tree that were used as a medicine for dogs, and that *dogberry* became *dogwood* in time. No link between the tree's wood and dogs has been found; we only know that in the past its wood was used to make toothpicks and that its crushed bark was thrown into the water to intoxicate fish and make them easy to catch by hand. John Ciardi proposes in *A Second Browser's Dictionary* (1983) that "Dog is a simple corruption of OE *dagge,* spit, skewer, because the wood of the European dogwood, being hard and smooth-grained, was commonly used for spitting meat." (See *Cornelian Cherry.*)

"Dogwood winter" is similar to a "blackberry winter." In 1907 an issue of *American Folklore* reported this explanation by a contributor: " 'Don't you know what dogwood winter is?' demanded a man from Hickory, North Carolina. 'There is always a spell of it in May, when the dogwood trees are in bloom. For several days there is cold disagreeable, cloudy weather, and often a touch of frost.' '' (See *Blackberries*.)

DOROTHY PERKINS'S ROSE. Ranking with Peace and Crimson Glory as the best known of American roses, the Dorothy Perkins is a pink rambler introduced by the famous Jackson & Perkins Nursery of Newark, New Jersey, in 1901. It is a small cluster-flowering type, and though ramblers have bowed in popularity to larger-flowered varieties, it remains a sentimental favorite often mentioned in literature. The rose was named for the wife of the firm's co-owner. (See *Rose*.)

DOUGLAS FIR. Only the giant sequoias and redwoods of California among North American trees exceed the Douglas fir in height and massiveness. The coniferous evergreens grow up to 300 feet tall and 12 feet wide, yielding more lumber commercially than any other American species. The Douglas fir or Douglas spruce, as it is sometimes called, was named for its discoverer, David Douglas (1798–1834), who came here from Scotland in 1823 to study American plants and collect specimens for the Royal Horticultural Society. The former gardener at Glasgow's botanical gardens collected more than 200 plants and seeds then unknown in Europe. His 11-year journal became historically valuable because he was one of the first travelers in the Pacific Northwest. The Douglas fir, which he first observed in 1825, is botanically of the pine family, and yields a hard, strong wood of great commercial importance. Douglas's death was a strange one: In 1834 he extended his travels to the Hawaiian Islands, where he was killed by a wild bull.

DUMBCANE. (See *Mother-in-law Plant*.)

DUMMY'S PLANT. The common and appropriate name for *planta del mudo*, "dummy's plant" is a Venezuelan herb that when chewed supposedly renders its user totally dumb for two days. (See *Mother-in-law Plant*.)

DURIAN. An old Malay saying has it that "When the durians fall, the sarongs rise." The lopsided, hard-shelled green fruit of the *Durio zibethinus* tree, volleyball size and covered with pods on its outer pod, is widely believed to be an aphrodisiac in Malaya, Thailand, Indonesia and the Philippines. The "emperor fruit" (or "king fruit" or "queen fruit") *fruit* (up to $10 apiece) is thought to be so rich in protein that pregnant women are advised to eat it only in moderate amounts for fear that they might produce a child "too large to come out." The durian is so well regarded in Asia that the ownership of just one tree (they often reach 80 feet high) can make a person prosperous. Owners, however, often have to sleep under their trees to guard them, for the fruit sometimes "falls ripe" at night and is devoured by rats. One sixteenth-century traveler claimed that the durian "surpasses in flavor all the fruits of the world." A. R. Wallace, a widely traveled naturalist, described it this way in 1872: "A rich butterlike custard highly flavored with almonds gives the best idea of it, but intermingled come wafts of flavor that recall to mind cream cheese, onion sauce, brown sherry and other incongruities; it is neither sweet nor juicy, yet no one feels the want of more of these qualities, for it is perfect as it is." At the height of its season in August, many Asians travel thousands of miles to eat the aphrodisiac durian. The best of its 100 varieties is said to be grown in Thailand, where the late President Sukarno of Indonesia, famous for his womanizing, kept a house near Bangkok for discreet visits during the height of the durian season. The only trouble with the durian is that it literally stinks. Addicts say that it is no more objectionable than Gorgonzola or Camembert cheese, but most non-Asians consider it among the foulest-smelling foods in the world; one gourmet wrote, "to say it smells like rotten garlicky cheese is generous." British author Anthony Burgess has compared eating durian to eating vanilla custard in a latrine, and walking through Bangkok markets in durian season has been compared to walking through a sewer. Airlines refuse to carry durians even in sealed containers, and Asian hotel rooms literally have to be fumigated after durian feasts. One husband is reported to have chased his wife out of bed making, her eat her prize specimen on their hotel fire escape.

EARWIG. The nocturnal earwig (*Forficula auricularia*) is a common garden pest, but it won't wiggle or wriggle into people's ears and then drill its way into the brain with the aid of its large pincers. Yet it was exactly this popular superstition that gave the earwig or ear-wiggle its name more than 1,000 years ago. One English writer even instructed: "If an earwig begotten into your eare . . . spit into the same, and it will come forth anon . . ." Good trick if you can do it.

To "earwig" someone is to fill his mind with prejudices by insinuations, by whispering into his ear and wriggling into his confidence.

EDELWEISS. The edelweiss (*Leontopodium alpinum*), well known in song and picture (the little Alpine flower is featured in many Swiss designs), takes its name from the German *edel*, "noble," and *weiss*, "white" or "pure." An Italian liqueur named edelweiss is flavored with extracts of this Alpine flower.

EGGPLANT. Eggplant of course, takes its common name from its supposed resemblance to a large egg in shape. The vegetable is generally known as the *aubergine* to the English. Its early reputation varied in Europe, where it was thought to induce insanity and was called the "mad apple," but it was also considered to be an aphrodisiac and, like the tomato, was dubbed the "apple of love." Native to India, the fruits range in size and in color from purple-black to white. The name *eggplant* is first recorded in 1767 in England, where the first cultivated eggplants were indeed white and shaped like eggs. An earlier folkname for the fruit was "Guinea squash." Vineland, New Jersey, advertises itself as the "Eggplant Capital of the World," and at its annual Eggplant Festival serves many eggplant dishes, including an eggplant wine. (See *Aubergine*.)

ELDERBERRY. He who cultivates the elderberry, says an old proverb, will live until an old age and die in his own bed. Amazing properties have long been attributed to the wine and other products made from *Sambucus nigra*. Said seventeenth-century English herbalist John Evelyn: "If the medicinal properties of the [elderberry] leaves, bark, berries, etc., were thoroughly known I cannot tell what our countrymen could ail for what he would not find a remedy, from every hedge, either for sickness or wounds."

ELDER TREE. (See *Judas Tree.*)

EMPEROR FRUIT. (See *Durian.*)

ESCAPE. The Latin word *excappare* (from *ex*, "out of," and *cappa*, "cloak") means "to slip out of one's cloak," and is the ancestor of our word *escape*, although the Greeks had a similar word meaning literally "to get out of one's clothes." The idea behind these words is probably someone slipping out of a cloak or coat held by a robber or jailer, and escaping, leaving the villain or keeper with the cloak in his hands. An escape in gardening terminology is any cultivated plant, such as phlox, daylillies or lily of the valley, that runs wild and propagates itself without further cultivation.

EUPATORIUM. Mithridates VI trusted no one, no one at all. Coming to the throne when only 11 years old, this king of Pontus (an area in Asia Minor along the Black Sea) eventually murdered his mother, several sons and the sister he had married in order to retain power. On one bloody evening he killed all his concubines to prevent his harem from falling into enemy hands. Eupator, "The Great," all his life guarded himself against poisoning by accustoming his body to small amounts of poison, rendering himself immune by gradually increasing these daily doses. Then, weary of another son's treachery, he decided to commit suicide and found that he had *mithridatized* himself far too well. No poison in any amount worked, for he had total immunity. Instead he had to have a mercenary or slave stab him to death. Such is the story, anyway, that the credulous Pliny the Elder tells us about Mithridates VI (120–63 B.C.) who was betrayed by the very poisons he himself had so often used to kill.

A *mithridate* is the antidote to all the poisons that Pliny claims Mithridates had developed. It contained 72 ingredients, some of them plants, and none of them given by the historian. The last ingredient, however, was to be "taken with a grain of salt," Pliny says, and it is from his

acceptance and presentation of Mithradates' story that that phrase probably originates. The botanical genus *Eupatorium,* comprising more than
500 species of chiefly tropical American herbs, is also named for Eupator, King Mithradates VI of Pontus. He is said to have used one of its
species for healing, or in his famous antidote.

EVERGREEN. (See *Deciduous.*)

EVERLASTING FLOWER. (See *Ageratum.*)

EVE'S DATE. Since we mentioned Adam's apple, it's only fair to
devote a few lines to Eve's date (*Yucca baccata*). Found in Mexico and
the southwestern United States, this little-known fruit can be eaten out
of hand. The dark-purple Eve's date probably takes its name because
it's shaped like a stubby banana; it is tempting and sweet in taste but
leaves a slight bitterness in the mouth.

FAIRY RINGS. Fairies dancing on the spot were once thought to cause the dead or withered circles of grass often found on lawns. The fairy rings are, sad to say, caused by more prosaic fungus below the surface that envelop the grass roots and prevent them from obtaining water.

FAVA BEAN. The *fava bean* takes its name from *faba,* the Latin word for "bean." It is often called the "broad bean," "horse bean," or "Windsor bean." Since antiquity this widely grown legume has been known to cause favism, a type of anemia, in people of African and Mediterranean origin with a certain enzyme deficiency; fava-bean poisoning sometimes proves fatal. (See *Beans.*)

FEIJOA. The delicious guava (*Feijoa sellowiana*) is native to South America and grown in Florida and California for its highly esteemed white-fleshed fruit. The small tree, introduced into southern Europe in 1890, is named *Feijoa* for Spanish naturalist J. da Silva Feijo. A member of the myrtle family, it is a small genus noted only for the pineapple guava, which is often called "feijoa." Closely related to the true guava, its fruit is used widely for jam and jelly. The oblong fruit, about two inches long and a dull green marked with crimson, has a delicate pineapple flavor that literally melts in the mouth.

FENNEL. *Finochio* or *fennel* can be traced to the Latin word *feniculum,* meaning "product of the meadow." "Florence fennel," a sweet variety, is often called "finochio." Anciently held to be an aphrodisiac, fennel was also emblematic of flattery, was thought to clear the eyesight and was said to be the favorite food of serpents. "To eat conger and fennel" (two supposed aphrodisiacs) was held to be especially stimulating.

FERTILIZER. The first mention of the word *fertilizer* came in 1661 when an English writer noted that "Saint-foime (Saint-foin) or Holy-hay [*Onobrychis sativa,* a member of the pea family, also called Holy Clover] . . . [is] a great Fertilizer of Barren-ground." Fertilizers, however, have been known since time immemorial. The word *fertile,* from which *fertilizer* derives, comes from the Latin *ferre,* to bear. While animal and plant fertilizers date far back in history, chemical fertilizers weren't developed until the first half of the nineteenth century.

Sewage has long been used as a fertilizer. Because cesspools used to be cleaned during the night in the eighteenth century, their contents were called "night soil" and the cleaners "night men." That the contents were sometimes added as fertilizers to soil at night could account for the *soil* in the expression.

FERULE. *Ferula communis,* or the giant fennel, is a plant that became famous as a switch or stick used in classrooms on disobedient students. This member of the fennel family takes its name from the Latin for "stick" and grows up to 8–12 feet high. It was grown by the Romans both for its handsome yellow flowers and the dried pith of its stems, which provided excellent tinder for starting fires. But by the sixteenth century the pliable stalks of the plant were being used as schoolroom switches, their name slightly changed to *ferule.* Eventually the name *ferule* was applied to "a sort of flat ruler, widened at the inflicting end into a shape resembling a pear . . . with a . . . hole in the middle, to raise blisters."

FETID FLOWERS. (See *Rafflesia.*)

FIG. When someone says "I don't care a fig," she or he isn't referring to the delicious fruit (whether she or he knows it or not), but to the ancient "Spanish fig," a contemptuous gesture made by thrusting the thumb forth from between the first two fingers. The insult is said to be an invitation to "kiss my ass."

"Nothing is sweeter than figs," Aristophanes wrote. Figs are mentioned in the biblical story of the Garden of Eden, and it was under a Nepal species of fig tree called the *Bo* that Buddha's revelations came to him. The ancient Egyptians trained apes to gather figs from trees.

The fig takes its English name from the Latin *ficus,* "fig," which became the Provençal *figa.* It figures in a number of phrases of its own. English, for example, features it in various expressions from the euphemistic "fig you" to far worse, and in French *faire la figue* means "to give the obscene finger gesture." The exclamation, "Frig you," has nothing to do with the "fig you" etymology, however, probably deriving from the Old English *frigan,* to love. The distinguished etymologist Laurence Urdang points out in *The Whole Ball of Wax* (1988) that the natural shape of the fig has much to do with its sexual inferences: "When one encounters fresh figs growing or even in a market, it becomes clear why their visual appearance has given rise to so many translinguistic metaphors: Not to mince words, a pair of fresh figs closely resembles in size and configuration, a pair of testicles. Pressed together, they resemble the external parts of the female genitalia."

According to the biblical story (Gen. 3:7), after the Fall, Adam and Eve covered their nakedness with fig leaves (or leaves of the banyan tree). It wasn't until times of Victorian prudery, however, that statues in museums were covered with fig leaves.

Fig Sunday is an old name for Palm Sunday, when figs used to be eaten to commemorate the blasting of the barren fig tree by Jesus on entering Jerusalem.

An old story that is incapable of proof but widely accepted is that the word *sycophant* for an "apple-polisher" originated in ancient Greece from the Greek *sukophantes* (*sulkon,* fig, and *phainen,* to show), which meant an informer who reported to the authorities growers who exported figs. At one time it was supposedly against the law to export figs from Athens and *sukophantes,* or sycophants, often turned in violators of the unpopular law for their own personal gain. These toadies were widely despised.

The Persian King Xerxes boasted that he would invade Greece, thoroughly thrash all the Greek armies and then feast on the famous fat figs of Attica. Ever since he was soundly defeated by the Greeks in 480 B.C. at the battle of Salamis, "attic figs" has meant wishful thinking.

Many gardeners go to great lengths to nurse their fig trees through cold northern winters, wrapping the trees in burlap, covering them with leaves and hay, and even growing them in portable tubs that can be wheeled into the garage or tool shed for the winter. (See *Judas Tree.*)

FILBERT. About the only connection between the Frankish Saint Philibert and filbert nuts is that the saint's feast day falls on August 22, the height of the nut harvesting season. This was enough reason, however, for Norman gatherers to name the nuts *philberts* in his honor. Saint Philibert, his name *Filuberht* in Old High German, was a Benedictine who founded the Abbey of Jumiéges in 684. What Americans call "filberts" are actually hazelnuts. Filberts are confined botanically to two European nut varieties; about 250 million pounds of them bear the saint's name each year.

A "Gilbert Filbert" was British slang for a very fashionable man-about-town early in this century, deriving from the popular song "Gilbert, The Filbert, Colonel of the Nuts," and "cracked in the filbert" meant eccentric or crazy. (See *Nut.*)

FLEUR-DE-LIS. The *fleur-de-lis,* or "flower of the lily," is the French name for the iris, whose striking colors reminded the Greeks of Iris, goddess of the rainbow, one of whose duties was to visit the deathbeds of dying women and bear away their departing spirits. After the Second Crusade, Louis VII (1137–1180) chose the iris to be emblazoned on the coat of arms of France. It was later called "the flower of Louis," and his name corrupted into *Luce.* The French symbol of empire since the twelfth century, the fleur-de-lis was chosen by the fourteenth-century Italian navigator Florio Gioja to mark the north point of the compass in honor of the King of Naples, who was of French descent.

FLORAL FIRECRACKER. (See *Brevoortia Ida-Maia.*)

FLOWER. In Anglo-Saxon times the word for flower was *blossom;* this changed after the Normans conquered England in 1066, and their *fleur* became the English flower. However, both words have the same common ancestor—the ancient Indo-European *blo,* which eventually yielded both *blossom* and *flower.*

Flour, the finely ground meal of any grain, is just a specialized use of the word *flower.* In fact, *flower* and *flour* were used interchangeably until the nineteenth century, as in Milton's *Paradise Lost,* where we find the line "O flours That never will in other climate grow." In French *fleur de farine* is the flower or finest part of the grain meal.

Still used today and one of the longest-lived modern-day slogans, the phrase "Say it with flowers" was coined for the Society of American Florists in 1917 by plantsman Patrick F. O'Keefe (1872–1934).

"Cut flowers" is an old term for flowers cut from the garden for bouquets or display. A visitor once asked George Bernard Shaw why he kept no vases of cut flowers. "I thought you were so fond of flowers," he said.

"So I am," Shaw retorted. "I'm very fond of children, too. But I don't cut off their heads and stick them in pots all over the house."

According to tradition, Saint Elizabeth of Hungary gave so much food to the poor that her own household didn't eat well. Her husband suspected this and when he saw her leaving the house one day with her apron full of something, he demanded to know what she carried. "Only flowers, my lord," Elizabeth said, and God saved her from her lie by changing the loaves of bread in her apron to flowers. (See *Quick Fence.*)

FORGET-ME-NOT. We have it on the authority of the little volume *Drops from Flora's Cup* (1845) that this flower (*Myosotis palustris*), also called the "mouse ear" due to the resemblance of its small leaves to the ears of a mouse, received its more popular name in the following way: In an age when ladies were ladies and gentlemen were gentlemen, sometimes to a fault, an engaged lady and gentleman were walking on the banks of the Danube when the lady spied a flower floating on the water. Knowing that she was sad to see the pretty flower lost, he waded into the water to retrieve it. But he stepped in over his head and couldn't get back to shore. With a last desperate effort he threw the flower at her feet, exclaimed "forget me not," and drowned. The flower's name since that time has been the same. The tale is not recorded elsewhere.

FORSYTHIA. The bloom of this handsome yellow-flowered shrub is the first obvious sign of spring in many places. The forsythia was named for William Forsyth (1737–1804), a Scottish gardener and horticulturist who became superintendent of the royal gardens at Saint James and Kensington in London. Forsyth introduced many unusual ornamental plants to England and may have personally brought the forsythia from China. The inventor of a plaster that stimulates new growth in dying, diseased trees, he received formal thanks from Parliament for this contribution. The *Forsythia* genus is especially valuable to gardeners because it is easy to propagate, requires little care and does well in partial shade.

FORTUNELLA. Fortunella, or the kumquat, is the only genus of well-known fruit trees to be named for a living person, and no more deserving person could be found than Robert Fortune (1813–1880), a Scottish botanist and traveler. Few men have equaled Fortune as a plant hunter. The author of *Three Years' Wanderings in the Northern Province of China* (1847) and other botanical books, he began traveling in Asia for the Royal Horticultural Society in 1842. A former employee in the Society's English gardens, his orders were to collect flora; he brought many beautiful plants back to Europe, including the kumquat, tree peonies, the Japanese anemone and a number of chrysanthemums. Fortune also introduced the tea plant into India for the East India Company, founding its cultivation there. The tallest species of *Fortunella* is only ten feet high, the smallest is a bush of about three feet. The kumquat fruit is orangelike but smaller, having three to seven cells or sections as opposed to eight to fifteen in the orange. The kumquat, which is eaten fresh or preserved, has been crossed with other citrus fruits into a number of strange hybrids like the *citrangequat* and *limequat*. (See *Kumquat.*)

FO-TI-TIENG. Legend has it that the Chinese herbalist Li Chung Yun was 256 years old when he died in 1933, just after marrying for the twenty-fourth time. Moreover, he had all of his own hair and teeth and looked about 50. Whether the story is true or not is highly debatable (one writer says that "it is a matter of record with the Chinese government that Li was born in 1677"), but there is no doubt that the venerable vegetarian heartily recommended fo-ti-tieng for those who desired a long active life marked with sexual vigor. Several scientists, including the French biochemist Jules Lepine, have found an alkaloid in the leaves and seeds of this low-growing plant of the pennywort family (*Hydrocotyle asiatica minor*) that they claim has a rejuvenating effect on the nerves, brain cells and endocrine glands. The Indian sage Nanddo Narian, then 107 himself, informed his faithful that fo-ti-tieng (which means "the elixir of long life" in Chinese) contained "a missing ingredient in man's diet without which we can never control disease and decay." Others have claimed that one-half teaspoon of the herb in a cup of hot water will remove wrinkles and increase sexual energy, and larger doses will act as an aphrodisiac. So off to the jungle marches of the Asian tropics, where the herb is found! And remember, too, Li Chung Yun's more general (and better) advice: "Keep a quiet heart, sit calmly like a tortoise, walk sprightly like a pigeon, and sleep soundly like a dog." Also, said the sage, eat only food that grows above the ground, with the exception of ginseng root. (See *Ginseng.*)

FOUR-LEAF CLOVER. (See *Clover.*)

FOXGLOVE. "Fairy glove" and "finger-flower" are two other popular names for the handsome foxglove (*Digitales purpurea*), which takes its scientific name from the Latin *digitus,* "finger." The flower's tubular blossoms resemble a finger or the empty finger of a glove, but no one knows where the *fox* in the popular designation comes from. The ground leaves of the plant are used to make the heart medicine digitalis.

FOX GRAPE. *The Theatre of Plants* (1640) by John Parkinson informs us that "The Foxe Grape . . . is white, but smelleth and tasteth like unto a Foxe," which is presumably why the American grape is so named. There are two species of wild fox grapes: *Vitis labrusca,* which is the source of many fine varieties of American grapes, and *Vitis rotundifolia,* also called the "scuppernong" or "muscadine." The wine term "foxy" refers to the pungent fruity flavor of Concord wine and other wines made from native American grapes: these wines are reminiscent of jelly or jam to many people.

FRANGIPANE. The Marquis Frangipani, a major general under Louis XIV, is said to have invented the pastry cake filled with cream, sugar and almonds called "frangipane" or "frangipani." The name is also applied to the fragrant but ugly *Plumeria rubra* tree or shrub, and to a perfume either prepared from or imitating the odor of its flowers. The perfume is usually associated with the name of its otherwise unknown inventor—possibly a Frangipani relative or the marquis himself. An alternate suggestion is that both pastry and perfume may have been introduced by an earlier member of the Italian Frangipani family, a relative who came to France with Catherine de Médicis a century before the marquis. Considering Catherine's many contributions to French cooking, this is not unlikely.

FRANKLIN TREE. The Franklin tree, or "Franklinia" is named after American statesman, scientist, writer, printer and inventor Benjamin Franklin. This species has an unusual history; introduced into cultivation from the wild in 1770 by America's first botanist, John Bartram, no one has been able to find it in its wild state since. Its scientific name is *Gormania altamaha*.

FREESIA. There is some question about the naming of this fragrant and beautiful genus of South African herbs. Containing three species but scores of horticultural forms, freesias grow from a bulblike corm, belonging to the iris family and bearing typically white or yellow flowers at the end of their stems. They are generally raised in greenhouses and are popular in floral arrangements. Some authorities, including *Webster's Biographical Dictionary*, say the genus was named for E. M. Fries (1794–1878), a Swedish botanist; others cite F. H. T. Freese, a pupil of Professor Klatt, the christener of the genus.

FUCHSIA. The color fuchsia, a vivid bluish or purplish red, takes its name from the ornamental fuchsia shrubs that honor German physician and botanist Leonhard Fuchs (1501–1566). These principally Mexican and South American shrubs, which are of the evening primrose family and can have purple, red, yellow or white flowers, were named for Fuchs in 1703 by the French botanist Charles Plumier. Dr. Fuchs was noted for his treatment of the "English sweating sickness," a plague that had spread to Europe. He became professor of medicine at the University of Tübingen in 1536, remaining there until his death more than three decades later. His herbal *De historia stirpium* (1542) was widely known, and this compendium of medicinal and edible plants was probably the main reason why the genus *Fuchsia* was named in his honor. The genus contains some 100 species, with the fuchsia shrubs only one of its many cultivated plants.

FUNKIA. This widely cultivated plantain lily or hosta is named after a real person, the German botanist C. H. Funkia. *Funkia* is actually one of the few words that is doubly eponymous, for its alternate name *hosta* honors Austrian botanists Nicholaus and Joseph Host. The plant, valued in the garden for its shade tolerance, is also known as the "niobe." Its genus name is *Hosta* and there are at least 14 species.

GARDEN. *Gardins* or *jardins* were originally fruit and vegetable plots that monks in medieval France enclosed, or guarded, to keep cattle and other animals away from their plants. By the early fourteenth century the word *gardin* was being used in England, but it wasn't spelled *garden* for another 100 years or so.

The term "garden bed" probably owes its origin to the beds we sleep in, being figurative from the shape or purpose of the garden bed. However, the word *bed* itself may come from a Teutonic word meaning "a dugout place, a lair," and the term "garden bed" could have come directly from there. English-speaking people have been using the expression since at least A.D. 1000. The expression "to bed out" plants is recorded as early as 1671 in a gardening manual but is probably much older. Shakespeare used the old phrase "bed of roses," and it may have been popular centuries before him. It seems to have first been employed by the poet Robert Herrick and means a situation of luxurious ease, a highly agreeable position of comfort or pleasure. A variant seldom heard anymore is "a bed of flowers."

There are, of course, thousands of outstanding gardens throughout the world. One of the most famous was the "Hanging Gardens of Babylon," one of the Seven Wonders of the World. The Hanging Gardens of Babylon were supposedly built by the biblical King Nebuchadnezzar to please his wife, Amytis, who had grown tired of northern Babylon's flat plains and longed for scenery that would remind her of her native home in the Median hills. Should you want to cultivate the same, build a square garden, 400 feet each way, rising in a series of terraces from an adequate river and provide it with enough fertile soil to hold even great trees. Vague directions, but the plans have been lost over the years.

Any place from a garden to a park to heaven can be called "paradise." The extensive parks and pleasure gardens of the Persian kings were the first paradises, for the word comes to us from the Greek *paradeisos*, meaning "park," "orchard" or "pleasure gardens," which the Greeks borrowed from a similar Persian word. Such gardens, and the word for them, were known more than 3,000 years ago in the Near East, where they were such prized retreats that they took on religious significance. The Septuagint translators of the Bible adopted the word as a name for the Garden of Eden, and later it was used by early Christian writers to mean heaven itself.

Truck, derived from the old French *troquer*, "to exchange," was another word for "country pay" in earlier times. Since trucks most often carried vegetables from gardens to market, the term "truck garden" came to refer to a vegetable garden.

The "Victory Garden" was a home vegetable garden popular in the United States during World War II; they were encouraged by the government to increase food production during a time of shortages. The idea helped revive the idea of home vegetable gardens, once known as "kitchen gardens," among many Americans who had lost touch with the land.

Voltaire coined the expression "cultivate your own garden," meaning tend to your own business. The origin of the common expression "to lead down the garden path" remains a mystery. Not recorded in print until 1926, it may be the creation of the novelist Ethel Mannin in whose book *Sounding Brass* it first appeared, though this seems unlikely. In the book, "to lead down the garden [path]" means seduction, but the expression's common meaning is to deceive in any way. The "garden path" suggests that the deception is done in a pleasant way, so that the victim suspects nothing.

One of the most famous U.S. gardens is Magnolia Gardens near Charleston, South Carolina, of which British novelist John Galsworthy wrote: "I specialize in gardens and freely assert that none in the world is so beautiful as this." Other noted U.S. gardens include: Middleton Place, near Charleston, South Carolina; Cypress Gardens, near Charleston, South Carolina; Bellingrath Gardens, near Mobile, Alabama; McKee Jungle Gardens, Vero Beach, Florida; Viscaya Art Museum, Miami, Florida; Dumbarton Oaks, Washington, D.C.; Lambert Gardens, Portland, Oregon; Pierates Cruze Gardens, Baltimore, Maryland; Winterthur, Winterthur, Delaware; Biltmore Estate, Asheville, North Carolina; Avery Island, Iberia, Louisiana; Descanse Gardens, La Canada, California; Orchid Jungle, Homestead, Florida; Brookgreen Gardens, Georgetown, South Carolina; Norfolk Botanic Garden, Norfolk, Virginia; International Friendship Gardens, Michigan City, Indiana and Golden Gate Park, San Francisco, California. (See *Garden of Eden*.)

GARDENIA. "Mr. Miller has called it Basteria. But if you will please to follow my advice, I would call it Gardenia, from our worthy friend Dr. Alexander Garden of S. Carolina."

"If Dr. Garden will send me a new genus, I shall be truly happy to name it after him, Gardenia."

These quotations from an exchange of letters between a friend of Linnaeus and the great botanist himself during 1757–58, reveal the politicking that is sometimes involved even in just naming something. Linnaeus did honor his promise to their mutual friend, and two years later dedicated a newly discovered tropical shrub to Dr. Garden, even though the amateur botanist did not discover the beautiful, sweet-smelling gardenia. Dr. Alexander Garden (ca. 1730–1791) a Scottish-American physician, resided in Charleston, South Carolina, where he practiced medicine and also devoted much of his time to collecting plant and animal specimens, discovering the Congo eel and a number of snakes and herbs. Garden carried on an extensive correspondence with Linnaeus and many other European naturalists, probably as much out of loneliness as for intellectual stimulation. An ardent Tory, he returned to England during the Revolutionary War, resuming his practice in London and becoming vice-president of the Royal Society. Dr. Garden was by all accounts a difficult, headstrong man. When his granddaughter was named Gardenia Garden in his honor, he still refused to see her. After all, her father had fought against the British!

GARDEN OF EDEN. The most famous garden of all. Directions: Turn right from the labyrinth and proceed to El Mezey near Damascus, where the waters of the Tege and Barrady divide into four streams that are said to be the four streams of Moses mentioned in Genesis. . . . But, on second thought, many places have been called the original Garden of Eden, among them Persia (Iran); Armenia; Chaldea; Basra; southern Iraq; Israel; Egypt; East Africa; Java; Ceylon; Sinkian, China; Lemuria; the Seychelles Islands; Sweden; and, yes, Mars, by Brinsley Le Poer Trench in his book *The Sky People*. In the late nineteenth century, Galesville, Wisconsin, was proposed as the site of the biblical garden, and in recent times Baptist minister Elvy E. Calloway has claimed the honor for Bristol, Florida, offering as "proof," among other evidence, the fact that Bristol, on the banks of the Apalachicola River, is the only place where gopher wood (the Torrey tree) grows, Noah having made his ark of gopher wood. In the seventeenth century a Swedish professor even wrote a book attempting to prove that the garden had been located in the Land of the Midnight Sun. At Al-Qurna in Iraq, the site of so much recent bloodshed, there is a sign that stands outside a little enclosure around a tree, reading: "On this holy spot where Tigris meets Euphrates this holy tree of our father Abraham grew symbolizing the Garden of Eden on earth. Abraham prayed here two thousand years B.C."

A "Garden of Eden" is sometimes termed a "Garden of Paradise,"as it is in Ceylon. There, Ceylonese point to the Adam's apple tree (*Tabernaemontana coronaria*) when claiming their country as the original Eden. The small tree or shrub bears an attractive fruit with a shape suggesting that a piece has been bitten off, and the Ceylonese say that it was delicious before Eve and Adam ate of it, though it became poisonous after their "fall." You can grow your own on the front lawn if you live in a subtropical climate. (See *Adam's Apple Tree*.)

GARDEN GODS. Gardeners have prayed to many garden deities through the ages. After a drought ruined crops in 496 B.C., Roman priests insisted that a new goddess named Ceres be worshiped and prayed to for rain. When the drought ended, Ceres became protector of the crops and the first grains harvested each year were sacrificed to her and called *cerealis*. From the Latin *cerealis,* meaning "of Ceres," came the English word *cereal,* which honors the goddess every morning on millions of breakfast tables. Ceres' Greek counterpart was Demeter, the goddess of fruit, crops and vegetables.

Pomona was a Roman goddess of fruit from whose name *pomology,* the science of fruits and fruit growing, derives. She was the wife of Vortumnus, a Roman god of orchards and fruit who presided over seasonal changes. Vortumnus, also called Vertumnus, courted Pomona in a variety of forms (as a reaper, ploughsman, pruner of vines, etc.). His name may derive from the Latin *vertere,* "to turn," as the god who changes his shape, or for the god of the turning or changing year.

Flora, the old Roman deity of flowers and fertility, had a temple erected to her near the Circus Maximus, where a special priest was in attendance. The public games at Rome called the *Ludi Florales* were held in her honor in the Circus from April 28 to May 3. Men decked themselves with flowers and women wore colorful dresses during this time of public merriment.

The name of the Greek and Roman god Priapus has come to mean a representation of a phallus, and the adjective *priapic* means "relating to or overly concerned with masculinity." Originally, however, Priapus, said to be the son of Aphrodite and Dionysus, was a fertility god of gardeners whose statue was often placed in home gardens. Represented as a grotesque, deformed creature with a huge penis, he was thought by the Roman poet Virgil to be "little more than a venerable scarecrow" used to keep birds and thieves away from the fruits and vegetables.

"Fiacres" are small horsedrawn cabs that take their name from an old town house called the Hotel de Saint Fiacre in Paris, where they were first rented out from a stand in 1648. The hotel, in turn, took its name from an image of Saint Fiacre that hung outside it. Saint Fiacre, who is invoked today as both the patron saint of gardeners and cab drivers, was an Irish prince who founded a monastery with a hospital and extensive gardens near Paris about 615. Legend has it that his bishop granted him as much land as he could turn over in a night and that the ground miraculously opened at the touch of his spade. It is also Saint Fiacre's fate to be invoked for perhaps the most unpleasant assortment of diseases that any saint is responsible for, including diarrhea, venereal diseases and even warts on the knees of horses. But this saint was the first man to restore people to mental health by hard work in the garden (what psychiatrists now call "horotherapy"), and he is thus best remembered as the patron saint of gardeners. His monastery eventually grew into the village of Saint Fiacre, and his day is August 30, appropriate for the harvest. French gardeners have observed his anniversary for generations, attending services in flower-decked chapels dedicated to him.

Here in the Americas gardeners might do better to erect shrines to Xipe than to Saint Fiacre. Xipe (pronounced *she-pay*) was the Aztec god of sowing and planting. Another name for this patron saint of gardeners is *Xipe Totec*. (See *Adam's Profession.*)

GARLIC. Owing to its resemblance to the leek, garlic, the herb that "makes men drink and wink and stink," takes its name from the Old English *garleac: gar,* "spear," and *leac,* "leek." The Romans believed garlic contained magical powers and hung it over their doors to ward off witches, just as some people wear cloves around their necks to protect themselves against colds, diseases and even vampires.

Pilgarlic is an interesting word that is no longer used to mean a "baldheaded man." It takes its name from the early English *pyllyd garleke,* "peeled garlic," for someone whose head resembles a shiny peeled garlic bulb. Since many baldheaded men were old and pitiful, the word came to take on the meaning of a person regarded with mild contempt or pity, an old fool or someone in a bad way. (See *Onion.*)

GAZEBO. A gazebo is a garden structure of Dutch origin that was originally built of stone or brick. It is now a small, wooden-roofed building that is screened on all sides and set apart from the house to provide an attractive view of the garden on all sides. The word's origin is uncertain. One unproved theory holds that this word for a garden lookout or belvedere is a humorous invention of some eighteenth-century wit, who modeled it on the word *gaze,* pretending that *gaze* was a Latin word (it is of unknown origin), which would make *gazebo* the future form "I shall see" of that hypothetical verb. Nor has anyone proved that the word is from some obscure Chinese source, as its brief first-recorded use in 1752 in an architectural book suggests to some etymologists: "The Elevation of a Chinese tower or Gazeba."

GENTIAN. Among the loveliest of wild flowers, the fringed gentian has been immortalized by William Cullen Bryant and other poets. The large *Gentiana* genus to which it belongs contains some 400 species and provides us with many valued alpine plants for rock gardens. Gentians take their name from the powerful monarch Gentius, who reigned as king of Illyria, an ancient seaport on the Adriatic, from 180 to 167 B.C. Pliny and Dioscorides wrote that Gentius was the first to experience the medicinal value of gentians. Since early times the roots and rhizome of the European yellow gentian (*Gentiana lutea*) have been used as a means of healing wounds, as a bitter tonic and counter poison, and to help cure diseases. Certain alcoholic beverages are made from the plant, too. The beautiful flowers, usually blue, despite *Gentiana lutea,* are generally found at high altitudes. Difficult to cultivate, they are nevertheless extensively grown in home gardens. Gentianaceae, the gentian family, consisting of 800 species and 30 genera, also bears the Illyrian king's name.

GERANIUM. The ancient Greeks thought the beaked seed pods of geraniums resembled the head and beak of a crane, and so they named the flowers after their word for "crane," *geranos.* This family of flowers, containing about 250 species, does not include the very popular common garden geranium (Pelargonium) so widely grown today, which was mistaken for it over the years and so shares its name. *Pelargonium,* however, is from the Greek for "a stork," in allusion to the shape of its fruit. (See *Cranberry.*)

GERMINATE. The Latin word *germen,* "sprout," is the ultimate root of germinate. Long before it meant the seed of a disease, a usage first recorded in 1803, *germ* meant "any portion of a living thing, animal or vegetable, that is capable of development into a likeness of that from which it sprang." This led to the botanical use of *germ* in germinate, meaning to develop from a seed into a plant.

GINSENG. Ginseng, which can cost up to $32 an ounce or $512 a pound for a piece of "heaven grade root," has surpassed the cost of even the truffle as a precious aphrodisiac. In the past it has been sold at $300 an ounce or $4,800 a pound, which is probably the all-time record for a food. One Chinese emperor reputedly paid $10,000 for a perfect man-figure ginseng root, or at least so the story goes. Similarly, it's said that Chairman Mao drank a ginseng tea made from $100-an-ounce ginseng root at least three times a week. At any rate, the herb still sells briskly in Asian markets for $200 a pound and despite the protests of modern pharmacologists, lovers throughout the world cling to the mystique of its so-called super powers.

Lovers have been fascinated by the "Man Plant" for more than 5,000 years. Like mandrake, the most potent ginseng roots are said to be shaped like a man's body (in fact, the plant takes its name from the Chinese *jen shen*, "man herb"), and the Chinese believe that even better results are obtained when the root is dug up at midnight during a full moon. The Chinese call ginseng, or *goo-lai-san*, the "elixir of life," "the herb that fills the heart with hilarity," and the "medicine of medicines." An American species of ginseng (*Panax quinquefolium*) is grown and gathered in this country, especially in the Ozarks and Appalachia. Diggers can earn $33 to $44 per pound of dried root, and our largest domestic dealer exports some 70,000 pounds of the herb annually. Such profits are nothing new, however; it is a matter of record that the first American ship to reach China in 1784, Major Samuel Shaw's *Emperor of China*, carried a cargo of the ginseng so dear to Chinese lovers. (See *Mandrake*.)

GLADIOLUS. Gladiolus were called "sword lilies" in twelfth-century England. Centuries before this the Romans named the flower *gladiolus*, "little sword," from the Latin *gladius*, "sword," because either their long brilliant spikes of flowers or the shapes of their leaves resembled the swords Roman gladiators used in the arena. "Corn lily" is another old name for gladiolus, of which there are more than 240 species.

GOLDEN APPLES. (See *Apple*.)

GOLDEN RICE. (See *Carolina Rice*.)

GOOBER. (See *Peanuts*.)

GOOSEBERRY. How the gooseberry got its name is a puzzle to historians and etymologists. One theory claims that *gooseberry* is a mispronunciation of "gorge berry," an early name for the fruit; however, *gooseberry* was used before "gorge berry," according to surviving records. For similar reasons, most word detectives do not believe that *gooseberry* is a corruption of *groseille,* the French name for the fruit, or the Dutch *kruishes,* which means "cross berry." Perhaps a better explanation is that *gooseberry* is a corruption of the German *Jansbeeren* ("John's berry," so named because it ripens during the feast of Saint John), which was corrupted into the German *Gansberren* and then translated into English as *gooseberry* because *gans* means "goose" in German. That, in fact, is the only thing linking geese with the berry or plant— the goose doesn't like berries; it isn't even averse to them, it just ignores them entirely. Neither were gooseberries customarily served with roast goose, as is sometimes stated. There is even a theory holding that the goose gave its name to a fool or simpleton (as in a "silly goose") and that the green berry (suggesting a "greenhorn" or fool) became known as a goose (or fool) berry.

No matter how its name evolved, the British have celebrated the gooseberry in song and story as well as in special events. Gooseberries were so common in Elizabethan England that Shakespeare used the expression "not worth a gooseberry." In early times there were "gooseberry shows," "gooseberry fairs," and "gooseberry feasts," and the fruit was used in scores of dishes. It was an old Norman practice to eat green gooseberry sauce with mackerel, and for this reason gooseberries were called *groseille à maquereau* in French to distinguish them from currants, both of the fruits being *groseilles.* Pigeons and other fowl were stuffed with gooseberries, which were, and still are, prized for eating fresh out of hand when dead ripe, as well as in gooseberry pies, tarts, pastries, puddings, jellies and jams. There is even a gooseberry wine celebrated in poems by Oliver Goldsmith and Charles Lamb.

One British writer thought fully ripe gooseberries tasted more like grapes than any other fruit, but that description leaves much to be desired. The truth is that gooseberries have a unique flavor of their own beyond compare. They have been paid compliments by many discerning writers, but the words of little Marjorie Fleming, "Pet Marjorie," the youthful prodigy of Sir Walter Scott, are most memorable. Wrote Marjorie in her quaint and charming diary shortly before her death at age seven: "I am going to turn over a new life and am going to be a very good girl and be obedient . . . here there is plenty of gooseberries which makes my teeth watter."

Probably the most famous dish made from gooseberries is "gooseberry fool," a dessert made of the fruit stewed or scalded, crushed and mixed with milk, cream or custard. Some say the *fool* in the dish is a corruption of the French verb *fouler,* "to crush," but this derivation seems to be inconsistent with the use of the word. More probably the dish is simply named after other, older fruit trifles, the use of *fool* in its name in the sense of "foolish or silly" being suggested by "trifle." In any case, "gooseberry fool" has been an English favorite since at least 1700. So widely known is the dish that another plant is named after it: The English call the willow herb *Epilobrium hirsutum* "gooseberry fool" because its leaves smell like the dessert.

In Victorian times summer was a dull period for British newspapers. So much space was left for reports of record-size vegetables and fruits grown by one gardener or another that it was nicknamed "the big gooseberry season."

GRAFT. The gardening term *graft* derives, ultimately, from the Greek *grapheion,* "a bone or wood pencillike instrument used for writing on wax tablets." The ancients apparently thought that a *grapheion* resembled a cut shoot used for grafting. *Graft* meaning the acquisition of money, etc., by dishonest means may be a special use of the horticultural term *graft,* in the sense that something is added from the outside. (See *Imp.*)

GRAPE. The grapefruit doesn't take its very misleading name because it grows in clusters (it doesn't) or because it tastes like grapes, as one early botanist suggested. The origin remains a mystery, but it may be a corruption of "great fruit," which was a nineteenth-century translation of a scientific name for the fruit, *Citrus grandi,* and refers, of course, to the fruit's large size. Grapes themselves look nothing like their namesakes. They were named for the *grape* or *grapple,* the small hook that the French used to grab or harvest them. The English called grapes "wineberries" until they imported the French word. (See *Shaddock.*)

Grapes figure in a number of memorable phrases. In Aesop's fable "The Fox and the Grapes," a fox spies luscious-looking grapes hanging from a vine. Everyone knows that he leaped a number of times trying to get them, failing by a few inches with each leap and gave up after rationalizing that they were probably sour and inedible anyway. La Fontaine, another great fabulist, later regarded the fox as admirable, remarking that his words were "better than complaining," but the fox's "sour grapes" have come to mean any belittling, envious remark.

Some 15 years after Samuel Morse transmitted his famous "What hath God wrought!" message, a long telegraph line was strung from Virginia City to Placerville, California. It was so crudely strung, according to legend, that people jokingly compared the line with a sagging grapevine. No record can be found of this, but, in any case, grapevines were associated with telegraph lines somewhere along the line, for by the time of the Civil War a report "by grapevine telegraph" was common slang for a rumor. The idea behind the expression is probably not rumors sent over real telegraph lines, but the telegraphic speed with which rumor mongers can transmit canards with their own rude mouth-to-mouth telegraph system.

A "vintage year" has come to mean a year notable for anything. The phrase originated with and still mainly refers to the year in which a good vintage, "gathering," of grapes was made into an excellent wine.

GRASS. All the words in the sentence *Grass grows green* come from one source, the Teutonic *gro*, which in turn derives from the Aryan *ghra*, to grow. Our word *graze* also ultimately comes from this source. Grasses are worldwide in distribution and a listing of them would fill a large book. It has been noted that the grass family supports the temperate and tropical world, containing as it does wheat, corn, rice, rye, barley, oats and sugar cane. But most people think of lawns or meadows when they think of grass, as is witnessed by common American sayings such as "don't let the grass grow under your feet"—don't be lazy, be active and energetic. Such grass is probably one of the few plants that almost everyone can identify, though not the many varieties of it.

"A little classic of the poetic imagination," the *New York Times* once called the saying "getting down to grass roots," but just whose poetic imagination we don't know. In 1935, when the Republican party was seeking a broader base of support among voters, John Hamilton of Topeka, Kansas, used the words in describing the "new" G.O.P. No one has tracked the phrase back further in print, but one respected etymologist testified that he heard the expression in rural Ohio in about 1885. A term dear to politicians, it simply means to get down to basic facts or underlying principles, its appeal becoming more nostalgic as more concrete replaces grass. *Grass roots* itself, for basics, fundamentals, has been traced to 1932 when used, appropriately enough, to describe the candidacy of Oklahoma Governor William H. (Alfalfa Bill) Murray for the Democratic presidential nomination. It, too, probably stems from the western prairies.

The old story that the synonym *grass widow* for a divorcee derives from *veuve de grace*, a divorcee or widow by courtesy or grace of the Pope, has no basis in fact—for one thing "grace widow" is nowhere recorded in English. Just as unlikely is the theory that the words originated with the custom of British officers in India sending their wives on vacation to the cool grassy hills during intensely hot summers, where, separated from their husbands, they were humorously referred to as "grass widows." There is also a yarn that forty-niners in America "put their wives out to grass," boarding them with neighbors until they returned from prospecting. The most plausible explanation of this old English expression, which dates back to at least the early sixteenth century, is that it formerly meant an unmarried mother and just changed in meaning over the years. "Grass" probably referred to the grass in which the grass widow's child might have been begotten, outside of the traditional marriage bed, and "widow" to the woman's unmarried state. We find the same parallel in many languages, including our current slang "a roll in the hay"; the German *Strohwiteve,* straw widow; the Middle Low German *graswedeue,* an obsolete word for a woman with an illegitimate child; and in the Southern mountains idiom "weed woman" for a loose woman or prostitute. (See *Lawn.*)

GRASSHOPPER. The very appropriate name for this common insect is more colorful in other languages. The Italian name for the grasshopper is *cavalletta,* "little mare," while the Spanish call it *saltamontes,* "jump mountains." For some reason the Germans call it *die Heuschrecke,* "the terrible hay-thing." In Greek mythology the sound of the grasshopper is said to be the voice of the handsome Tithonus, who married Aurora, the goddess of dawn. Aurora asked Zeus to grant her husband immortality, which the great god did, but she neglected to ask Zeus to keep him forever young. Time passed and the handsome Tithonus fell victim to its ravages, while Aurora remained young and beautiful. She eventually took pity on the old doddering man and turned him into a grasshopper and locked him in a palace room. Tithonus has since been heard every evening at his palace window crying for his lost Aurora.

"Knee-high to a toad," first recorded in 1814, was the original of the Americanism "knee-high to a grasshopper," and "knee-high to a mosquito" as well as "knee-high to a frog" appeared before "knee-high to a grasshopper" came on the scene some 37 years later. But "knee-high to a grasshopper" has outlasted all the others, including the more recent "knee-high to a duck." It is generally used in comparisons, emphasizing youth, smallness or remoteness in time. There are some 120,000 varieties of grasshoppers, and to be literally knee-high, or tibia-high, to a grasshopper a person would have to range from one millimeter tall to little more than an inch tall. (See *Gull.*)

GREAT MAIDEN'S BLUSH. (See *Blushing Thigh of the Aroused Nymph.*)

GREEN BEAN. (See *Beans.*)

GREENGAGE PLUM. (See *Plum.*)

GREEN THUMB. Nobody, it seemed, knew why the Italian monk Fra Antonio could make plants grow so well in the cloister garden. But one day an elderly monk watching Fra Antonio observed that he had a green thumb on his right hand, which made him an excellent gardener—the green thumb, no doubt, colored by the plants he had been handling. This is a nice little story, but so far as we know the term "green thumb" doesn't go back to medieval times. In fact, it is first recorded in 1925 by Dean Middleton, a BBC broadcaster and gardening book author. It is probable that Middleton merely popularized the phrase, which many people remembered hearing in about 1910 and is probably a generation older. A variation on the term *green thumb* for an excellent gardener is "green fingers."

"Mr. Green Thumb" is a nickname for horticulturist Luther Burbank, who created hundreds of vegetables, fruit and flower varieties. He once said of his creations: "Can my thoughts be imagined when . . . I look upon these new forms of beauty on which other eyes have never gazed." (See *Burbank Potato.*)

GUANO. A rich, natural manure composed mostly of the excrement of seabirds found on small islands near the Peruvian coast, guano takes its name ultimately from the Quechua Indian *wanu*, meaning "dung," for fertilizer or fuel. Beds of guano on these rocky islands are sometimes as deep as 60 feet. The word *guano* has also come to mean any similar natural fertilizer, and in the southern United States also means commercial chemical fertilizer.

GULL. What is the gull doing in a gardening word book? Read on. Actually, gulls, comprising some 44 species that often live inland, far from any ocean, should not be called *sea*gulls. The gull, the only bird ever to have a monument erected to it, is intimately connected with American horticultural history. All gulls take their name from the Breton *gwylan* for the bird, which derives from the Breton *gwela*, "to weep," in reference to the bird's cry. The species prominent in American folklore is the California gull (*Larus californicus*). In 1848 an invasion of grasshoppers threatened to destroy all the crops of Mormon settlers near the Great Salt Lake; the people were saved from starvation only by the appearance of flocks of California gulls that devoured the grasshoppers after all other means had failed. The Sea Gull Monument on Temple

Square in Salt Lake City is dedicated to the species, "in grateful remembrance of the mercy of God to the Mormon pioneers." In a similar 1947 incident, black-headed gulls destroyed a plague of caterpillars in Scotland. (See *Boll Weevil*.)

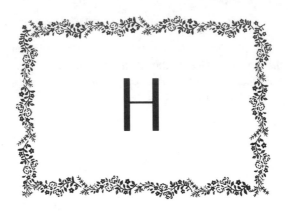

HABANERO. (See *Chili Pepper.*)

HARVEST. The harvest was so important in ancient times that the word *haerfest*, or *harvest*, became the Old English term for autumn as well as for the gathering in of crops. This usage prevailed well into the tenth century, when *harvest* began to be used exclusively to mean the gathering in of wheat (called "corn" in England) and finally crops in general. The German word for autumn is still *Herbst*, which is related to the English harvest. *Harvest* is cognate with the Latin *carpere*, to pick.

A number of English words have their roots in the harvest, words that most people would not expect to have a botanical heritage. In Roman times, for example, harvested grain was ground with a heavy roller called the *tribulum*. Being ground under and pressed out by this machine soon suggested the word *tribulation* to those who felt that they were under similar pressure.

The Anglo-Saxons had a harvest ceremony called the *threscan* in which people stamped on piles of dry wheat, separating the grain from the stalks. This action resembled the stamping of feet when people cleaned their shoes against the sills of wood or stone that marked the doorways of houses and soon the sill came to be called the "threshold" of a house.

Misappropriation of money or funds by an official trustee or fiduciary is called *defalcation*. This word has its roots in the Latin *falculus*, sickle, which yielded the verb *falcare*, to cut. The Latin *de*, down, plus *falcare*, means to cut down. Someone guilty of defalcation thus cuts down someone else's possessions as a farmer might cut down grain with a sickle when he harvests it.

The *after mowth*, which later came to be pronounced "aftermath," is the second or later mowing, the harvest of grass that springs up after the first hay mowing in early summer when the grass is best for hay.

This term was used as early as the fifteenth century and within a century *aftermath* was being applied figuratively to anything that results or follows from an event.

A confused mixture, a hodgepodge, or mixture is a "farrago." The word comes from the Latin *farrago* meaning a mixed harvest of feed grains. "Farraginous," heterogeneous or mixed, as in "A farraginous mixture of random ideas," comes from the same source. Both words were first recorded in England in the early seventeenth century.

According to one story, *calamus* was a principal crop of hay, straw or wheat in early Greece. When this crop failed for any reason, large scale suffering almost surely resulted and such disasters came to be called *calamitas* after the poor harvest. Unfortunately, this story and others similar to it are not accepted by many authorities, including the *Oxford English Dictionary*, which says *calamity* may derive from a lost Greek word, *calamis*, meaning injured or damaged. Others trace calamity to the Greek *klambos*, mutilated. No one really knows and the first story is possibly true. (See *Season*.)

HA-HA. Here is an exclamation that became a word that has one of the most peculiar derivations. A ha-ha is "an obstacle interrupting one's way sharply and disagreeably, a ditch behind an opening in a wall at the bottom of an alley or walk." It is used in English gardens as a boundary that doesn't interrupt the view from inside but can't be seen from the outside until you come very close to it—is in effect a sunken fence, the inner side of the ditch perpendicular and faced with stone, while the outer side is turfed and sloping. When these ditches or fosses were first used extensively in the seventeenth century, etymologists tell us, people out for a stroll in the country were frequently surprised to find a sudden and unperceived check to their walk. Their exclamations of "ha-ha!", "ah-hah!" or "Hah-hah!" in expressing their surprise became the name of the ditch or sunken fence.

HAW. The fruit of the Old World or English hawthorn (*Crataegus monogyna*), which can be red or yellow, is called "haw" or "hall." These names are also used for hawthorns themselves. In the language of flowers, hawthorn is the symbol of "good hope" because it is a spring flowering tree that shows winter is over. Commonly called the "thornapple" for its thorny trunks, which make impenetrable barriers, the hawthorn's lovely flowers were used to crown Athenian girls at weddings, and the Romans placed leaves of the hawthorn on the cradles of newborn infants to ward off evil spirits. In China, the fruit or haws of the Asiatic hawthorn is considered a delicacy.

HEARTS-A-BUSTIN'-WITH-LOVE. A lovely little-known Southern name for the burning bush (*Euonymus americanus*), hearts-a-bustin'-with-love has seedpods that burst open to reveal many scarlet seeds. It is also known as "strawberry bush," "swamp dogwood," "arrowwood" and "spindle bush."

HEDGE. The word *hedge*, in the form of *hegge*, is recorded in English as early as 785, referring to rows of bushes or trees, such as privet or hawthorn, planted in a line to form a boundary. In time the word *hedge* came to mean a "safeguard," and by the sixteenth century writers were using the word as a verb meaning to protect oneself with qualifications, to avoid committing oneself. Shakespeare was the first to use the word in this way, in *The Merry Wives of Windsor*.

HELIOTROPE. Many plant leaves and flowers turn toward the sun. The ancient Greeks noticed that the fragrant, vanilla-scented perennial flower *Heliotropium arborescens*, often called "cherry pie" today, did so, and called it the *heliotrope* from the Greek *heleos*, "sun," and *trepos*, "turning to go into it." Another fragrant flower sometimes called heliotrope, and also called "cherry pie" for its blossoms, is common valerian (*Valeriana officinalis*), probably named scientifically for the Roman emperor Valerian.

A Greek legend says the god Apollo loved the ocean nymph Clytie but abandoned her for her sister, and she died of sorrow. A remorseful Apollo changed the dead Clytie into a living flower that always turns toward the sun, but the legend does not mention the flower's name.

Today we also use the word *heliotrope* for any plant that bends toward light.

HELL. *Hell* is a colorful name for thick tangles of rhododendron or laurel so vast that people become lost in them. Their huge thickets are also called "laurel hells," and they are most common in mountain areas of the South, where this term seems to have been coined.

HEPATICA. These charming little wildflowers have three-lobed leaves that resemble the human liver. Noticing this, someone in medieval times named them from the Greek *hepatikos*, "of the liver." A member of the buttercup family, they are also called "liverleaf" and "liverwort." Some gardeners grow them in shadier parts of the flower garden.

HERBA SACRA. Vervain (*Verbena officinalis*) was the *herba sacra* or "divine weed" of the Romans, who believed that, among other things, it cured the bites of rabid animals, arrested the progress of snake bite, cured the plague and scrofula, reconciled enemies and warded off witches. The Romans so esteemed vervain that they held annual feasts called *Verbenalia* in its honor, and ambassadors in ancient times wore vervain as a badge of good faith.

HERB OF GRACE. Rue is called the "herb of grace" because it is the symbol of repentance due to its extreme bitterness. Shakespeare used the expression in *Richard II*, and there are many old records telling of the use of rue in ceremonies of exorcism.

HERCULES' CLUB. The club carried by the mythological strongman Hercules was hewn from a thick wild olive branch, but somehow *Aralia spinosa*, a small, spring-trunked ornamental tree of the ginseng family, came to be known as Hercules' club. The prickly plant, which also goes by the name of "angelica tree," "prickly ash" and "the devil's walking-stick," has a medicinal bark and root, and hedges of Hercules' club form a strong impenetrable barrier. Creating some confusion, however, is the fact that *Zanthoxylum clava-herculis*, commonly known as the "prickly ash" and the "toothache tree," is also called Hercules' club. (See *Apples*.)

HICKORY. *Pawcohiccora* was the name American Indians near Jamestown, Virginia, gave to the milky liquor they obtained from nuts of a tree that abounded in the area. Colonists called the milky liquor and nuts "hiccora" or hickory, abandoning the first part of the Indian word, and eventually applied *hickory* to the useful tree the nuts came from, which supplied them with a stony, tough wood good for many purposes. "Old Hickory" was the nickname of American President Andrew Jackson, a man acknowledged by all to be as "tough as hickory wood" in both his military and political campaigns.

HOLLY. The Romans used holly as a decoration in their wild festival of *Saturnalia* long before the early Christians in Rome adopted it for Christmas. Related to the word *holy*, *holly* derives ultimately from the Anglo-Saxon *holen* for the tree. There are some 400 species of holly trees and hundreds of named varieties.

HOLLYHOCK. The old favorite garden flower wasn't introduced to England by the crusaders and named after the Holy Land as legend has it. *Hollyhock* is a corruption of "holy hock," which the plant was first called. *Hock* is an old name for "mallow," and the plant probably became "holy" because it had been known as "Saint Cuthbert's cole" at one time. Saint Cuthbert, who lived in the seventh century and also has an eider duck named for him, was, of course, holy and had his retreat on Holy Island (the Isle of Farne) off the English coast as well. He lived in a hermit's cell on the island, where the mallow grew in marshes, and pilgrimages were made there as early as the ninth century.

HOLLYWOOD. The film capital of the world, laid out in 1887, is probably named for the California holly or toyon (*Heteromeles arbutifolia*), a large shrub that isn't a tree holly, but whose scarlet berries, borne from Christmas to Easter, suggest the holly and are much used for Christmas ornaments. Hollywood may, however, be the transferred place name of another Hollywood named for a tree holly, someplace where the holly is a native tree. There is no proof for the tale that the town was first called "Holywood" by its pious founders, the name corrupting to Hollywood as the town degenerated morally.

HOLY CLOVER. (See *Sainfoin.*)

HONEYDEW MELON. *Honeydew* is a popular shortening of "honeydew melon" (*Cucumis Melo inodorus*), a variety developed around 1915 and so named because of its sweetness. Honeydew can also either be the sweet material that exudes from the leaves of certain plants in hot weather or a sugary material secreted by aphids and other insects. In either case, it gets its name from its sweetness coupled with its dewlike appearance. Spenser wrote of it in *The Faerie Queene:*

> *Some framed faire lookes, glancing like evening lights,*
> *Others sweet words, dropping like honey dew.*

HONEYSUCKLE. This plant was named in error in ancient times, when it was thought erroneously that bees extracted honey from the plant. The name is applied to several other plants but mainly to the more than 180 species of woody vines and shrubs belonging to the *Lonicera* genus, named for sixteenth-century German botanist Adam Lonitzer.

HORSERADISH. There is apparently no truth to old tales that the fiery horseradish (*Cochlearia armoracia*) is so named because it was once used to cure horses of colds, or because it made a good seasoning for horse meat. *Horse* is used as an adjective before a number of plants to indicate a large, strong or coarse kind. Other examples include the "horse cucumber," "horse mint" and "horse plum." The horseradish is, of course, hotter than the ordinary radish, and has a much larger root and leaves than that vegetable.

Many plants *are* named after the horse because they were used to feed or train horses or because they resemble the animal. The "horse bean" is used as horse feed; "horse bane" was supposed to cure palsy in horses; the "horse-eye bean" was thought to resemble a horse's eye; and the pods of "horse vetch" are shaped like horseshoes.

The "horse chestnut," John Gerard says in his famous *Herball* (1597), bears its name because "people of the East countries do with the fruit thereof cure their horses of the cough . . . and such like diseases." But the horse-chestnut nut is big, too, and when a slip is cut off the tree "obliquely close to a joint, it presents a miniature of a horse's hock and foot, shoe and nails."

Incidentally, Samuel Pepys in his *Diary* mentions a "horse-radish ale," flavored with horseradish, which must have been hot indeed.

HOSACKIA. Few people know that New York's Rockefeller Center was once the site of the famous Elgin Gardens, one of the first botanic gardens in America. The Elgin Gardens were established by Dr. David Hosack (1769–1835) who subsequently deeded them to Columbia University, which became the landlord of Radio City. Hosack, a professor at Columbia, is remembered as the physician who attended Alexander Hamilton after his fatal duel with Aaron Burr. He served on the first faculty of Columbia's College of Physicians and Surgeons and helped found Bellevue Hospital, as well as founding and serving as first president of the now-defunct Rutgers Medical College. Hosack wrote a number of medical and botanical books, including a biography of Casper Wistar. *Hosackia,* a genus of more than 50 species of perennial herbs of the pea family, is named for him. Its most cultivated species is *Hosackia gracilis,* "witch's teeth," a rock garden plant about 12 inches high with pretty rose-pink flowers borne in small umbels.

HOTBED. *Hotbed,* a gardener's term for a glass-covered bed of soil heated by decaying manure or electrical cables in which seedlings are raised early in spring, has since the eighteenth century been used to mean a place favoring rapid growth of something disliked or unwanted. At that time one writer called theater "the devil's hotbed." The gardening term "hothouse," an artificially heated greenhouse for the cultivation of tender plants, also does double duty, meaning "overprotected, artificial or unnaturally delicate," as in "He grew up in a hothouse environment."

HOUSELEEK. An attractive succulent that often grows on the roofs of thatched cottages in England, the houseleek or "roof houseleek" (*Sempervivum tectorum*) was originally planted on house roofs because it was believed to ward off lightning, fever and evil spirits. The emperor Charlemagne decreed that each of his subjects must grow the houseleek on his roof. Wrote Thomas Hill in the early sixteenth century *Natural and Artificial Conclusions:* "If the houseleek or syngreen do grow on the housetop, the same house is never stricken with lightning . . ." The plant is also called "Jove's beard" and "Juniper's beard." It is no relation to the onionlike vegetable called a leek. (See *Leek*.)

HUCKLEBERRY. When the first American settlers noticed the wild huckleberry, they compared it to the English bilberry, and first called it a "hurtleberry" or "hirtleberry," from which its present name derives. Huckleberries were so little, plentiful and common that "a huckleberry" became early-nineteenth-century slang for "a small amount" or "a person of no consequence," both of these expressions probably inspiring Mark Twain to name his immortal hero Huckleberry Finn. The berry was also used in the colloquial phrase "as thick as huckleberries," meaning "very thick," and "to get the huckleberry" meant to be laughed at or ridiculed, a predecessor of sorts of the raspberry (razz) or Bronx cheer. "To be a huckleberry to someone's persimmon" meant, in nineteenth-century frontier vernacular, to be nothing in comparison with someone else.

The huckleberry, which is not a true berry but a drupe fruit, belongs to the *Gaylussacia* genus, named in honor of French chemist Joseph-Louis Gay-Lussac (1778–1850). One species of the genus, *Gaylussacia brachycera*, the wild box huckleberry, holds the world record as the plant covering the greatest area from a single clonal growth: a colony that began an estimated 13,000 years ago and covers an area of 100 acres was found in 1920 near the Juniata River in Pennsylvania.

HUMUS. The word *humus*, the dark organic material in soils familiar to all good gardeners, comes from *humus*, the Latin for "ground" or "soil." Less apparent is the derivation of the word *humble*, which also comes from *humus*, via the Latin adjective *humilis*, "on the ground," or "lowly."

HYACINTH. The hyacinth is named for the handsome youth Hyacinthus of Greek legend, loved by the gods Apollo and Zephyrus. When Hyacinthus favored Apollo, Zephyrus, the god of the winds, blew a quoit thrown by Apollo as he played with the young man, and it struck and killed Hyacinthus. From Hyacinthus' blood sprang a flower marked with the letters *AI*, meaning "alas." This "sanguine flower inscribed with woe" of Milton was called the hyacinth, and its name came to be attached to the hyacinth we know today, even though the flower in question was probably a small purple iris with markings similar to the letters *AI*.

HYBRID. The offspring of a tame sow and a wild boar was called a *hybrida* by the Romans, and this Latin word came into English in the early seventeenth century to describe such animal offspring. *Hybrid* wasn't applied to plants until almost 200 years later. A hybrid is, strictly speaking, the offspring of a cross-fertilization between parents differing in one or more genes, and a great many, possibly the majority of cultivated plants, have resulted from either natural or artificial hybridization.

HYDRANGEA. The Greeks of old thought this plant's seed capsule looked like a "water cup" and named it from the Greek *hydr*, "water" and *angos*, "seed" or "capsule." Long one of the most commonly grown shrubs in America, the hydrangea consists of some 80 species, usually with large, showy pink, white or blue blooms. Pink-flowered specimens can be changed to blue by burying bits of iron or aluminum in the soil.

IMP. A graft or plant shoot was called an *impian* by the Anglo Saxons. Shortened to *imp,* this word came to mean offspring or a child. At first *imp* meant any child, but the word is now almost always applied to a bright mischievous child, like the child named in this book's dedication. (See *Graft.*)

IMPERATRICIS ROSES. (See *Lapageria.*)

INOCULATE. *Inoculate* derives from the Latin *inoculare,* "to graft by budding," "implant." The word was first recorded in this sense at the beginning of the fifteenth century and wasn't used in the medical sense of inoculation, to plant a disease agent or antigen in a person to stimulate disease resistance, until 1722. (See *Graft.*)

INSANE ROOT. Banquo says to the witches in Shakespeare's *Macbeth:*

> *Were such things here as we do speak about?*
> *Or have we eaten on the insane root*
> *That takes the reason prisoner?*

Either henbane (*Hyoscyamus niger*) or poison hemlock (*Conium maculatum*), the hemlock that killed Socrates, is the insane root that was supposed to deprive anyone who ingested it of his senses. No one is sure which plant is the villain.

INSEMINATE. Our word for "to impregnate," *inseminate* first meant to sow or implant seed into the ground. It was first recorded in English in this sense in 1623, and is derived from the Latin *seminare,* "to sow" or "to plant."

IODINE. This common antiseptic is, oddly enough, named after the violet. *Iodine* derives from the Greek word *iodes,* "like a violet," which in turn comes from the Greek *ion,* "violet." The iodine we commonly use is rust-colored, but when heated it forms a dense violet-colored vapor.

IRIS. Iris, the Greek goddess of the rainbow, gives her name to the colored portion of the eye called the iris and to the iris flower, which has varieties in all the colors of the rainbow. The orris is an iris species (*Iris germanica florentina*) with a very fragrant rootstock. *Orrisroot* is a powder used in perfume and other products that is made from the roots of the orris.

IVY. The ivy of the Greeks bore golden berries and was probably not the plant we call ivy today. Thought to prevent drunkenness, it was also given as a wreath to the winners of athletic contests. *Hedera helix,* the common English Ivy so widely cultivated in temperate climates, is regarded as a symbol of everlasting life because it remains green in all seasons.

The colleges originally referred to as the "Ivy League" are Harvard, Yale, Princeton, Dartmouth, Cornell, Brown, Columbia and the University of Pennsylvania. They are all "old-line institutions" with thick-vined, aged ivy covering their walls. The designation was at first applied specifically to their football teams. Sportswriter Caswell Adams coined the term in the mid-1930s, at a time when Fordham University's football team was among the best in the East. A fellow journalist compared Columbia and Princeton to Fordham and Mr. Adams replied, "Oh, they're just Ivy League," recalling later that he said this "with complete humorous disparagement in mind."

JACKFRUIT. The enormous edible fruit of this tropical tree in the mulberry family often weighs up to 70 pounds. The fruit of *Artocarpus integrifolia* is perhaps the largest tree fruit known, far larger than that of its close relative the breadfruit tree (made famous by Captain Bly). (See *Blighia sapida*.)

JACK-IN-THE-PULPIT. The upright spadix of *Arisaema triphyllum* is arched over by a green or striped spathe, which to early American settlers made it look like a man (Jack) standing in a pulpit, resulting in the common name *jack-in-the-pulpit*. In parts of Great Britain it is known, perhaps more aptly, as "priest's pintle," the latter word meaning "penis."

JACOB'S LADDER. The biblical Jacob (Gen. 28:12) saw a ladder reaching to heaven in a dream. Sometime in the early eighteenth century an imaginative English gardener saw a resemblance to this biblical ladder in the paired leaflets (one above the other) of *Polemonium caeruleum*, a blue–flowered member of the phlox family, and dubbed it "Jacob's ladder."

JACOB'S ROD. The asphodel of the ancients so frequently encountered in poetry is *Asphodeline lutea*, a perennial yellow-flowered herb that for reasons unclear is sometimes called "Jacob's rod." In ancient times the dead were thought to sustain themselves on the roots of asphodels so the flowers were often planted on graves. Interestingly, the much-better-known daffodil bears a name that is a corruption of *asphodel*. (See *Daffodil*.)

JASMINE. The jasmine vine with its fragrant flowers is native to Eurasia and Africa and was introduced into England in 1548. It takes its name from the Persian *yāsmin* for the plant. According to a legend recounted in the rare eighteenth-century book *The Sentiment of Flowers:*

> *This beautiful plant grew in Hampton Court garden [England] at the end of the seventeenth century; but, being lost there, was known only in Europe in the garden of the Grand Duke of Tuscany, at Pisa. From a jealous and selfish anxiety that he should continue to be the sole possessor of a plant so charming and rare, he [the Duke] strictly charged his gardener not to give a single sprig, or even a flower, to any person. The gardener might have been faithful if he had not loved; but being attached to a fair, though portionless damsel, he presented her with a bouquet on her birthday; and in order to render it more acceptable, ornamented it with a sprig of jasmine. The young maiden, to preserve the freshness of this pretty stranger, placed it in the earth, where it remained green until the return of spring, when it budded forth and was covered with flowers. She had profited by her lover's lessons, and now cultivated her highly-prized jasmine with care, for which she was amply rewarded by its rapid growth. The poverty of the lovers had been a bar to their union; now, however, she had amassed a little fortune by the sale of the cuttings from the plant which love had given her, and bestowed it, with her hand, upon the gardener of her heart. The young girls of Tuscany, in remembrance of this adventure, always deck themselves on their wedding day, with a nosegay of jasmine; and they have a proverb, that "she who is worthy to wear a nosegay of jasmine is as good as a fortune to her husband."*

JEQUIRITY BEANS. The scarlet seeds of the jequirity (*Abrus precatorius*), or "Indian licorice" as it is also called, are often used for making rosaries to sell to tourists in tropical climes. Deadly rosaries they are indeed, for jequirity beans are extremely poisonous.

JERUSALEM ARTICHOKE. The Jerusalem artichoke does not come from Jerusalem, is not an artichoke and does not taste anything like an artichoke. The starchy underground tuber (a good potato substitute) was called *girasole articiocco,* "sunflower artichoke," by northern Italians because it is a member of the sunflower family and resembles a sunflower in leaf and stem. To Englishmen hearing the word, *girasole* sounded like *Jerusalem,* and they mistakenly translated the name as "Jerusalem artichoke." (See *Artichoke; Jerusalem Cherry.*)

JERUSALEM CHERRY. Despite its common name, this plant (*Solanum pseudo-capsicum*) is not a cherry and does not grow in or near Jerusalem. A popular greenhouse plant grown for its scarlet, globe-shaped fruits, it is native to Brazil. The name "Jerusalem" is attached to a number of plants not native to the area, including the "Jerusalem cowslip," "Jerusalem oak," "Jerusalem sage," "Jerusalem thorn" and "Jerusalem artichoke." It seems that, except in the last case, *Jerusalem* was bestowed simply as a vague name for a distant foreign place the plant was thought to hail from. (See *Jerusalem Artichoke*.)

JIMSONWEED. "Jamestown-weed" was the original name of jimson-weed, or the thorn apple, a plant that can be poisonous when its foliage is wilted. *Datura stramonium* was named Jamestown-weed because it was first noticed growing in America near Jamestown, Virginia; in fact, soldiers among the insurgents in Bacon's Rebellion of 1675 are said to have eaten this weed when defeated and driven into the wilderness, many almost dying of it. Over the years *Jamestown-weed* was slurred to *jimsonweed* in pronunciation, which by the nineteenth century was the common name for the plant.

JIZZYWITCH. (See *Katydid*.)

JOB'S-TEARS. In the Philippines, the annual grass Job's-tears (*Coix lacryma-jobi*) is the source of the nourishing cereal food *adlay*. The tear-shaped seeds are found on the white or dirty-white female flower clusters, and inside of each tear are the edible kernels that have long been used in the Far East for grain. Grown in western nations as an ornamental, the 3- to 6-foot-high, sword-shaped grass is named *Job's-tears* after the biblical Job, whose great misfortunes were borne with proverbial patience, but who must have shed many tears.

JOE-PYE WEED. A weed, according to an old saying, is only an uncultivated flower. Sometimes it's even more. The joe-pye weed, for instance, may have been named for an Indian medicine man because he "cured typhus fever with it, by copious perspiration." The tall, common plant with clusters of pinkish flowers might well be the only weed ever dedicated to a real person. Records from 1787 prove the existence of a Joseph Pye, or Shawquaathquat, who was possibly a descendant of the original Salem, Massachusetts, healer, but the colorful Joe Pye has not yet been unequivocally identified.

JONATHAN APPLE. The Jonathan apple is named after Jonathan Hasbrouck, an American judge who died in 1846. Fifth in order of commercial importance in America, it is a late fall ripening apple that is bright red and often yellow striped. The Jonathan, grown mainly in the Northwest, is one of many apple varieties named to recognize their growers or other notables. The Gravenstein, Grimes Golden, McCoom and Stayman are a few others that come to mind. (See *Apple.*)

JONQUIL. We no longer pronounce the name of this pretty flower (*Narcissus jonquilla*) the way it was originally intended. "Junkwill" is the proper pronunciation if we consider the word's Latin ancestor *juncus,* meaning "rush," named for its long and rushlike leaves. But in the nineteenth century *jonquil* began to be pronounced "John–quill," which certainly sounds much better to the English or American ear. (See *Daffodil.*)

JOVE'S BEARD. (See *Houseleek.*)

JOY O' THE MOUNTAIN. This colorful name is given to trailing arbutus in the mountains of the South. Trailing arbutus (of the *Epigaea* genus) is probably the most fragrant of all wildflowers. This evergreen plant is difficult to cultivate in home gardens, but thrives in the wild.

JUDAS TREE. An old Greek tradition has it that after betraying Christ, Judas hanged himself from what is popularly called the "Judas tree" (*Cercis siliquastrum*), a leguminous tree of southern Europe that flowers before its leaves appear. Other legends claim that Judas hanged himself from a fig tree or an elder tree. In fact, the mushroomlike growths occurring on the back of the elder are called "Judas's ears."

JUNIPERBERRY. The berries of several junipers were used by American Indians for food and for the aromatic oil obtained from certain species. Probably the most famous of the juniperberries is that of the common juniper (*Juniperus communis*), which has been used for centuries to flavor gin and game dishes like wild boar. However the western juniper, or yellow cedar, a plant that can be a shrub or a tree 60 feet high, bears oval, blue-black berries that are widely known to be edible and high in vitamin C; they were, in fact, used in the past to prevent scurvy. Junipers are unusual in that the female flowers are made up of little scales that become fleshy, grow together and form a sweet, berrylike fruit. In certain species the small, pearl-shaped berries take three years to ripen.

JUNIPER'S BEARD. (See *Houseleek.*)

KALE. *Kale* is both twentieth-century American slang for money and a vegetable. The word derives from the Middle English *cale*, a variant of *cole*, for "cabbage." American settlers called this primitive member of the cabbage family "colewarts." Money is possibly called kale because banknotes are green like the vegetable.

KATYDID. John Bartram, America's first great botanist, first recorded *katydid* (or a word similar to it) in 1751 as the name of the large, green arboreal insect of the locust family known scientifically as *Microcentrum rhombifolium*. The word is of imitative origin; the chattering noise the long-horned grasshopper makes sounds like "Katy did! Katy did!" The katydid is sometimes called the "jizzywitch" in the South.

KENILWORTH IVY. Sir Walter Scott's novel *Kenilworth* (1821) takes its name from the English town of Kenilworth and its castle in Warwickshire. The climbing vine *Cymbalaria muralis* may have been named "Kenilworth ivy" in honor of the town, or possibly for Scott's novel, in which case it would be the only plant so named. It is also called "Coliseum ivy," "Aaron's beard" and "climbing sailor."

KIDNEY BEAN. The "haricot bean" takes its name from the French *haricot*, which derives from the Nahuatl Indian *ayacotl* for the bean. It is better known as the "kidney bean" because its shape resembles a kidney, this name dating back at least a century.

KING DEVIL WEEDS. In the late nineteenth century several European yellow-flowered hawkweeds of the genus *Hieracium* were inadvertently introduced into northeastern North America. Although very showy and handsome, they became such troublesome weeds that they were rechristened "king devil weeds." The two worst species of them, orange hawkweed and mouse-eared hawkweed, are regarded by experts as among the fifty worst garden weeds.

KING FRUIT. (See *Durian.*)

KISSING-COMFIT. This name is given to the candied root of the sea holly (*Eryngium maritimum*) that is used as a lozenge to sweeten the breath. This handsome rock garden plant is of the carrot family. There are more than 100 species of the *Eryngium* genus, most of them bluish in color and thriving in a moist, rich soil.

KIWI. New Zealanders are called "Kiwis" after their native kiwi bird. Their name, in turn, was given to the kiwi fruit, also known as the "Chinese gooseberry" (though it is not a true gooseberry) and *yangtao*, which has been cultivated in China for centuries. The Australians, however, did greatly improve the fruit with their Hayward variety, developed by nurseryman Hayward Wright, creating a world market for the large, luscious kiwi fruit that tastes of strawberry, lime and a touch of banana. Incidentally, the kiwi bird takes its name from the Maori *kiwi-kiwi* for the bird, which is also called an "apteryx" (after its scientific name, *Apteryx australis*) in crossword puzzles.

KUDZU. (See *Beautiful Nuisance.*)

KUMQUAT. The Chinese dialect *gamgwat*, "gold citrus fruit," is the origin of the name of this shrub of the genus *Fortunella*, which yields golden citrus fruits, with sweet rinds and an acid pulp, that are used chiefly for preserves. (See *Fortunella.*)

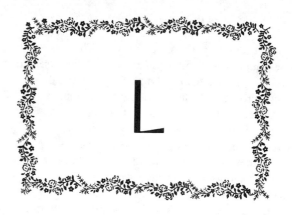

LADYBUG. Originally a lady was just "the head farmer's wife," derived from the Old English *hlæfdigue*, "a woman who kneads bread." But by the seventeenth century a lady was "a woman of pleasure" who made her bread in other ways—and you didn't call a lady "a lady" then. In ladybug the *lady* is associated with the original meaning, as the beneficial garden insect is named in honor of "Our Lady," the Virgin Mary. Not named in the erroneous belief that all ladybugs are female, these brightly colored beetles of the family Coccinellidae feed on aphids and other destructive garden pests, and should fly away home if warned that their houses are on fire and their children will burn—too many children believe this for it not to be true. In England the beetles are called "ladybirds," due to a British aversion to the word *bug*, which is associated there with buggery or sodomy. Some American Southerners favor the British word, which is why Claudia Taylor Johnson, our former First Lady, bore this familiar Southern nickname. In Germany ladybugs are considered such good luck that replicas of them are used as Christmas tree decorations. (See *Beetle*.)

LADY'S MANTLE. According to one old gardening manual, lady's mantle (*Alchemilla*) is a flowering plant whose large, serrated, and many-lobed leaves resemble "the mantle of Our Lady." The delicate lady fern (*Athyrium filix–femina*) does not refer to the Virgin Mary as is commonly believed, but takes its name from the legend that possession of its seeds could render a woman invisible. The *Alchemilla* genus of plants derives its name from the Arabic word *alkemlych*, which refers to its ancient use by Arabian alchemists who, for some reason unknown to science, collected dew from their leaves for medicines and potions.

LAELIA. A candidate English botanist John Lindley may have had in mind when he named the *Laelia* genus was a vestal virgin of that name, in allusion to the delicacy of these flowers. The vestal virgins, six in number, were daughters of the best Roman families, trained in youth to serve the goddess of hearth and home in her temple in Rome, where they prepared sacrifices and tended a perpetual sacred fire. Their vows included obedience and chastity, and after serving Vesta for 30 years they were allowed to leave the temple and marry, which they seldom did. The virgins were influential and even had the power to pardon criminals, but if they broke the vows of chastity the penalty was a public funeral followed by burial while they were still alive. Needless to say, most remained vestal virgins.

But these tropical American orchids, comprising about 35 species and prized for their showy flowers, may be named for Gaius Laelius, a Roman statesman and general who died about 165 B.C., or for his son Gaius Laelius, a Roman consul nicknamed "Sapiens, or the wise." Both father and son were soldiers and excellent orators; the father was the best friend of Scipio Africanus Major, and the son was known for his friendship with Scipio Africanus Minor. The younger Laelius was also a close friend of Cicero, who wrote that he and Scipio used to like to go on holidays to the seaside, "where they became incredibly childish and used to collect shells and pebbles on the beach." Sapiens probably had a hand in writing the plays of Terence, and his vast knowledge was admired throughout Rome.

LAPAGERIA. French Empress Josephine, Napoleon Bonaparte's first wife, was born Marie-Josèphe-Rose Tascher de la Pagerie. A Creole of French extraction, she had been married to Viscount Alexandre de Beauharnais, who was guillotined after the French Revolution. Josephine escaped the blade herself only because of powerful friendships. The empress brought Napoleon much happiness, including two children from her first marriage—Eugène, later viceroy of Italy, and Hortense, who became Queen of Holland—but her numerous love affairs caused him to consider divorce several times. On one occasion, it is said, the glass cracked over the picture of Josephine that Napoleon always carried. The emperor turned pale and declared, "My wife is either sick or unfaithful," and his latter premonition proved true. Napoleon finally did have his marriage with Josephine annulled in 1810 on the grounds of sterility and married Marie Louise of Austria.

Josephine lived out her life in retirement at her private retreat, La Malmaison, near Paris, and the emperor continued to consult her on important matters as he always valued her keen mind. She died in 1814 at the age of 51. An avid botanist as well as an ardent lover (her garden at Malmaison contained the greatest collection of roses in the world), the beautiful Josephine has the monotypic genus *Lapageria*, containing only one species, named for her. This showy Chilean vine of the lily family is among the most attractive climbing vines. Its flowers are rose-colored, trumpet-shaped and, unlike Josephine Lapageria, usually solitary. The French government is now renovating Josephine's rose garden at Malmaison; most of the roses in it bear the species name *Imperatricis* after the empress.

LARKSPUR. The lark is noted among birds for its long, straight rear claw or spur. Since the spur-shaped flower called "larkspur" resembles the claw, it took the bird's name. Larkspurs, of which there are some 200 species, are just as commonly called "delphinium." (Scc *Delphinium*.)

LARVA. One meaning of *larva* in Latin is "a mask." Linnaeus first used the term as the scientific (yet poetic) word for a caterpillar because, as one writer put it, "such a creature wears a disguise, the future insect is not recognizable in the present grub, its form a 'mask' which will one day be cast off."

LASTHENIA. Among the students who attended the philosopher Plato's lectures at the Academy in Athens was a woman named Lasthenia, who sneaked in by disguising herself as a man. Little more is known of her, but centuries later her story inspired the Italian naturalist Cassini to name the plant genus *Lasthenia* for this persistent pupil. The small genus contains only three species, two native to California and the other to Chile. Tender annual herbs, the showy flowers are yellow, on long, often nodding, stalks.

LAURELS. Laurels or bay leaves have symbolized victory since the winners at the Pythian games in ancient Greece were crowned with wreaths of laurel. The usage is still common in such expressions as "win the laurels," "to rest on one's laurels" and "to look to one's laurels."

The Greeks did not give wreaths of leaves from the bay laurel tree to Olympic game victors, who were awarded wreaths made of wild olives. (Winners of the Nemean games were given wreaths of green parsley, and Isthmian game victors received wreaths of dry parsley or green pine needles.) In any case, "winning the laurels" or "crowned with bays" has come to mean a reward of victory. Laurel is a symbol of peace, too, and of excellence in all the arts. The bay laurel tree (*Laurus nobilis*) grows up to 60 feet in Greece but is most popular in the United States grown in tubs and kept pruned to a desired shape.

In Greek legend Apollo fell in love with and tried to seize Daphne, the daughter of a river, and at her own request she was turned into a bay laurel tree, which became sacred to Apollo. The god ordered that laurel be awarded as the prize for poets and victors. This led to the belief that laurel leaves communicated the spirit of poetry (the ancients put laurel leaves under their pillows to acquire poetic inspiration while they slept) and to the tradition of laurel symbolizing excellence in literature. The first laureates were university graduates in poetry and rhetoric who were presented laurel wreaths and called "doctors laureate" and "bachelors laureate."

Before the title "poet laureate" was conferred upon any poet in England there were a number of court poets: King Henry I (1068–1135) had a Versificator Regis (King's versifier) named Wale. Ben Jonson was granted a pension by James I in 1616 and was a poet laureate in the modern sense, and Chaucer, Skelton, and Spenser had been called laureates before him; but it wasn't until John Dryden was appointed poet laureate by Charles II in 1668 that the position became official. Today the poet laureate is chosen by the sovereign from a list of names submitted by the prime minister when the position falls vacant. Appointments are for life, and by custom the poet laureate composes odes for the New Year and for the sovereign's birthday. Since 1987 the United States, too, has had a poet laureate. (See *Bay Laurel Tree.*)

LAVENDER. In medieval Latin the name for the lavender plant is *livenendula,* from *livere,* "to make bluish." However, the plant was long used for scenting linen, and it was associated with *lavare,* "to wash," which was probably combined with the former name to give it the name *lavender.*

The aromatic lavender plant (*Lavandula spica*) has been cultivated for centuries. Its many uses include its addition to bath water and the use of its branches to beat just-washed clothes. In allusion to this, "lay out in lavender" first meant to give someone a physical beating, to knock someone down or unconscious. In time, however, the phrase came to mean to give someone a verbal beating or to chastise, as in "If I debate him, I'll lay him out in lavender."

LAWN. The lawns we maniacally manicure today take their name from the obsolete word *laund,* which is a borrowing from Old French *lande,* "moor," and was first recorded in the early fourteenth century. *Laund* meant merely "a woodland glade" and its first definition in 1548 described "a place void of trees." *Lawn* is simply a variant spelling of that word, but it isn't until the early eighteenth century that we find *lawn* used to mean a plot of grass kept closely mown, usually by gardeners with scythes or by grazing animals. However, Chinese emperors had lawns as far back as 157 B.C., and the Maya and Aztec royalty made lawns, as did the ancient Romans, who used sheep to maintain them. Writing in the *Smithsonian* magazine (June 1991), Richard Wolkomir remarks on our passion for lawns despite the backbreaking and mind-bending troubles they cause us:

> *Grassophilia has deep roots. A former Smithsonian ecologist, John H. Falk, once studied people's terrain preferences. He found that, whether they live in the United States, Africa or India, the great majority prefer grassy savannas over all other landscapes, even if they've never seen a savanna. He had theorized that grasslands were the early humans' preferred habitat, and that preference seems to be genetically ingrained in Man today.*

The word *lawnmower* isn't recorded until 1875, while *lawn sprinkler* made its appearance 19 years later. However, the lawn mower was invented around 1830 by English textile plant foreman Edwin Budding, who patterned his invention on factory machinery used at the time to shear the nap of woven cloth to a uniform height. Close to a century passed before retired American army colonel Edwin George in 1919 invented the first motorized lawn mower, using the gasoline engine from the family washing machine for his invention. Then came the riding lawn mower upon which all adults look ridiculous, though some people take them seriously—especially the forty or so people who compete in the Twelve-mile Riding Lawn Mower Race held in Twelve–Mile, Indiana, on July 4th of every year, the winner usually breaking 45 minutes. Such people might be called "mownomaniacs." *Mownomaniac* is a new word for someone obsessed with caring for, and especially mowing, his or her lawn. Mownomaniacs have been around for about a century and a half now (there were few lawns as we know them before 1850), but the word was apparently coined by author Richard Wolkomir in his article quoted above. (See *Grass*.)

LAWSONIA. Linnaeus probably named *Lawsonia inermis*, the mignonette tree and the source of the dye henna, for John Lawson, a traveler in North Carolina said to have been burned alive by Indians. Lawson came to America from England in 1700 and traveled about 1,000 miles through unexplored territory, recording his observations of native flora and fauna in his *A New Voyage to Carolina* (1709). A founder of what is now Bath and New Bern, North Carolina, he was appointed Carolina's surveyor general in 1708 but was captured and put to death in the Tuscarora uprising three years later. It is not known whether Linnaeus related "red men" and death by fire to the red dyestuff taken from the eastern tree's leaves, though the connection is not impossible. However, at least one authority claims that the Swedish botanist named the plant for a Dr. Isaac Lawson, a Scottish botanical traveler who published an account of a voyage to Carolina in 1709.

LEAVES. (See *Oak*.)

LEEK. The national emblem of Wales takes its name from the Old English *leac*, for this member of the onion family. But the plant is native to central Asia, and many peoples have had different names for it. Nero, for example, was nicknamed "Porrophagus" (leek) because he ate so many leeks, believing that they improved his singing voice. The leek has only recently been identified as the fabled storgehenge that the Greeks considered a love potion. Saint David, patron saint of the Welsh, is said to have commanded his countrymen to wear a leek in their caps to distinguish themselves from their Saxon foes. "To eat the leek" is an English term meaning "to eat your own words."

LEMON. Lemons were probably initially grown in the Middle East, for *lemon* is first recorded as the Persian and Arabic word *limun*, which became the Old French *limon*. *Limon* passed into English when the French exported the fruit there, and by the mid-seventeenth century the fruit was being called the lemon.

Lemon, meaning something defective or inferior, derives from the sour taste of a lemon and is apparently an Americanism dating back to the turn of the century, as is lemonade (a drink the British call "lemon squash").

"Lemon sole" has nothing to do with lemons, except that lemon juice might be squeezed on the fish before eating it. The term is an established redundancy; when we say "lemon sole," we are saying "sole, sole," because the lemon part is a corruption of the French *limande*, "sole." (The sole was so named because its shape was thought to resemble the sole of the foot.)

In the seventeenth century the French called a cut piece of lemon peel added to a drink to give it flavor a "zest," a term that may have derived ultimately from the Latin *scistees*, "cut," but can only be traced back as far as the French *zest* meaning "the skin that divides the inside of a walnut," and "orange or lemon peel." *Zest* passed into English and came to mean anything agreeable to piquant in flavor and, finally, hearty enjoyment or gusto, as in "zest for life."

LESPEDEZA. Japanese or bush clover, sometimes called the "hoop-coop plant" but widely known as "lespedeza," is believed to have been brought to America in the early nineteenth century with a cargo of tea that was unloaded at Charleston or Savannah. The plant became an escape that was first identified at Monticello, Georgia, in 1846. This initial collected specimen is now preserved at Harvard's Gray Herbarium. A member of the pea family, lespedeza has become a very important crop, not only for hay and forage but for improving poor soils. It has been shown that corn and cotton crops can be increased from 10 to 30 percent by turning under a crop of lespedeza previous to their plantings.

The genus *Lespedeza* contains 125 species, of which Japanese clover (*Lespedeza striata*) is only one. Many of these species are native to America, and it was to them that the French botanist François André Michaux referred when he named the genus in 1803. *Lespedeza* was named in honor of V. M. de Zespedez, Spanish governor of Florida in 1795, whose name Michaux misread as *Lespedez*. The Japanese clover species of *Lespedeza* is supplemented by a number of others, including a Korean species (*Lespedeza stipulacea*) better adapted to northern areas, and *Lespedeza cuneata*, a perennial. In fact, the chief belt of production in this country is planted to Korean lespedeza. Only in America is the group used extensively for agricultural purposes, although lespedeza plants and shrubs are cultivated as ornamentals throughout the world.

LETTUCE. Lettuce probably takes its name from a form of the Latin *lactuca*, "milky juice," in reference to its milky fluids when it goes to seed. The Roman gourmet Apicius watered the lettuce in his garden with mead every evening so that it would taste like "green cheese cakes" when he picked it in the mornings. (See *Bibb Lettuce*.)

LETTUCE BIRD. A popular name for the goldfinch (*Astraglinus tistis tistis*) is "lettuce bird" because lettuce seed is among its favorite foods. A good way to draw this attractive yellow bird to the garden is to let some lettuce plants bolt, blossom and bear seed. Because of its musical abilities the goldfinch is also called the "wild canary."

LIGHT ON A BUSH. An old name for the bayberry (*Myrica pennsylvanica*, often called *Myrica caroliniensis*), "light on a bush" originated among American pioneers in the seventeenth century. You can make your own candles from these berries. In fact, in colonial times September 15th was known as "Bayberry Day," a time, according to one old account, "when old and young sallied forth with pail and basket, each eager to secure his share in the gift of nature." For although the bayberry isn't good to eat, beyond the use of its root bark as a medicine, the "candleberry," as it was also called, was considered to be "light on a bush," its small, aromatic, gray berries yielding wax for candles.

LILACS. There are white, blue, pink, red and purple lilacs, in many variations, but the word *lilac* means "blue." *Lilac* began as the Persian word *nilak,* "bluish," for the flower; it passed into Arabic as *laylak,* became *lilac* in Spanish and came into English in the same form. The flower's most famous use in American literature is in Walt Whitman's elegy on the death of Lincoln, "When Lilacs Last in the Door Yard Bloom'd," first published in 1865.

LILY. There are hundreds of lily species and varieties of many colors, but the flower is usually associated in English with the color white, as indicated by the expressions "lily white" (very white) and "the lily truth" (the pure truth).

Everybody knows that the expression "to gild the lily" is wrong and hackneyed as well, but it is still used to describe something superfluous and usually comes to mind first as "gild the lily" even to most of those fastidious few who correctly say "paint the lily." The fault lies, of course, in confusing what Shakespeare really wrote in *King John,* when the Earl of Salisbury makes his protest against the king's second coronation:

> *Therefore, to be possessed with double pomp,*
> *To guard a title that was rich before,*
> *To gild refined gold, to paint the lily,*
> *To throw a perfume on the violet,*
> *To smooth the ice, or add another hue*
> *Unto the rainbow, or with taper-light*
> *To seek the beauteous eye of heaven to garnish*
> *Is wasteful, and ridiculous excess.*

Since "to gild" comes first in the pertinent line and it is just as ridiculous to gild a beautiful flower as to paint one, the phrase was often remembered as "to gild the lily." Perhaps the old phrase to "gild the pill" also helped create the confusion. It meant to coat a bitter pill with sugar and gave *gild* wide currency as a word meaning to cover over, to paint (*not* to paint with gold necessarily). As for King John, he was far from "ridiculous." The unscrupulous king, who had unjustly seized the throne after the death of his brother Richard in 1199, wanted a second coronation because like any shrewd politician he knew that the awe-inspiring spectacle would win him more support among his subjects.

The liver, the largest gland in our bodies, was once believed to be the seat of passion. It was also thought that the liver of a coward contained no blood, not as much "as you find in the foot of a flea," since a coward wasn't capable of passionate violence. Hence the expression "white-livered" and "lily-livered" for cowardly. Shakespeare wrote of cowards with "livers white as milk" and later came lusty expressions like "a lily-livered, action-taking knave" based in part on a pale white flower.

Scholars believe that the bibical "lilies of the field" were actually red anemones.

LIMA BEANS. Named for Lima, Peru, by early European explorers who found them there, tender lima beans are often called "butter beans" in the United States. The succotash made from them (and corn) derives from the Narraganset Indian *msiquatash*, literally meaning "fragments."

LIME. Limes have been cultivated for thousands of years and take their name ultimately from the Persian *liman* for the fruit. As far back as 1795, lime juice was issued in the British navy as an antisorbutic, to protect against scurvy. After about 50 years, Americans and Australians began calling English ships and sailors "lime-juicers," and later "limeys." The term "limey" was eventually applied to all Englishmen, and today the designation and the story behind it are widely known. Originally a contemptuous term and an international slur, *limey* is now considered a rather affectionate designation.

LINCOLN BUG. Anti-Lincoln feelings died hard in the American South after the Civil War, as the name of this little bug demonstrates. Even as late as 1901, this foul-smelling destructive insect, also known as the "harlequin cabbage bug," was commonly called the "Lincoln bug" or "Abe Lincoln bug" in Georgia and other southern states. But then Lincoln himself was called "The Ape," "Seward's Ape" and much worse. Happily, *Abe Lincoln bug* is seldom heard today; unfortunately, no giant species of a plant honors this giant of a man.

LINDEN TREE. (See *Linnaean System*.)

LINNAEA. Named for its flowers in pairs at the end of slender, upright stalks, the twinflower was scientifically called "Linnaea" by Linnaeus himself. The great botanist apparently chose this humble genus, consisting of two species, out of modesty, describing the twinflower as "a plant of Lapland, lowly, insignificant, disregarded, flowering but a brief space—from Linnaeus who resembles it." (See *Linnaean System*.)

LINNAEAN SYSTEM. Linnaeus, most famous of all naturalists, not only dubbed us *Homo sapiens*, but chose the names for far more things than any other person in history, classifying literally thousands of plants, animals and minerals. Carl von Linné—*Carolus Linnaeus* is the Latin form of his name—showed an early love of flowers that earned him the nickname "the little botanist" when he was only eight years old. The son of a Lutheran minister who cultivated his interest in nature, he became an assistant professor of botany at Uppsala University, then studied medicine in Holland, where in 1735 he wrote his *Systema Naturae*. Linnaeus was only 28 at the time, and his masterpiece was followed by *Genera Plantarum* in 1737 and *Species Plantarum* 16 years later. These books marked the beginning of taxonomy, a system of scientific nomenclature that would be elaborated on in more than 180 works.

The Linnaean system the naturalist developed divided the kingdoms of animals, vegetables and minerals into classes, orders, genera, species and varieties, according to various characteristics. It adopted binomial nomenclature, giving two Latin names—genus and species—to each organism. In this two-name system all closely related species bear the same genus name, e.g., *Felis* (Latin for "cat") *leo* is the lion, and *Felis tigris* is the tiger. The system Linnaeus invented provided scientists with an exact tool for the identification of organisms and is standard today, although many old popular names for plants and animals linger on. Further, it recognized all organisms as part of a grand scheme, a unique concept at the time. Linnaeus continued to practice medicine and headed the botany department at Uppsala, naming thousands of plants that he collected and classifying hundreds more that professional and amateur botanists sent him from all over the world. He named some plants for their characteristics alone, some for prominent people and others for their discoverers, but in every case the designation he applied remains intact. Linnaeus was 71 when he died at Uppsala in the cathedral in which he is buried. His garden at the university, where he grew many of his plants, is still visited by pilgrims from all over the world.

The handsome linden, or lime or bass wood tree (*Tilia*), makes excellent shade plantings, but is also of interest here because of its connection to the greatest of botanists. The story is best told by the American botanist L. H. Bailey in his classic but unfortunately out-of-print treatise *How Plants Get Their Names* (1933):

Carl Linnaeus was born in southern Sweden in 1707. His father, Nils Ingermarsson, took a Latin surname when he began his school and university career to become a scholar and eventually a churchman, adapting it from a certain famous lind, the lime-tree or linden. It was custom in those days for persons to choose a Latin name or to Latinize the patronymic. The family of the cousins of Linnaeus chose the name Tiliander from the same tree, *Tilia* being Latin for the lindens. Another branch of the family became Lindelius. The particular lind tree, it is written, "had acquired a sanctity amongst the neighbours, who firmly believed that ill-fortune surely befell those who took even a twig from the grand and stately tree." Even the fallen twigs were dangerous to remove, and they were heaped about the base of the tree. It had perished by 1823.

To the people the name Linnaeus was rendered Linné, the accent preserving the essential pronunciation of the word. Linnaeus, for his part, wrote that "Linnaeus or Linné are the same to me; one is Latin, the other Swedish." His great Latin books were written naturally under the name Linnaeus, and thus is he mostly known to naturalists. In later life a patent of nobility was granted him and he was then Carl von Linne. We find him signing himself as Carolus Linnaeus Smolander, his province or "nation" being Smoland and Carolus being the Latin form of Carl or Charles; also as Carl Linnaeus, Carl Linne, and Carl v. Linne. This much is by way of preface to explain the forms in which the name of this marvellous man appear.

(See *Linnaea*.)

LOBELIA. Linnaeus named more than 1,000 plants, including hundreds that have come to be household words. Many of these names honored people. Indeed, by labeling species as well as genera, the Swedish botanist sometimes commended two people with the same plant. This is the case with *Lobelia dortmanna*, the water lobelia. Linnaeus named the plant's family Lobeliaceae and its genus *Lobelia* after Matthias de l'Obel, or Lobel (1538–1616), a distinguished Flemish botanist and physician who lived a century before Linnaeus. But he called *Lobelia dortmanna*, one of its 300 species, after an obscure druggist named Dortmann whom he met while studying in Holland. Nothing is known about Dortmann, but Lobel had been both physician and botanist to England's learned King James I. A native of Lille, Lobel tried to classify plants according to their leaf formations long before Linnaeus and wrote several of the earliest botanical books. The Lobeliaceae family commemorating him contains 24 genera and more than 700 species, some of which are trees and shrubs, but its *Lobelia* genus consists of about 300 species of annual or perennial herbs widely grown for their mainly blue, red, yellow or white flowers. The species *Lobelia inflata* was used by American Indians like tobacco and has a tobaccolike odor; it was also employed as the base for a popular home remedy, though it is considered poisonous in quantity. *Lobelia siphilitica,* the blue syphilis, was used by the Indians to treat syphilis; it was even introduced into Europe centuries ago for this purpose.

LOBLOLLY PINE. *Lob* in British dialect means "to boil" and *lolly* means a "soup" or "stew." *Loblolly* is first recorded in 1597 in Gerard's *Herball* as a thick gruel or stew. It is probably an onomatopoeic word, one writer noting that "it describes a semi-liquid state" and "itself shakes in pronunciation like jelly, which is most nearly what it describes." In America settlers began to apply *loblolly* to muddy places and called *Pinus taeda,* a long-leaved Southern pine, the "loblolly pine" because it commonly grew in such swampy areas, and because it is commonly used to make paper pulp where the wood cooked into a thick "stew" in one stage of its transformation. The name is first attested in about 1730. There is also a loblolly bay (*Gorclonia lasianthus*), and in nineteenth-century America any mudhole was humorously called a loblolly.

LOCOWEED. Various plants of the genera *Astragalus* and *Oxytropis* native to the Southwestern United States are called "locoweed" (from the Spanish *loco,* "insane") because when eaten by horses, cattle and sheep they cause irregular behavior, including weakness, impaired vision and paralysis. In the West a person who acts crazy is sometimes said to be "locoed," that is, crazed as if from eating locoweed.

LOGANBERRY. California Judge James Harvey Logan (1841–1928), who had been a Missouri schoolteacher before working his way west as the driver of an ox team, developed the loganberry in his experimental home orchard at Santa Cruz. Logan, the former Santa Cruz district attorney, was serving on the superior court bench in 1881 when he raised the new berry from seed, breeding several generations of plants to do so. Though a respected amateur horticulturist, he never adequately explained how the berry was developed. One account claims that the loganberry originated "from self-grown seeds of the Aughinbaugh [a wild blackberry], the other parent supposed to be a raspberry of the Red

Antwerp type.'' Other experts believe that it is a variety of the western dewberry, or a hybrid of that species, crossed with the red raspberry. The dispute may never be resolved, but experiments in England have produced a plant similar to the loganberry by crossing certain blackberries and red raspberries. In any case, there is no doubt that the purplish-red loganberry is shaped like a blackberry, colored like a raspberry and combines the flavor of both—or that it was first grown by Judge Logan and named for him. Its scientific name is *Rubus loganobaccus,* and the trailing blackberrylike plant is grown commercially in large quantities, especially in California, Oregon, Washington and other places that have fairly mild winters.

LONG ROW TO HOE. Rows in American home gardens today, usually 15 feet or so in length, can't compare to the long rows of corn, beans and other crops on early American farms and in early American gardens. These rows, which often stretched out of sight, had to be weeded by hand and approaching one hoe in hand was dispiriting to say the least. The expression ''a long row to hoe'' was probably well-established for any time-consuming, tedious task many years before Davy Crockett first recorded it in 1835. It is still heard in a day when mechanized equipment has replaced hoes on farms, perhaps because of the great national passion for vegetable gardening—according to a recent poll, more than 100 million Americans grow vegetables.

LOOSESTRIFE. One incredulous author wrote that the Romans put loosestrife flowers under the yokes of oxen to keep the animals from fighting with each other. Many people believed similar myths about loosestrife (*Lysimachia*) in ancient times. The plant's name is derived from the Greek *lusi,* from *luein,* ''to loose,'' and *mache,* ''strife.'' Loosestrife is said to have been named *lusimachon* by the Greeks from the name of one of Alexander the Great's generals, who supposedly discovered it.

LOTUS-EATER. A daydreamer, someone who leads an indolent, dreamy life of easy indifference to the busy world, is sometimes called a ''lotus-eater.'' In the *Odyssey* Homer writes that the Lotus-eaters or Lotophagi were a people who lived on the northeast African coast and ate what later Greek writers identified as the fruit of the shrub *Zizyphus lotus,* which made them dream all day, forget their friends and family and lose all desire of ever returning to their homes. Any traveler who ate the sweet fruit or drank a wine made from it wanted only to live in Lotus-Land. Lotus, however, is a name given to many plants. The Chinese make a lotus seed dessert called *pinh tan lian tye* reputed to be an aphrodisiac, and the delicious sugarberry or hackberry (*Celtis australis*) grown in the northern United States has been called the fabled food of the lotus-eaters. Even jujubes, long a favorite candy, were once thought to be flavored with lotus fruit.

LOVE APPLE. Why tomatoes were dubbed "love apples" is a matter of some dispute. A cornfield weed that was first cultivated by the Mayans and called the *xtomatl,* the tomato was named the *pomi del peru* and *mala peruviane* when Cortes brought it to Europe from America. That they hailed from exotic climes and were a scarlet shapely fruit undoubtedly helped, but the designation "love apple" owes just as much to semantics as sexuality. All Spaniards at that time were called Moors, and one story has it that an Italian gentleman told a visiting Frenchman that the tomatoes he had been served were *pomi dei Moro* (Moor's apples), which to his guest sounded like *pommes d'amour,* or "apples of love." However, another version claims that "apples of love" derives in a similar roundabout way from the Italian *pomo d'oro,* "golden apple," and a third tale confides that courtly Sir Walter Raleigh presented a tomato to Queen Elizabeth, coyly advising her that it was "an apple of love." In any case, the tomato quickly gained a reputation as a wicked aphrodisiac and, justly or not, it has held this distinction ever since. In Germany the tomato's common name is still *liebesapfel,* or "love apple," and the expression "hot tomato" for a sexy woman is common in many languages. (See *Tomato.*)

LOVE-LIES-BLEEDING. (See *Amaranth.*)

LYCORIS. Mark Antony is mainly remembered for his fatal romantic entanglement with Cleopatra, so it is often forgotten that he led a riotous life while a youth, having had four wives—Fadia, Antonia, Fulvia and Octavia—before he committed suicide for his Egyptian queen. One of his outside interests was Lycoris, a Roman actress who became his mistress. Centuries later an English botanist named the six lovely, fragrant flowers of the *Lycoris* genus after this beautiful woman. The amaryllislike *Lycoris* grow from a bulb and are lilac-pink or pink, with the flower cluster a loose umbel. Native to China, Japan and Central Asia, they are generally grown in greenhouses in the United States and England.

MACADAMIA TREE. Not a true nut but a seed, the macadamia nut grows on the macadamia tree, so named for Dr. John Macadam, secretary of the Victoria Philosophical Institute in the late nineteenth century. Also known as the "Queensland nut," it is native to Australia but grown in Hawaii, California and Florida as well. (By the way, Dr. Macadam is not the engineer—inventor John Loudan McAdam after whom macadam roads are named.)

THE MAGIC FLOWER. No one knows the name of the magic flower of Greek myth that Flora gave to the goddess Juno to make her pregnant. According to the myth, Juno was jealous about the birth of the goddess Athena without a mother and was determined to have a child by herself. (Athena's father, Zeus, had swallowed his pregnant wife Metis, because he feared she would give birth to a son stronger than himself; Athena sprang from the head of her father when the god Prometheus split his head open with an axe.) Flora's magic flower enabled Juno to have a child without a father, and she gave birth to Mars, who was a god of vegetation sacred to farmers, and later became the god of war. (See *Garden Gods*.)

MAGNOLIA. Like Matthias de l'Obel, for whom Linnaeus named the lobelia, Pierre Magnol (1638–1715) was a French physician and botanist who published a book that classified plants. A professor of botany at Montpelier University, Magnol had somehow obtained an education despite the fact that he had been denied entrance to French colleges because he was a Protestant. Through his teachings in botany his name became celebrated, and Linnaeus honored him by naming the beautiful magnolia tree after him. The magnolia had been introduced into Europe from Japan in about 1709, but it wasn't named for the professor until after his death. Linnaeus owed much to Magnol, who originated the system of family

classification of plants, and picked a large plant family to honor him—
Magnoliaceae, which includes ten genera and more than 100 species.

Native to South Asia and the southeastern United States, Magnoliaceae
contains some of the most beautiful garden shrubs and trees. Its lemon-
scented fragrance was once used by the Chinese to season rice. The
tree's huge showy flowers that grow up to ten inches across are commonly white, yellow, rose or purple, and appear with or before the first
leaves of spring. The magnolia grows to heights of up to 100 feet. The
leaves of one species, the Southern umbrella tree, are often two feet
long, and the attractive leaves of *Magnolia grandiflora* are used to fashion funeral wreaths. Mississippi calls itself "The Magnolia State" because of its abundance of magnolias. Houston, Texas, is called the
"Magnolia City" for the same reason.

MAGUEY. (See *Century Plant.*)

MAHERNIA. One of the most unusual of eponymous words, the plant
genus *Mahernia* is an anagram of *Hermannia,* another genus to which
it is closely allied. Linnaeus must have been in a playful mood when he
coined the word from *Hermannia,* which he had also named. In any
event, it is probably the only botanical anagram that is an eponymous
word. Linnaeus named *Hermannia* for Paul Hermann (1645–1695), a
professor of botany at the University of Leyden, who is surely the only
man to be honored by two genera in this odd way. *Hermannia* is a large
genus that includes some 80 species of ornamental evergreen shrubs with
yellow flowers. The genus *Mahernia* includes about 30 species of pretty
greenhouse herbs or small undershrubs of which the yellow, fragrant
honey-bell (*Mahernia verticillata*) is most notable. Both genera are native
to South Africa.

MALPIGHIAN. His name is not well known outside scientific textbooks, but the Italian physiologist Marcello Malpighi (1628–1694) deserves recognition as the founder of microscopic anatomy and for his
pioneer work in the study of plant and animal tissues. As the discoverer
of the movement of blood through the capillaries, he completed the
theory of circulation proposed by William Harvey. Malpighi, a professor
of medicine at Messina University, later served as private physician to
Pope Innocent XII. He was one of the first people to use the microscope
to study animal and vegetable tissues and the first to attempt an anatomi-
cal description of the brain using this instrument. He is commemorated
by several words, including the Malpighiaceae family of ornamental tropical plants. The technical terms "Malpighian corpuscle," "Malpighian

layer," "Malpighian tube" and "Malpighian tuft" recall his important work in anatomy.

MANDARIN ORANGE. This fruit takes its name from either the flowing orange robes of Chinese mandarin officials or the superiority implied in the title "mandarin." The word is first recorded in an 1816 botanical treatise. (See *Tangerine*.)

MANDRAKE. The "magical" mandrake (which, incidentally, gave its name to the old comic book hero Mandrake the Magician) was at first known as the "mandragora," because its root uncannily resembles a miniature man, and it was as magical and awe-inspiring as a dragon. But in medieval times the word for dragon was *drake,* so the plant became known as "mandrake." Like ginseng roots, and even peony roots to some extent, the roots of the mandrake were associated with many fantastic beliefs. One claimed they were an aphrodisiac (especially if shaped like a woman), another held that they caused barrenness in women and yet another claimed they could cure any illness. Many people believed that mandrake would shriek like a human being when uprooted and that a person should not touch the roots when pulling them up. To avoid the latter, a dog was actually tied to the plant to tug it out of the ground!

Mandrake's curious history can be traced back to biblical times, where the herb is mentioned in both Genesis and the Song of Solomon. In Gen. 30:14–17 we find that Rachel has allowed her husband to spend the night with her own sister for a few highly prized mandrakes. The Song of Solomon shows that the roots were in great demand among men, too. The "Phallus of the field" (as the ancient Egyptians called mandrake) is really a member of the potato family. It is popularly believed to be shaped like both the male and female figure, and in fact one ancient writer describes how medieval con men preyed on this belief:

> *Imposters carve upon these plants while yet green the male and female forms, inserting millet or barley seeds in such parts as they desire the likeness of human hair to grow on; then, digging a hole in the ground, they place the said plants therein, covering them with sand till such time as the little seeds have stricken root, which, it is said, would be perfectly effected within twenty days at furthest. After that, disinterring the plants, these imposters, with a sharp cutting knife, so dexterously carve, pare, and slip the little filaments of the seeds as to make them resemble the hair which grows upon the various parts of the human body.*

Dudaim, which comes from a Hebrew word meaning "pleasures of love," has been another name applied to the mandrake, and the Greeks often called Aphrodite, their goddess of love, "she of the mandrakes" or *Mandragoritis.* The Greeks also thought that Circe possessed the plant. A passage in the *Odyssey* tells of this infamous witch adding the "love apples" to her nefarious brews. Interestingly, the famed physician Dioscorides, who served as an army surgeon under Nero, used mandrake wine as a sedative in surgical operations and noted in his *De materia medica* that it was used in love potions. But centuries later Celsius went much further, stating that after eating a little mandrake root even female elephants "are seized with so irresistible a desire for love as to run eagerly, in every direction, in quest of the male."

In ancient times, the mandrake served both as a fertility and virility symbol. A woman who wore a male specimen around her neck was guaranteed to become pregnant by her favorite lover, and after having worn the root to lure a man into bed, women wore it again in childbirth to ease the pains of labor. The dark-leaved, purple-flowered plant with its little yellow fruits was also highly touted as a tonic. So well known was "the half-man root" that Saint Hildegard of Bingen wrote in the twelfth century, "In mandragora the influence of the devil is more present than in other herbs; consequently man is stimulated by it according to his desires, whether they be good or bad." Three centuries later Machiavelli was much more enthusiastic about the love herb in his comedy *La mandragola.* "You must know," he wrote, "that nothing is so sure to make women conceive, as a draught composed of Mandragora. This is a fact which I have verified upon four occasions, and had it not been for the virtues of this plant, the Queen of France, as well as many noble ladies of that kingdom, would have proved barren."

Diverse medieval superstitions about mandrake became ingrained in the public mind and reinforced its reputation as a magic plant. Shakespeare recounts one such belief in *Romeo and Juliet* (act 4, scene 3) when Juliet says, "And shrieks like mandrakes' torn out of the earth,— that living mortals hearing them run mad," because it was "common knowledge" at the time that the mandrake shrieked when pulled from the ground, and anyone hearing its cry went mad. To gather the love-apple plant a man had to blow on a horn to drown out the shriek while pulling, or employ an animal to do the job. "Therefore they did tye some dogge or other living beast unto the roote thereof with a corde," one herbalist explained, "and in the mean tyme stuffed their own ears for fear of the terrible shriek and cry of the mandrake. In whych cry it doth not only dye itself but the feare thereof killeth the dogge."

Another superstition that enhanced the mandrake's reputation was the belief that it sprang up from under the gallows where criminals, especially rapists, ejaculated sperm or urinated at the instant they died. No such beliefs linger today, but mandrake is still widely used as a love stimulant, even in the form of a modern drug called *Mandragorine*. The roots themselves are sold all over the world, particularly in Italy and Greece, as remedies against impotence and infertility, and U.S. mail-order sales remain high. In the United States the May apple (*Podophyllum peltatum*) is sometimes called mandrake, but the true species is *Mandragora officinarum* of southern Europe, also known as "the devil's apple." Both of these species can be poisonous, so collectors should beware. In any case, it's highly unlikely that you'll find a mandrake with phallus and testicles clearly shown, or a "female mandrake" showing the ovaries. More likely your specimen will simply have thick tuberous roots divided into two leglike branches. As for its effects . . . well, "potatoes are cheaper."

MANGETOT. (See *Pea.*)

MANGO. One of the most important of tropical fruits, mango varieties number in the hundreds. Some of the notable dessert mangoes are the *Alphonse* of Bombay, the *Ferdandin* of Goa and the *Kimayuddin* of South India. The delectable fruit, whose name derives from the Portuguese *manga*, is grown in the American South, but these varieties can't be compared to tropical ones in taste. One Indian poet described mangoes as "sealed jars of paradisical honey"; the Buddha was given a grove of them so that he could sit in the shade and meditate; and a Hindu god, Subramanya, renounced the world because he couldn't obtain a mango he desired. The mango isn't a difficult fruit to eat once you get the hang of cutting the pulp away from its large central seed, but it might be better to eat it naked in a bathtub to avoid the explosion of juice that is common to novices.

The nutritious mango tastes something like a peach, but the comparison is wholly inadequate. An attractive bright yellow and red fruit, it hangs like a pendulum from its long stem. A building in Angkor that dates to A.D. 961 bears the following quotation under one of its most beautiful female figures: "Drawn by the flower of its glory to the fruit of the beauty of the mango tree of her body . . . the eye of man could nevermore tear itself away."

MANURE. The French word *manovrer*, from the Latin *manu operare*, "to do work by hand," meant "to cultivate land." This verb became *manouren* in French and in about 1400 the English borrowed the term.

They used *manouren* to mean "to cultivate," and in time developed the noun *manure* from it to describe the animal dung used to help fertilize the land.

MARIGOLD. The W. Atlee Burpee Co. lobbied to make the marigold America's national flower and offered a $10,000 prize to anyone who could grow a pure white marigold variety, but neither endeavor came to fruition. Although the French and African marigolds usually grown here are not French or African at all, but Mexican natives, the marigold does not take its name from the genus generally grown in American gardens. There are several genera whose flowers are called marigold; the chief ones are *Tagetes,* which includes among its 30 species the misnamed French and African marigolds, and *Calendula,* a genus that counts the popular "pot marigold" among its 20 species. The pot marigold was found in the Holy Land by the early Crusaders and brought back to Europe, where it was probably named after the Virgin Mary and the color gold, being called "Mary's gold" or "Marygold" before it became *marigold*. Linnaeus gave the pot marigold its scientific designation, *Calendula officinalis,* but he merely used a name that had been given to the plant centuries before. The herbalist Gerard remarks that the name *Calendula* was bestowed upon the plant because it supposedly bloomed regularly "in the calends" or first days of almost every month (*calends* mean the first of the Roman month). The pot marigold was once used as a poultice for wounds and is still grown as a flavoring for soups and other dishes. *Calendula officinalis* differs from the so-called French and African species (*Tagetes*) mainly because its leaves are not strong-smelling. But the flowers of the *Tagetes* genus, also herbs, do resemble the pot marigold, so early American settlers gave them the same name. *Tagetes* possibly honors the Etruscan god Tages, though this is not certain. All flowers of the genus are native from North Mexico to the Argentine, which does make the marigold an ideal candidate for the U.S. national flower.

Flowers in other genera also called "marigolds" include the European corn marigold (*Chrysanthemum segetum*), which when dried is often used as hay; the "marsh marigold" (*Caltha palustris*); the "cape marigold" (*Dimorphotheca*), which is native to Africa; and the "fig marigold" (*Mesembryanthemum*), whose 2,000 species are also found mainly in South Africa. The much-cultivated "ice plant," whose leaves are sometimes used like spinach, is a species of the last group.

MARJORAM. Marjoram is any of several mints, including "sweet marjoram" and "pot marjoram." The old saying "as a pig loves marjoram'' (that is, not at all) is still heard occasionally. *Marjoram* is an alteration of the Latin *amaracus* for the herb. Oil from sweet marjoram is used in perfumes, and its leaves are used as a cooking seasoning.

MARMALADE. Though made today of oranges and lemons, the conserve called marmalade takes its name from the Latin *milimelum* or "honey apple," which was some variety of apple grafted on quince stock. The Latin for "honey apple" became the Portuguese word for "quince," and the first marmalades recorded, in the early sixteenth century, were made of quinces and brought to England from Portugal. But over the centuries there have been plum, cherry, apple and even date marmalades as well. "Natural marmalade" is the fruit of the marmalade tree (*Lucuma mammosa*).

MARROW. *Marrow* is a British term that is sometimes used in America. It means "a long, green squash," and has its origins in the use of *marrow* as the term for the pulp of a fruit, which dates back to at least the tenth century. Squash was often called "marrow-squash" in eighteenth-century America.

MCINTOSH. Like many fruit varieties, the McIntosh apple was discovered accidentally. It is named after John McIntosh, a Canadian farmer from Ontario, who found the late red apple in 1796 while clearing woodland in Dunclas County and was so impressed by it that he began to cultivate the variety. Today the "Early McIntosh," one of the best early red apples, bears the same name, as does the "Sweet McIntosh," regarded by many as the sweetest of all red varieties. The original McIntosh is still grown; however, it is a late type with whitish-yellow flesh and a superb though slightly acidic taste. McIntosh account for about 10 percent of apples grown in the United States, but they constitute about 75 percent of the New England harvest and 50 percent of the New York State crop. Most connoisseurs rate them superior in taste to the Red and Golden Delicious apples that have become the dominant American varieties.

METHUSALEH TREE. (See *Bristlecone Pine*.)

MEXICAN JUMPING BEAN. These are seeds of plants of the Mexican genera *Sebastiania* and *Sapium* of the spurge family. What causes the seed or "bean" to "jump" are the movements of a moth larva inside it. The seeds will jump more if put in a hot place.

MICAH ROOD'S APPLE. This apple has streaks of red running through its white flesh. The tale begins on a spring day in 1693 when a jewelry peddler visited old Micah Rood's farm in Franklin, Pennsylvania. Shortly after, the peddler was found murdered under an apple tree in Rood's orchard, but his jewelry was never recovered. Rood wasn't convicted of the crime. According to legend, though, all the apples harvested from the tree that autumn had streaks of blood inside. Rood died of fright after seeing them, and the "damned" spots or streaks were called "Micah Rood's curse" from that day on. When recounting this story, don't ruin it by quibbling that apples with red streaks running through the flesh were common before Rood's time, that they are simply "sports," or mutations like the famous Golden Delicious variety and many others. There seems to be no record of a farmer named Micah Rood, but two peddlers were murdered around that time.

MIDSUMMER MEN. The orpine (*Sedum telephium*), also known as "live-forever," is called "midsummer men" because it used to be potted and hung in the house to tell young women if their sweethearts were true. The plant's leaves supposedly bent to the right if they were faithful, to the left if they were untrue. The plant is a perennial with reddish-purple flowers.

MIMOSA. *Mimosa* comes from the Greek word meaning "to mimic," in allusion to the collapse of the leaves in some species of this tree, which was once thought to be a mimicking of the motions of animals. The mimosa's reaction to shock or cloudy weather is one of the strangest cases of physiological response among plants: Its leaflets fold up face-to-face at the slightest irritation, and its leaves collapse entirely if the shock is sufficient.

MIMULUS. These showy flowers were once thought to resemble a monkey's face and were thus named from the Greek *mimo*, "face." Other names for them are the "monkey flower" and the "cardinal monkey flower." Experts are at a loss to explain why the flower mysteriously lost its perfume toward the end of the nineteenth century. One species, *Mimulus moschatus*, is called "monkey musk," but it actually has no smell at all.

MINNIEBUSH. Often planted in rock gardens, this small shrub of the heath family is so named not because it's a little bush, as some people believe, but because it honors the Scottish surgeon and botanist Archibald Menzies (1754–1842).

MINT. *Mint* is derived from the name of the Greek nymph Minthe, who was transformed into the herb by Proserpine, the jealous wife of the underworld god Pluto. Wild mint (*Mentha sativa*) has been chewed since early times and is often regarded as an aphrodisiac. Aristotle forbade the chewing of mint by Alexander the Great's soldiers because he felt it aroused them erotically and eliminated their desire to fight, disposing them to make love, not war. According to early writers, mint leaves left potential lovers in mint condition, "stirring up the mind and taste to a greedy desire." There are many varieties of the plant, including the pungent peppermint used in making crème de menthe and cordials. Fresh mint has been highly regarded as a sauce for lamb, just as mint jelly is today. The versatile mints flavor many drinks, including juleps and tea, as well as candies and chewing gum. In days past, mint tea was made strong: One pint of boiling water was left standing for one minute and then poured over one ounce of the leaves.

MIRACLE FRUIT. When chewed together, the berrylike fruits of the African shrub *Synsepalum dulcificum* and *Thaumatococcus daniellii* make sour substances taste sweet. For this reason they are called the "miracle fruit," "miracle berry," "miraculous fruit" and "serendipity berry." Another African shrub, *Dioscoreophyllum cumminsii* goes by the same names for the same reason.

MISTLETOE. Kissing under the mistletoe might not seem so romantic to those who know one possible origin of this word. According to some authorities, *mistletoe* derives from the Old English word *mistiltan; tan* means "twig" and *mistil* means "dung." It seems that in olden times people thought mistletoe twigs sprang from bird droppings. Another theory is that *mistil* means "bird-lime" and refers to a sticky substance used to catch birds that was made by boiling mistletoe twigs. Mistletoe, long known to be poisonous, was used in connection with human sacrifices by the Druids, which is why the early Christian church forbade its use in church decoration. Kissing under the mistletoe is an English custom dating back to the early seventeenth century. Few people know that each kiss requires the plucking of a berry from the mistletoe and that the kissing is finished when the last berry is picked. The berries should not be eaten. They are poisonous.

MOLY. According to Homer, the Greek god Hermes gave the mythical herb moly to Ulysses as an antidote against the sorceries of Circe. A number of plants bear the name *moly* today, but none has been identified as the moly of legend.

MORNING GLORY. Because the morning glory only opens its flowers in the morning, it has been used as a synonym for a person who begins something brilliantly but does not fulfill his or her promise. The expression dates back almost a century in American sports. The honeysuckle (*Ipomoea purpurea*) takes it genus name from the Greek for "worm" and "similar," in allusion to its twining habit.

MOTHER-IN-LAW PLANT. A common name for *Dieffenbachia seguine,* which itself honors nineteenth-century German botanist J. F. Dieffenbach. *Dieffenbachia* is called the "mother-in-law plant" and "dumbcane" because an irritating enzyme in the leaves of this houseplant causes swelling of the tongue and temporary speechlessness should they be chewed. But no one should wish Dieffenbachia poisoning on a mother-in-law or anybody else; it is a dangerous, painful condition requiring prompt medical care.

MOURNING TREE. Once cut, the cypress never grows again, which probably led to its being dedicated to Pluto, the king of the infernal regions in Roman mythology. The tree often referred to as the "mourning tree" is the beautiful *Cupressus funebris,* which was often planted in cemeteries along the Mediterranean. Its wood was used to make coffins. (See *Cypress.*)

MULBERRY. An Asian legend recounted in Ovid's *Metamorphoses* tells how mulberries became red. Pyramus, a Babylonian youth, loved Thisbe, the girl next door, and when their parents forbade them to marry, they exchanged their vows through an opening in the wall between their two houses. Thisbe agreed to meet her lover at the foot of a white mulberry tree near the tomb of Ninus outside the city walls. But on reaching their trysting place she was frightened by a lion and dropped her veil when she fled deep into a cave. The lion, its mouth red from another kill, ripped the veil, covering it with blood, and when Pyramus arrived and found the bloody veil, he thought that Thisbe had been killed and devoured by the beast. Throwing himself on his sword, he committed suicide just as Thisbe emerged from the cave. Distraught at the sight of her dying lover, Thisbe, too, fell upon his sword and committed suicide, the blood of young love mingling and flowing to the roots of the white mulberry, which thereafter bore only red fruit.

Legend also has it that the mulberry takes its botanical name, *Morus,* from the Greek *morus,* meaning "a fool." This has no connection with the Pyramus myth, according to the *Hortus Anglicus,* but is related to the fact that it "can't be fooled," that the tree "is reputed to be the wisest of all flowers as it never buds till the cold weather is past and gone." As for the word *mulberry* itself, which should properly be *morberry,* it more prosaically derives from the Latin *morus,* which became *mure* in French. The English called the berry the "mureberry" at first, but this was difficult to pronounce (too many *r*'s) and was eventually corrupted to mulberry in everyday speech.

Far from being an unknown fruit, as it is today, the mulberry was much celebrated in literature. Considered a harbinger of spring ("Whensoever you see the Mulberie begin to spring—you may be sure winter is at an ende"), the tree became part of ancient song and story. In the *Seven Champions,* Eglantine, daughter of the King of Thessaly, was transformed into a mulberry tree. Shakespeare mentions mulberries in both *Venus and Adonis* and *A Midsummer Night's Dream,* the latter play making the Pyramus and Thisbe myth the subject of a brief scene that is a travesty of the beautiful legend. And no one knows when children began playing the perennial English-American game where they hold hands and sing: "Here we go round the mulberry bush, / the mulberry bush, the mulberry bush. Here we go round the mulberry bush / On a cold and frosty morning."

It's even said that Ludovico Sforza, patron of Leonardo da Vinci and one of the most powerful and unscrupulous princes of the Renaissance, called himself *Il Moro* after the mulberry, because he prided himself on his prudence, which he felt equaled the mulberry tree's caution in blooming each spring. Sforza could just as well have been called *Il Moro* because he was as swarthy as a Moor, but fortunately the mulberry is well known enough without him.

There has always been a Mulberry Gardens in London, and America had Mulberry streets and Mulberry corners as far back as colonial days. Here, in addition to the white and black mulberries imported from Europe, we have our native red mulberry, *Morus rubra,* which has not only been eaten out of hand and used in recipes for syrups, wines, jams, tarts and other desserts but has been considered an important food for poultry and pigs in the South. So ubiquitous is the red mulberry in America that it was often used as a synonym for "raspberries" in colonial times. Longfellow wrote of mulberry trees in one of his poems, and well into the twentieth century ripe mulberries ready to be picked were a common sight just a few yards from main streets in cities. Many writers after Longfellow praised mulberries, including D. H. Lawrence. In fact, Lawrence liked to take off his clothes and climb into mulberry trees to meditate. Probably the best proof of the berry's popularity is the fact that it was chosen as the code name for the engineering feat of installing prefabricated harbors off the coast of Normandy prior to the landing there by Allied forces in World War II. "Operation Mulberry" made the supply of Allied forces far more efficient, and hastened the end of the Second World War.

Much has been written about international *tulipomania* but almost none of our history books mentions our American "mulberry mania" of the 1830s. This was a craze for planting the Philippine white mulberry variety *Morus multicaulis* ("many stemmed") with the expectation of making great profits in the silk industry. The leaves of these trees, used by the Chinese in sericulture and even tried by the British under James I, were said to be superior to all others for silkworm feeding, and millions of them were planted in the "multicaulis fever" that ensued. Although Ben Franklin had tried to establish a silk industry in Philadelphia, the fever really began in Connecticut, where the seven Cheney brothers founded America's first silk mill at South Manchester in 1838 after having experimented with silk culture for five years. One year, from 300 mulberry trees laid horizontally in the ground, there sprang 3,700 shoots, or enough to feed 6,000 silkworms. This meant bushels of cocoons and yards of much-wanted silk. Many farmers followed the Cheneys' example, and across America books and articles were published about raising mulberry trees. Silk societies were formed and bounties offered. Prices escalated crazily. In 1838 two-and-a-half-foot cuttings skyrocketed from $25 to $500 per hundred. In Pennsylvania alone as much as $300,000 changed hands for mulberry trees in a week, and trees were frequently resold by speculators at great profits. But by 1840 mulberry trees glutted the market, and were valued at only five cents each. When speculation collapsed and the so-called "golden-rooted trees" were uprooted from plantations in 1839, disgruntled investors coined a new word, *multicaulished,* meaning "run out," "good for nothing," "disliked."

The only mulberry tree speculation that rivaled the mulberry mania would come almost a century later when a promoter conned investors into buying mulberry trees by promising that he could guarantee "a precolored silk" by providing "rainbow-hued silkworms" that had actually been injected with dyestuffs. Needless to say, these trees did not deliver on that promise. (See *Tulip.*)

MUNG BEAN. The Asian mung bean takes its name from the Tamil *mungu* meaning "the same." These are the beans that are easiest to sprout, taking barely three days, and are used as Chinese bean sprouts.

MUSHROOM. When Englishmen in the fifteenth century tried to pronounce the French word for this succulent fungus, *moisseron,* it came out *muscheron.* Over the years this became *mushroom,* a pronunciation probably influenced by the common English words *mush* and *room*. All in all, they may have been better off with their native name for the edible fungus: "toad's hat." Toad's hat is no longer heard, but "toadstool" is, of course, still the name for inedible, poisonous mushrooms. The French word *moisseron* is generally accepted as a derivative of *mousse,* "moss," upon which mushrooms grow. Cities that sprang up rapidly, as mushrooms do overnight, were called "mushrooms" in England as early as 1787. Within another century the name became a verb meaning "to spread out," applied first to bullets that expand and flatten, then to fires, and then to almost anything that grows rapidly.

The Greek city Mycenae may take its name from *mykes* or "mushrooms," the legend being that a hot and thirsty Perseus picked a mushroom and drank the water flowing from it, then expressed his gratitude by naming the city in its honor. Most famous of all Greek mushrooms is the poisonous red-capped hallucinogenic species called *Amanita muscaria,* or *fly agaric.* Symbolic of the erect penis, it was used as a sacrament in fertility rites and is still sacred to certain Indian tribes. British author Robert Graves suggested that the Greeks held this species sacred because they had a taboo against eating any red food whatsoever. He further contended that Soma, the mysterious legendary drink celebrated in Vedic poems by the Aryans who invaded India in the second millenium B.C., was not mead, wine or hemp as has been suggested, but *Amanita muscaria.* In his articles in the *Atlantic,* which relied heavily on the works of ethnomycologist Gordon Wasson, Graves made a strong case for the species being Soma. He pointed out that *Amanita muscaria* is the hallucinatory mushroom nibbled by Alice in Wonderland, Lewis Carroll having read about the species before writing his classic. Not all of the hallucinogenic agents in the fly agaric are absorbed into the bloodstream; some lodge in the kidneys and mix there with urine. Thus, it is said that certain Lapps and Finns get high on the filtered urine of reindeer that have eaten the mushroom. Various Siberian tribes and a small Mongol enclave in Afghanistan reportedly go one step further; they eat *Amanita,* urinate in a pot and use the sheepskin-filtered urine as a drink (mixed with milk or curds) at weddings and other festive occasions. Poachers in Scotland don't go quite so far but are reported to mix *Amanita muscaria* and whiskey together in an intoxicating drink called the "Cathie," in honor of that insatiable lover Catherine the Great of Russia, who is said to have favored it.

The Romans served mushrooms at wedding feasts to loosen the libido, and they were a favorite of the Emperor Nero, who called them a divine food—perhaps because he used them to poison his predecessor, the Emperor Claudius, as Rabelais suggests. It is more likely that Agrippina, the wife of Claudius, poisoned the monarch by lacing his favorite *Amanita caesara* dish with the juice of the poisonous *Amanita phalloides* species. Later, when Nero was told at an orgy that mushrooms were reputed to be the food of the gods, he is said to have replied, "Yes, they led to the deification of my father."

Mushrooms have become increasingly popular in America. In the last 30 years, consumption has increased from 44 million pounds to more than 231 million pounds. Most of these are cultivated white varieties and descend from a clump of white mushrooms Lewis Downing of Downingtown, Pennsylvania, found among his cream-colored plants in 1926. The majority of U.S. production (60 percent) is centered within a 30-mile radius of Kennett Square, Pennsylvania, which became our mushroom capital during the Civil War when a greenhouse grower in the region discovered that he could raise the fungi under benches of commercial flower crops. The French, however, were the first to grow mushrooms. Louis XV raised them in miles and miles of caves and tunnels outside Paris. Today there are those who believe that even the most legendary of gourmet mushrooms, the small, pitted, spongy-capped morel, can be "factory produced." Most spores for commercial mushrooms are in fact being spawned in laboratories.

One-hundred-pound mushroom specimens have been recorded, and others are so small that they can't be seen by the naked eye. Some 50,000 varieties exist throughout the world, about 1,000 of which are found in the United States. Many of these are delicious, but few people are expert enough to hunt them. Each summer brings a rash of deaths and illnesses from mushroom poisoning, which has plagued man through the ages. Among those whose deaths were attributed to eating poisonous mushrooms are Alexander the Great, the wife, two sons and daughter of the Greek dramatist Euripides, the Roman emperors Tiberius and Claudius, Czar Alexander I, Pope Clement VII and France's Charles V. Be aware that *there is no way to tell a poisonous wild mushroom from a safe one except by knowing the species.* You can't tell a morbid fungi by dropping a silver coin or spoon into a saucepan where your wild mushrooms are cooking—*it will not turn black*—and onions that come in contact with poisonous fungi *will not turn brown.* Neither is it true that a mushroom is edible because animals or insects eat it with impunity. Slugs, for example, frequently feed on *Amanita phalloides,* which is so deadly that even smelling it can bring on a violent attack in humans.

Yet, despite the fact that doctors beginning with Hippocrates have warned against collecting wild mushrooms, gourmets persist in hunting down such delicious species as the morel, puffball, chicken mushroom and shaddmane (the so-called "fool-proof four") and the rare honey mushroom (*Armillaria mellea*). The best advice is to join a mycological society and hunt with experts, but then someone has pointed out that "experts" are usually the ones who die from poisoning.

To leave a lasting impression on anyone still wanting to collect wild mushrooms, consider the following from Lucy Kavaler's *Mushrooms, Molds and Miracles:*

> *Several years ago workmen were moving a group of early fifteenth-century mummies from a medieval cemetery in France to a new resting place. The men crossed themselves and muttered to one another with horror about the expression of unendurable pain on the faces of one family of seven. Doctors came to look and diagnosed the cause of death: the dread Death Cap had done its work all those hundreds of years ago and left its record of suffering.*

(See *Caesar's Mushroom.*)

MUSKMELON. (See *Cantaloupe.*)

MUSTARD. Mustard takes its name from the *must* or "new wine" that was first used in mixing the paste, which is made from various plants of the *Brassica* genus, including, chiefly, *Brassica nigra,* "black mustard," and *Brassica hirta,* "white mustard."

Frederick the Great believed mustard did so much for his masculinity that he invented a drink made with powdered mustard, champagne and coffee. The history of hot mustard as an aphrodisiac is a long one. Rabelais, for example, writes that his lusty Demisemiquaver friars "began their meal with cheese, ending it with mustard and lettuce, as Martial tells us the ancients did. As each received a dishful of mustard after dinner, they made good the old proverb: Mustard after dinner / is good for saint and sinner."

"The rougish mustard," as it has been called, is made by adding turmeric to the mustard plant's black and white seeds. Indispensable to the American hot dog, mustard has been used for some unusual mustard plasters indeed. One sexologist notes that colleagues "cured an atony of the virile member of 3 or 4 years duration by repeated immersions of that organ in a strong infusion of mustard seed." Most men and women would no doubt dispense with such dippings for a frank with mustard and sauerkraut.

MYRRH. "A bundle of myrrh is my well-beloved unto me; he shall lie all night betwixt my breasts," says the Song of Solomon. Unfortunately, the aromatic herb sweet cicely (*Myrrhis odorata*) that is common to Europe is not the fabled myrrh of the Bible. The word *myrrh* comes from the Greek name for perfume, but the biblical myrrh, which is still used to make incense and perfumes, was probably obtained from the spiny shrub *Commiphor myrrha*. Myrrh's age-old reputation is shown in the classical myth of Myrrh, a daughter of King Cinyras, whom the gods changed into a myrrh tree for having incestuous relations with her father. (Their child Adonis was born from the split trunk of the tree.) Frankincense has a similar reputation and is also still used in incense and perfumes. This biblical aromatic generally comes from the Asian and African species *Boswellia carteri*.

MYRTLE. In Greek legend, Phaedra, the wife of Theseus, fell in love with her stepson Hippolytus, but he rejected her advances. While awaiting his return one day she sat under a myrtle shrub (*Myrtus communis*) and whiled away the time by piercing its leaves with a hairpin. This is why the leaves of the myrtle reveal many little punctures when viewed under a strong light. Phaedra hanged herself after falsely accusing Hippolytus as her seducer. Theseus then banished Hippolytus and caused his son's death.

Myrtle, which originated in western Asia, is believed by the Arabs to be one of the three things (along with a date seed and a grain of wheat) that Adam took with him when he was cast out of Paradise. According to Roman mythology, Venus wore a garland of myrtle when she rose from the sea, and when satyrs tried to watch her bathing in the nude she hid behind a myrtle bush.

Myrtle takes its name from *mýrtos,* the Greek word for the plant. Myrtle crowns were awarded to victors of the Greek Olympic games, and the plant has been a symbol of strength and love since ancient times. The Romans offered myrtle to Priapus as tokens of their gratitude for success in sexual affairs. The ancient Britons dedicated the plant to their goddess of love, always including myrtle in bridal bouquets and often planting myrtles near the homes of newlyweds. Mentioned in Petronius's *Satyricon,* myrtle berries, leaves and flowers were used in many love potions, and the plant's aromatic leaves and flowers have long been employed in perfumery. There are more than 100 species of myrtle from both the Old and New Worlds, but only a few are of interest to the gardener. Besides tree myrtle (*Myrtus communis*) there is a form with three leaves instead of two at every joint that is used by Jews for religious ceremonies, such as the Feast of Tabernacles.

NAKED BOY. "Naked boy" and "naked lady" are folk names for the meadow saffron or autumn crocus (*Calchicum autummale*), on which the flowers appear before the leaves. More poetically, the meadow saffron is called "the leafless orphan of the year" because the flowers are destitute or orphaned of leaves.

NARCISSUS. Like Hyacinthus, Narcissus was a handsome youth of Greek mythology. The nymph Echo (who could speak only when she heard another voice) wished that he would fall in love with himself after he spurned her love. When Narcissus chanced to see his own reflection in a still pool of water, that is just what he did, and then he drowned in that pool trying to reach his beautiful image. After his death the gods changed his body into the flower that has been called a narcissus ever since. Narcissus's name is also remembered in "narcissistic" self-love and in "narcotic," named after the narcissus because some narcissus varieties contain substances that induce sleep. (See *Daffodil; Hyacinth*.)

NARCOTIC. (See *Narcissus*.)

NASTURTIUM. The name *nasturtium* (from the Latin *nasus*, "nose," and *torquere*, "to twist") was given by the Romans to watercress (*Nasturtium officinale*) because of its pungency. "It received its name from tormenting the nose," Pliny said of this plant that the English later called "nosesmart." In the sixteenth century *nasturtium* was applied to the showy orange-colored flowers we call by that name today. The flower is now considered part of the genus *Tropaeolum*; its scientific name is no longer *Nasturtium indicum*, but it is still popularly called "nasturtium" while watercress never is.

NAVEL ORANGE. The first navel orange was a "bud-sport" that originated for reasons unknown from the bud of an otherwise normal orange tree in a monastery garden in Bahia, Brazil. Imported into the United States in 1870, this sweet, usually seedless, orange takes its name from the depression in its rind resembling a human navel, which contains an aborted ovary that appears as a small secondary fruit within the fruit. Many other varieties, however, exhibit this characteristic at times.

NECTARINE. (See *Bramley's Seedling.*)

NEMATODE. Novice gardeners might be puzzled by the term *nematode-resistant* that is affixed to many plants, especially tomatoes. A nematode is simply a small, microscopic worm that attacks the roots of plants and often causes great damage. The word is a learned borrowing from the Greek word for "thread" applied to threadlike things like these tiny unsegmented worms. Some plants have a better ability to repel these worms than others and are called nematode-resistant.

NERO'S CROWN. Cruel, vindictive, dissolute, profligate, treacherous, tyrannical, murderous—it would take a far longer string of adjectives to describe Nero, the last of the Caesars. Among the Roman emperor's countless victims were the rightful heir to the throne, Britannicus (Nero poisoned him); his own mother, Agrippina (Nero had her killed by his soldiers after failing to drown her); his first wife, Octavia; his pregnant second wife, Poppaea (Nero is said to have kicked her to death); the son of his benefactor Lucan; and a woman who refused to marry him. Nero may well have set fire to Rome in A.D. 64 because he wanted to see what Troy looked like when it burned, although there is no trustworthy proof of the story. And that Nero fiddled while Rome burned is essentially true, though he probably sang and played the harp, not the fiddle, while regarding the spectacle with cynical detachment. The tyrant rebuilt Rome, including a grandiose "Golden House" for himself, blamed the blaze on the Christians and persecuted them with such fury that they regarded him as the Antichrist. With such a record it's hard to understand why anyone would name a beautiful flowering plant after him, but someone did. Nero's crown (*Tabernaemontana coronaria*) is named for the bloody-minded, spindle-shanked, pot-bellied tyrant. Better to call the fragrant shrub "crape jasmine" or "Indian rose bay."

NEWTON'S APPLE. Almost everyone who has eaten an apple knows the story of Sir Isaac Newton sitting under an apple tree pondering the question of gravitation when a pippin popped him on the head and inspired the train of thought that led to his law of universal gravitation. But the particulars are usually omitted in this tale. According to Voltaire, who first told the story and got it from Newton's niece, the apple fell in his mother's garden at Woolsthorpe where he was visiting her in 1666. Even the name of the apple is known; it was a red cooking variety called the Flower of Kent. (If you want to sample it, plant the same tree Newton sat under—grafted scions of the tree have been taken over the years since 1666 and are available from English nurseries.) The apple that bopped Newton must have inspired a long train of thought, for the law of universal gravitation didn't come to fruition for nearly 20 years. Such charming stories have become part of the Newton legend whether they are reliable or not. Perhaps the greatest figure in the history of science, Newton said of himself: "I do not know what I may appear to the world, but to myself I seem to have been only a boy playing on the sea-shore, and diverting myself in now and then finding a smoother pebble or a prettier shell than ordinary, whilst the great ocean of truth lay all undiscovered before me."

NIP IN THE BUD. To obtain larger peonies or tomatoes or to get larger flowers or fruit of any kind, gardeners have long pinched off excessive blossoms on plants, nipped them early in the bud to channel all a plant's strength into the few remaining buds, which will then yield large flowers or fruit. No fruit comes from a nipped-off bud, of course, and so the gardening term "to nip in the bud" became proverbial in Elizabethan times for calling a halt to something before it has a chance to develop, especially in regard to bad habits or plans with little chance of success.

NOISETTE. A cross of the moss rose and the China rose, the hardy, widely grown garden rose named the noisette originated in America in about 1816. It was named after an early cultivator (not the originator) of the hybrid, Philippe Noisette of Charleston, South Carolina. It is less often called the "Champney rose" after its discoverer, John Champney of Charleston.

NOSEGAY. A bunch or bouquet of sweet-smelling flowers has been called a nosegay since at least the early fifteenth century. *Nosegay* has survived because it reminds us of how the nose delights in or is made gay by the smell of flowers, but the charming, playful "tussie-mussie" or "tuzzy-muzzy" for the same (as well as a gold or silver representation of a bunch of flowers) is practically extinct now. "Posy," for a bunch of flowers or flowerlike words, is little heard, but lives on in the language forever thanks to Christopher Marlowe's *Passionate Shepherd,* who rhymed: "And I will make thee beds of roses / And a thousand fragrant posies."

NUT. Due to the round shape of many nuts, *nut* has long been slang for "head," which led to the expression, "he's off his nut," meaning "he's crazy," which in turn gave us *nuts* for "crazy" and *nut house*, meaning "insane asylum." The word *nut* can be used for a sum of money, and figures in many other expressions as well, including "a hard nut to crack" (a tough problem to solve) and "from soup to nuts," meaning "complete."

To give someone a brief summary of something is "to put it in a nutshell" and obviously refers to the small size of a nutshell. The phrase has been with us at least since Pliny wrote that the *Iliad* had been copied in so small a handwriting by a contemporary of his that the whole work fit in a walnut shell. This feat has been duplicated several times over the years.

Since there are no nuts to be gathered in May, the old children's song with the words, "Here we go gathering nuts in May" seems to make no sense—and indeed, it may have been intended as a nonsense song. But "the nuts" in the phrase has been explained as being "knots" of May, that is, bunches of flowers. In Elizabethan England, Queen Elizabeth herself gathered knots of May in the meadows, one author tells us, and this is a plausible explanation even though there are no recorded quotations supporting the use of *knots* for "flowers," except possibly the English "knot gardens" of herbs.

Yankee peddlers who worked the rural South before the Civil War were known as far away as Europe for their trickery, especially for their fabled wooden nutmegs. It is doubtful that anyone would take the trouble to carve wooden nutmegs (it took an expert woodcarver a full day to make just *one* in a recent experiment) when these seeds of an East Indian evergreen tree (*Myristica fragrans*) cultivated extensively in the Spice Islands sold for less than a penny apiece. But whether carved wooden nutmegs ever existed or not (no one has ever turned up an authentic one), many country people did believe that Yankee peddlers sold them, along with carved wooden hams painted pink ("Basswood hams"), carved cigars and wooden pumpkin seeds! Connecticut is still called "the Nutmeg State" for this reason, and the warning, "Don't take any wooden nutmegs," probably influenced the coining of the still current phrase, "Don't take any wooden nickels."

Butternut was a Civil War term for Confederate soldiers, because their uniforms were often homespun colored brown with dye made from butternut tree bark.

English playwright William Dimond's melodrama *The Broken Sword* (1816) is all but forgotten, along with its characters, plot and dialog, and the author himself isn't remembered in most guides to literature. Yet Dimond has found immortality of sorts in the expression "an old chestnut," a stale joke or story, which probably derives from an incident in his play. *The Broken Sword*'s principal character is crusty old Captain Xavier, who is forever spinning the same yarns about his highly unlikely experiences. He begins to tell the following one to Pablo, another comic character:

> CAPTAIN XAVIER: *I entered the woods of Golloway, when suddenly from the thick boughs of a cork tree—*
> PABLO: *A chestnut, Captain, a chestnut!*
> CAPTAIN XAVIER: *Bah, I tell you it was a cork tree.*
> PABLO: *A chestnut; I guess I ought to know, for haven't I heard you tell this story twenty-seven times?*

Fame didn't come immediately. The lines lay at rest in Dimond's play for almost seventy years before American actor William Warren, Jr., repeated them at a stage testimonial dinner in Boston, after hearing another speaker tell a stale joke. Other actors present adopted Warren's chestnut, elaborated on it, and it became the time-worn "old chestnut."

O

OAK. Oaks, venerated by the Druids, were regarded as sacred to the god of thunder in ancient times because the trees were believed to be more likely struck by lightning than any other kind of tree. The origins of the oak's name are lost in history; the word was first recorded in the sixth century, but it is undoubtedly much older. One oak still standing in England is said to be 1,600 years old. In case you've ever wondered, a large oak has about 250,000 leaves, so if you have four on your property, you have a million leaves to admire and rake up every fall.

"Charles' oak" is a historically famous old oak that grew near Boscobel House in England. When Charles II fled the Parliamentary army after the Battle of Worcester on September 3, 1651, he climbed down into the hollow tree and hid there with a colonel of the royal guard until it was safe to proceed; his supporters lowered food and drink to him.

If the oak leafs out in spring before the ash tree, it will be a good, abundant year, according to the old proverb: "Oak before ash, in for a splash; Ash before oak, in for a soak." But if the ash leafs out before the oak, there will be flooding in the summer and a poor fall harvest.

An "oak winter" is a cold spell in the spring that occurs after small leaves have appeared on the oak trees. (See *Blackberries, Dogwood Tree.*)

OKRA. Okra was so valuable in ancient Angola that tribes made knife raids into neighbors' fields to steal the vegetable and killed anyone who stood in their way. *Okra* derives ultimately from the Tshi *nkruman*. The Arabs held it to be a rare delicacy fit for weddings and other special occasions, naming it *uehka*, which means "a gift." Okra is sometimes called "ladyfingers" in England because of the shape of the pods.

OLD FIELD PINE. Various pine trees, including the loblolly, sand and yellow pines, are called "old field pines" because they grow best on the exposed mineral soil of old farms. The term is an expression often heard in the South but has some currency in other regions as well.

OLIVE. "Wine within, oil without," was the Roman formula for a happy life, and the oil with which they anointed their bodies was, of course, olive oil. Olives themselves were believed to stimulate drinking by the Romans, whose word *oliva* for the fruit became our *olive.* So interwoven is the olive with history—Noah's biblical olive branch the symbol of peace; some of the ancient olive trees in the Garden of Gethsemane possibly growing there since the time of Christ's betrayal; Athens named for the goddess Athena after she gave the olive to man—that books have been written about the fruit. The olive tree, which has been known to live well over 1,000 years, was simply a staple of life, yielding both food and light and grown also for its symbolism of joy, happiness and peace. Green olives are those picked early; the black ones are picked ripe. Both are very bitter indeed before they are soaked in a lye-and-salt solution and readied for market.

According to legend, the Athenian hero Academus helped Castor and Pollux rescue their little sister Helen when she was kidnapped by the Athenian Prince Theseus. Academus revealed Helen's hiding place and she was spared marriage with Theseus. She grew up to become the famous "face that launched a thousand ships," in reference to her later abduction by Paris, which caused the Trojan War. As a reward for his help, the Spartans gave Academus an olive grove on the outskirts of Athens; the place later became a public park called the "Grove of Academus" in his honor. Much later, about 387 B.C., the philosopher Plato had a house and garden adjoining this park and opened a school of philosophy there. He walked and talked with his students in the peaceful olive grove for the rest of his life and was buried near it. His peripatetic successors taught there as well, so his school of philosophy became known as the "Academia" after the olive grove honoring the eponymous hero Academus. Renaissance scholars later adopted the name *academe* or "academy" for any institution devoted to learning, from the learning of philosophy to the learning of war, and it is from the word *academy* that our word *academic* derives. The English poet John Milton seems to be responsible for the wide use of the poetic fancy "groves of Academe" for institutions of higher learning; these words occur in his *Paradise Regained,* among other places:

> *The olive grove of Academe,*
> *Plato's retirement, where the Attic bird*
> *Trills her thick-warbl'd notes the summer long.*

ONION. *Onion* comes from the Latin word *unio*, "oneness" or "union," in reference to the many united layers in an onion. The Romans used the same word for the multilayered pearl; thus our "pearl onion" would have been a Roman *unio unio*. Onions were fed to the Egyptian laborers who built the great Cheops pyramid, dispensed by Alexander the Great to his troops to promote valor, and were praised by General Grant, who once wired the War Department that he would not move his army farther without onions. The onion is believed by some to be an aphrodisiac as well as a strength-giver, though as Shakespeare wrote, "Eat no onions nor garlic, for we are to utter sweet breath."

ORANGE. The Sanskrit word *narange* became the Latin *aurangia*, "golden apple," from which our *orange* derives. "Portugals" is a name still used for sweet oranges in Greece, Albania, Rumania, Italy and the Middle East, for bitter oranges were the only oranges known in Europe until Portuguese ships brought sweet oranges back from India in 1529. Later, in 1645, still sweeter Chinese oranges reached Lisbon, and they are responsible for the scientific name of the modern sweet orange, *Citrus sinensis* (*sinensis* is Latin for "Chinese"). Sweet oranges were a luxury enjoyed mainly by royalty until the mid-nineteenth century. Thousands of varieties of fruits are named after their developers, and in this regard the orange is no exception. The best-known eponymous orange variety is the "Temple," named after its early propagator, Floridian William Chase Temple. Others include the "Murcott Honey orange," named for Florida grower Charles Murcott Smith, and the "Parson Brown," which honors Nathan L. Brown, a Florida clergyman. The United States is by far the largest grower of oranges, producing more than 25 billion a year. An orange's color, incidentally, has nothing to do with its ripeness. Oranges turn orange only as a result of cold weather, which breaks down a membrane protecting their green chlorophyll. This is why summer oranges are often dyed and stamped with the words "color added."

Long the traditional decoration for a bride in England, the orange blossom is said to indicate purity because of its white blossoms, and fruitfulness because the orange tree is so prolific. (See *Navel Orange; Tangerine.*)

ORCHARD. "Hortyard," one of the old spellings of *orchard*, best explains its origins. The word originally meant "garden yard," deriving from the Old English *geard*, "yard," and the Latin *hortus*, "garden."

ORCHID. Orchids were once called "ballock stones," "sweet cods," "fox stones," "goatstones," "dogstones" and similar names—all because their tubers resemble human male testicles. Indeed, the name orchid derives from *orchis,* the Greek for "testicle," and the plant is called "priest's balls" in French and "boy plant" in German. (See *Avocado; Bubby Bush; Butterfly-pea; Jack-in-the-pulpit; Mandrake; Orchis; Papaya; Vanilla; Venus's-flytrap.*)

ORCHIS. The identity of the prodigious true male orchis of the Greeks and Romans has never been established. Mystery still surrounds this magic plant whose root was dissolved in goat's milk by the ancients. One drink of this goat milk, wrote an incredulous historian, and a man could perform sex as many as 70 consecutive times. Orchis is supposed to have been the main ingredient of *satyrion,* the love food of those lecherous satyrs of Greek mythology. It is a Greek word meaning "testicle," supposedly used because of the root's resemblance to that male organ. The orchid, the Turkish *Orchis morio,* the truffle, the mandrake and several other plants have been credited with being the male orchis of the ancients, but the true identity of satyrion is probably lost for all time. (See *Orchid.*)

PALMA CHRISTI. The large castor-oil plant (*Ricinus communis*) is called palma Christi because its leaf shape resembles the palm of the hand and in early times it brought to mind the image of Christ's hand nailed to the cross. The name is first recorded in an herbal published in 1548, but it is certainly older. The seeds of the castor-oil plant are used to make the purgative castor oil long hated by children.

PALM TREES. Palm trees take their name from the Latin *palma,* "palm of the hand," because the tree's fronds resemble a spread hand. Palm Sunday, the Sunday before Easter, is named after Christ's triumphant entry into Jerusalem, when people strewed his way with palm branches and leaves. The palm was a symbol of victory in Roman times, and "to bear the palm" meant to be the best, after the Roman custom of awarding a palm branch to a victorious gladiator. This led to the expression "palmy days," "prosperous" or "happy" days, as those days were to a victorious gladiator when he received a palm branch. Incidentally, the palm of the hand had its own Old English word, *folm,* which was used until Middle English times even while *palm* was used for the palm tree. It wasn't until then that the French *paume,* a derivative of the Latin *palma,* was borrowed and altered slightly to palm to mean both "palm of the hand" and "palm tree."

PANAMA HAT PLANT. This is the popular name of *Carludovica palmata,* the tropical American palmlike plant from whose young leaves Panama hats are made. The plant is also called "jipijapa" after Jipijapa, Ecuador, where it grows in abundance. The Panama hat made from the plaited leaves of *Carludovica palmata* is something of a misnomer. The hats originated in Ecuador, but have been called Panama hats since they were first recorded in English in 1833, probably because Panama was the major distribution center for them.

PANSY. The French *pensée,* meaning "thoughtful," is the source of this flower's name, probably because some unknown poet in ancient times believed that the flower had a thoughtful, pensive face. A cultivated violet, the flower was called the "pensée" in English during the early sixteenth century, but changed gradually in pronunciation and spelling to *pansy.* Other fanciful names for the pansy (*Viola tricolor hortensis*) have included "heartsease," "call-me-to-you," "three-faces-under-a-hood," "love-in-idleness," "kiss-me-at-the-garden-gate," "forget-me-not," "tri-colored violet" and "lady's delight." *Pansy* may have become slang for a male homosexual because of its similarity in sound to "Nancy," an older slang term for a gay male, or it may have its roots in an old English custom of men wearing sprigs of violets when they swore never to marry. None of many theories has been proved.

PAPAYA. The versatile papaya, or "tree melon," is a staple food in many parts of the world. Its enzyme papain aids in the digestion of food, which is one reason why its leaves are used as a meat tenderizer in some countries and its fruit is the basis for commercial tenderizers. Indians of Central America gorge themselves with "paw paw" so that they can eat large quantities of food at their feasts without becoming ill. The word *papaya* is a corruption of a Carib Indian word. In Cuba and some other Spanish-speaking countries the large fruit (it sometimes weighs up to 20 pounds) is called *fruta bomba* or "bomb fruit." Papaya itself has come to be widely used slang for "the female fruit," or "breasts," and in these countries it isn't used in polite conversation. (See *Avocado; Bubby Bush; Butterfly-pea; Jack-in-the-pulpit; Mandrake; Orchid; Vanilla; Venus's-flytrap.*)

PARADISE SHOOTS. The popular name of the lign aloes (from the Latin *lignum aloes,* "wood of the aloe"), "paradise shoots" are believed to be the only plant remaining from the Garden of Eden. Legend holds that Adam took a shoot of this aromatic tree when he left Paradise and all lign aloes were propagated from it. Numbers 24:6 mentions "The trees of lign-aloes which the Lord hath planted." Prized for the pleasant aroma of its wood, it is also called the "East Indian aloe tree."

PARSLEY. "Parsley grows for the wicked, but not for the just," according to an old English proverb. Parsley takes its name ultimately from the Greek *petrosélinon* for the herbs. This member of the celery family began earning its shady reputation even before the Romans, who wore curly-leaved parsley garlands in their hair not only because they were attractive but because they believed that nibbling on parsley sprigs enabled one to drink more wine without becoming drunk. The Greeks crowned winning athletes with parsley at their Nemean and Isthmian games, and used the herb as a flavoring. The Romans fed it to their horses on the theory that it made them swift. The plant is described by Seneca, who tells how the tempting sorceress Medea gathered parsley and other forbidden herbs by moonlight.

PARSNIP. The proverb "fine words butter no parsnips," meaning that words or promises without action are meaningless, dates back to at least the eighteenth century when English dramatist Arthur Murray used it in his play *The Citizen.* "Parsnips," declares an old English cookbook, "are best left in the ground," but the sweet nutty flavor of this member of the carrot family has been enjoyed by millions since long before the time of the Roman emperor Tiberius, who was so addicted to parsnips that he imported them from Germany. The English word *parsnip* is said to derive from the Latin *pastinaca* for the vegetable, acquiring the *ip* in its name from its association with the turnip. The Latin word comes from *pastinare,* "to dig or trench the ground," and *napus,* "turnip," in reference to the fact that the vegetable was thought to be a kind of turnip that the ground had to be trenched for (so that it would grow straight). Incidentally, the Russian word for parsnip is *pasternak,* so the Nobel Prize–winning Russian poet's name translates as Boris Parsnip.

PASSIONFLOWER. The purple-colored passion fruit (*Passiflora edulis*), which is borne on vines covered with striking white and purple passionflowers, is widely grown in the tropics for the table, especially in Brazil. It is not cultivated commercially in the United States, although another species grown here, *Passiflora incarnata,* or "the maypop," bears an edible fruit. Granadillas, as passion fruit are also called, are too perishable to be shipped, so it's off to Brazil for anyone hankering after one. The passionflower was so named by Spanish Catholic missionaries because its parts are said to resemble Christ's instruments of passion; its corona is the crown of thorns, and the five sepals and five petals represent the ten apostles (Peter and Judas not counted). Symbols of the crucifixion borne on the flower include:

Leaf	spear
Five anthers	five wounds
Tendrils	whips
Column of the ovary	pillar of the cross
Stamens	hammers
Three styles	three nails

Fleshy threads with the flowers	crown of thorns
Calyx	the glory of nimbus
White tint	purity
Blue tint	heaven

PEA. The word *pea* comes indirectly from the Latin *pisum*, "pea"; the early English singular for pea was *pease*, hence the old rhyme "pease-porridge hot, / Pease-porridge cold, / Pease-porridge in the pot, / Nine days old." Quite a mania for peas existed in seventeenth-century France. Madame de Maintenon, Louis XIV's mistress, called it "both a fashion and a madness," and it was at this time that the celebrated *petits pois à la française* was invented. Incidentally, it was quite proper at the time to lick green peas from their shells after dropping the whole pod in a sauce, so eating peas off a knife isn't so bad after all! Chinese sugar or snow peas, eaten pod and all, are sometimes properly called *mangetout* ("eat all").

"Till the last pea's out of the dish" is a Southern Americanism meaning "till the end," or "a long time." Red Barber popularized the Southern expression "tearing up the pea patch" for "going on a rampage" when he broadcast Brooklyn Dodger baseball games from 1945 to 1955, using it often to describe fights on the field between players. Barber came from the South, where the expression is an old one, referring to the prized patch of black-eyed peas, which stray animals sometimes ruined.

"English peas" is a term used in the South for green peas to distinguish them from the black-eyed or brown-eyed varieties. (See *Black-eyed Peas*.)

PEACH. Peaches were the "persian apples" of the ancient Romans. Their name, *Persicum*, became *pessica* in Late Latin, *pesche* in French and finally came into English as *peach*. The word for the fruit, which is luscious to look at, touch and taste, has been used to describe a pretty young girl at least since the ancient Chinese used it as slang for a young bride centuries ago. But the Chinese and the Arabs, too, also regarded the peach's deep fur-edged cleft as a symbol of the female genitalia and used *peach* in a number of slang expressions referring to sexual love. "Venus owns this tree . . . the fruit provokes lust," English herbalist Nicholas Culpepper wrote in 1652, and language reflects that people around the world shared his opinion. In Europe the French have used their word *peche* in similar sexual expressions, and "a peach house" was once common in English slang as a home of prostitutes.

The Elberta peach, the most widely sold of American peaches, was probably imported from Shanghai in 1850, but more than one source records a story that shows more imagination. According to this tale, Samuel Rumph of Marshallville, Georgia received peach tree buddings from a friend in Delaware, planted them and eventually harvested a good crop. His wife, Elberta, accidentally dropped a few pits from these peaches in her sewing basket and when their grandson wanted to start an orchard ten years later, she dug them out and asked her husband to plant them. By 1870 trees from the pits were flourishing, and by an accidental cross-pollination a new golden variety resulted, which Samuel named for his spouse. Elbertas, however, aren't considered good eating peaches by those who know their peaches.

"Georgia Peach" was the popular nickname of baseball great Ty (Tyrus) Cobb (1886–1961) because he was born in Narrows, Georgia, and he was to most baseball players as superior as the famed Georgia peach is to other peaches.

PEANUTS. Peanuts take their name from their resemblance to peas in a pod. They go by numerous descriptive aliases, including "monkey nuts," and "ground peas," but their most common synonym, "goober," is a corruption of *nguba,* a Bantu name plantation slaves gave to the peanut and one of the few African words still retained in English. "Pindar," another name slaves gave the peanut, comes from the Kongo *npinda.*

Peanut butter is an easily digested, high-protein food that nutritionists say provides an adequate survival diet when combined with a citrus fruit like the orange. Four out of five American homes are said to stock a jar of it on the shelf. Americans aren't as partial to "peanut butter soup," or to the dish called "Young Monkey Stuffed with Peanuts" invented by futurist chef Jules Maincave during World War I.

The "peanut gallery," usually the cheapest seats in the house, was the gallery or "second balcony" high up in Gay Nineties theaters, so high up that the crowds seated there were sometimes called the "gallery gods." Peanuts were the movie snack of the day, and the occupants of these cheap seats often rained peanut shells on performers who displeased them, thus earning the seats their name.

PEAR. One of the earliest cultivated fruits, pears are among the few fruits that ripen better after being picked. (The Chinese often ripened them in rooms filled with incense.) This fruit shaped like a Rubens nude goes incomparably well with cheese desserts. Rabelais wrote: "There is no match you could compare / To Master Cheese and Mistress Pear." The Old French *piere,* derived from the Latin *pirum,* gave us our word *pear.* Of the more than 3,000 pear species, the Bartlett is perhaps the best known. (See *Bartlett Pear.*)

PEAT. The word *peat* was first applied to the small bits of this substance used to burn in peat fires. Keeping this in mind, it is easy to see the derivation of *peat*, from the English *piece,* which may come from the Latin *pecia,* "a bit." Peat, of course, is an organic material found in marshy ground, composed of partially decayed vegetable matter and is much used by gardeners in improving garden soil.

PEONY. The gods wounded in the Trojan War were cured by the physician Paeon, according to Greek mythology. Thus many plants once prized for their curative powers were named for Paeon, including the beautiful flower called the "peony" with its hundreds of varieties. Because they believed the god Apollo often disguised himself as Paeon, the Greeks sang hymns of thanks and tribute to him that came to be called *paeans;* these are the source for our expression "paeans of praise." The species of peony called the "tree peony" (*Paeonia suffruticosa*) is called the "King of Flowers" by the Chinese and is widely regarded as one of the most beautiful of all garden plants. (See *Mandrake.*)

PEPPER. (See *Chili Pepper.*)

PERIWINKLE. In Italy the periwinkle is called *fiore di morto* because it used to be wreathed around dead infants. *Periwinkle* does take its name from the Latin *pervinca,* "to bind around," but whether it was so named because it was used in such burials is unknown. The periwinkle species *Vinca minor,* often called "blue-star periwinkle," is one of the best ground covers for shady places.

PERSIMMON. Ripe persimmons are among the sweetest, most delicious fruits, while green unripe ones are so astringent they are almost a synonym for "sour." Though there are Japanese as well as native species, the fruit takes its name from a Cree American Indian word for it.

'*Simmon* is a shortening of *persimmon.* '*Simmon* and *persimmon* figure in many old proverbs: "The longest pole takes the simmons," "We all come down like simmons after frost," "To be a huckleberry over someone's persimmon" (to be beyond someone's capacity), "To bring down the persimmon" (to win the prize), "To be a jump above someone's tallest persimmons" "To walk off with or rake up the persimmons" (to win the prize) and "a huckleberry to a persimmon" (nothing in comparison to something else). "He looks like he's eatin' a green simmon" refers to the unripe fruit's storied astringency and describes someone with a sour look on his face.

PETITS POIS. (See *Pea.*)

PETUNIA. This popular funnel-shaped flower is botanically related to the tobacco plant, hence its name from the Portuguese word *petum,* meaning "tobacco." The Portuguese had taken the word from the Tupi-Guarani South American Indian word *petyn. Petum* became the French *petún,* which passed into English as *petun,* an archaic word for tobacco. Toward the end of the nineteenth century, the name of the genus *Petunia* was formed in New Latin by botanists from the French *petún* because it was so closely related to tobacco. It wasn't long before the flower of the genus was being called the petunia.

PHILODENDRON. In its tropic homes our common houseplant the philodendron is a tree-climbing plant. Noticing this, the first botanists to observe the tree-loving plant named it after the Greek *philos,* "loving," and *dendron,* "tree." There are more than 200 species and hundreds of varieties of philodendron grown today.

PHOENIX TREE. The *Phoenix dactylifera,* the scientific name of the Egyptian date palm, reflects the ancient superstition that the tree will rise up like the legendary phoenix bird from its ashes fresher than ever if it is burnt down or dies of old age. Shakespeare referred to this in *The Tempest:* "Now I will believe / That there are unicorns; that in Arabia / There is one tree, the phoenix' throne; one phoenix / At this hour reigning there." *Phoenix dactylifera* is popularly called "the phoenix tree," and can be grown in any warm, frost-free part of the United States or in a conservatory. (See *Date.*)

PIEDMONT RICE. An old story holds that Thomas Jefferson stole seeds of Piedmont rice while traveling in the Piedmont region of Italy and smuggled them home in his pockets, despite the fact that Italy wanted to continue its monopoly on this type of rice and had made the crime of stealing the seeds punishable by death. Jefferson's introduction of the rice was important because Piedmont rice can be grown without irrigation. (See *Carolina Rice*; *Wild Rice.*)

PINEAPPLE. The Spanish conquistadores named this fruit *piña* because of its pine-cone shape, and the English translated *piña* to "pineapple," which they also used for the cones of the pine tree. Pineapples are called *anana* in France and many other countries, from a Guarani word meaning "excellent fruit." At one time in England the fruit was called the "Kingpine."

PINK. Several plants of the *Dianthus* genus, including the carnation, are popularly called pinks, because the edges of the flower petals are pinked or notched, as if clipped by pinking shears or scissors. The designation has nothing to do with color. (See *Carnation.*)

PIP. *Pip* is a shortening of *pippin*, which is used for an apple of good quality, hence the phrase "It's a pip!" The English word has its immediate roots in the French *pepin*, which probably comes from the French *petit*, "small." Sometimes pip is used as a nickname for a small boy, as it was for the cabin boy in Herman Melville's, *Moby Dick.* (See *Apple.*)

PISSABED. Dandelions were called "pissabeds" because of the old folk belief that they made people urinate—a belief perhaps associated as much with their golden color as their diuretic property. John Gerard recorded the word first in his 1597 *Herball.* *Piss* is an old word, first recorded in the thirteenth century, probably onomatopoeic (forming words by the sounds of their acts) in origin, and used by Chaucer, Shakespeare, Dryden and Burns, among other great writers. (See *Dandelion.*)

PISTIL. Apothecaries in ancient times used a club-shaped instrument called the "pistillum" to pound herbs and drugs in their mortars. Eventually, the name of this instrument was abbreviated to pestle, but when botanists named the similar-shaped female organs of flowers after it they more carefully followed the old Latin name and called the female organs pistils.

PLANT. Seeds and saplings were tucked into the soil and then stamped down into the ground by early Roman farmers just as they are by gardeners today. From this process grew the word *plant*, which derives from the Latin *planta*, for "sole of the foot."

The Latin word *plantatio*, "propagation of a plant, as from cuttings," is the source of our word *plantation*, used to describe a large estate or farm, or any area under cultivation. *Plantation* used in the sense of the early-American "Plimoth Plantation" extended the word to mean the planting of a colony in a new land or country.

PLANTAIN. One of our worst lawn and garden weeds, plantain takes its name from its leaves, which resemble the sole of the foot (the Latin word for "sole of the foot" is *planta*). The bananalike fruit called "plantain" doesn't share this derivation; its name is a corruption of the native West Indian word for the fruit. The eastern "plane tree," however, does have broad leaves and takes its name from the Greek *platanos*, "broad." (See *Plant*.)

PLEACH. As a word meaning "fold" or "intertwine," *pleach* has little general use today, no matter what its merits, but the Old English word does survive in the current language of gardeners as well as in old poems. To pleach is to prune and train plants to make a hedgelike wall. Two such walls with a path between them are called *pleached allés;* one of the finest in the world is the pleached plane trees at the Schönbrunn Palace in Vienna. *Pleach* was mainly a poetic word used in the past to mean "fold" or "intertwine" by Tennyson and Swinburne, among others. Shakespeare wrote in *Antony and Cleopatra:*

> *Would'st thou be window'd in great Rome and see*
> *Thy master thus with pleach'd arms, bending down . . .*

PLOW. Plowing, or turning over the soil for planting with an agricultural implement, is one of the world's oldest farming operations, and the English word *plow,* in the form of *plough,* is recorded before A.D. 1000. Few gardeners plowing their gardens with rototillers are aware of the many words and phrases that derive from this ancient operation.

Who would guess, for example, that "prevarication," meaning a lie, has its roots in plowing. In Roman times farmers who plowed crooked ridges were called *praevaricors,* their name deriving from the Latin verb for "to go zig-zag or crooked." The next step was to apply the word to men who deviated from the straight line and gave crooked answers in courts of law, which gave us our word *prevarication,* or lie.

Neither would many people suspect that "delirium" derives from plowing. In Latin *lera* means the ridge left by plowing, so the verb *delerare* means to make an irregular ridge. A *delirus* was one who couldn't make a straight furrow when plowing and thus came to mean a crazy, disoriented person whose mind wandered from any matter at hand. The state of such a person was called *delirium,* which remains our word for the condition today.

A balk, deriving from the Old English *balca,* was a ridge between two furrows made in plowing. Since the balk was an obstacle, the word *balk* was applied figuratively to any obstacle, and "to balk" came to mean "to place obstacles in the way of," to stop short as if at an obstacle and stubbornly refuse to go on.

To "plow-back" is a recent term meaning to reinvest profits back into a business or enterprise, while "to clean one's plow" means to beat someone up thoroughly, badly in a fight. The last expression originated among Ozark farmers and is used throughout the United States today, especially in the South. It probably derives from the practice of farmers cleaning their plows by running them through coarse gravel, scratching the plows up badly in the process.

PLUM. The plump, juicy fruit called the plum gives us the expression "a plum" for the best part of anything or a real prize, as in "That's a plum of an assignment." Originally, however, the expression was English slang meaning a very large sum of money, specifically 100,000 pounds. The Old English *plume,* derived from the Greek *proumnon* for the fruit, is the source of the English word *plum.* "Burbank plums" are probably the most famous in America, and take their name from the noted plant breeder Luther Burbank, who developed some 60 varieties of plums besides the Burbank, including a cross between a plum and an apricot that he called a plumcot. The Damson plum, another favorite, is named for the place where it originated. According to tradition, Alexander the Great first brought it to Greece from Damascus, Syria, and the Romans called it the plum of Damascus, *prunum damas cenum,* which became *damascene plum* and finally "damson plum" in English. The renowned "Greengage plum," which is actually yellow with a tinge of green, was brought from Italy to France in about 1500, where it was named the *Reine-Claude* after Claudia, *la bonne reine,* queen to Francis I. About 1725, Sir William Gage, an amateur botanist, imported a number of plum trees from a monastery in France, all of which were labeled except the *Reine-Claude.* A gardener named the unknown variety after his employer, and the *Reine-Claude* has been the Greengage in England and America ever since.

POINCIANA. The tropical royal poinciana with its brilliant, long-clawed scarlet or yellow-striped flowers is probably the most striking of all cultivated trees. Popular in Florida and California as well as its native Madagascar, the broadheaded tree grows from 20 to 40 feet high and is sometimes called the *Delonix* (Greek for long claw) and the "peacock flower." *Poinciana regia,* as well as the entire *Poinciana* genus, which contains several showy plants of the pea family, was named by Linnaeus in honor of Monsieur de Poinci, a seventeenth-century governor of the

French West Indies, where the tree is also much grown and admired. Another more descriptive name for the tree is "flame-of-the-forest."

POINSETTIA. This bright red flower, a symbol of Yuletide, could not have been named for a more fiery personality. Joel Roberts Poinsett (1779–1851) had much of the Christmas spirit in him, too, for he had a great love for the oppressed and a romantic, revolutionary desire to better their lives. Poinsett, whose rich father indulged his brilliant but sickly son, was born in Charleston, South Carolina, and educated in Europe, but dropped out of both medical and legal courses to devote himself to travel for seven years. His poor health did not prevent the young man from meeting Napoleon, Metternich, Queen Louise of Prussia and even the czar, who sent him on an official tour of southern Russia from which only Poinsett and two others came back alive.

After he returned to the United States, Poinsett was sent to South America by President Madison in 1809 to investigate the progress of countries struggling for independence. But he did much more than investigate. Officially the consul to Buenos Aires, Chile and Peru, he made himself an ambassador of revolution. His support of Chilean revolutionaries inspired the British to call him "the most suspicious character" representing the United States in South America, and "a scourge of the American continent" who was "contaminating the whole population." Declared persona non grata when the War of 1812 broke out, he managed to make his way back home. Poinsett served as a member of the South Carolina legislature and as a congressman for a number of years, but found himself more in his own element again when he was appointed the first American minister to Mexico in 1825. Here his revolutionary ardor was so excessive that he lasted only four years; his recall was first demanded by the regime that he helped overthrow and then by the republican regime that replaced it. By this time Poinsett was a familiar public figure, and when he sent specimens of the large, fiery flowers to the United States, they were inevitably named after him. Poinsett hadn't discovered the plant, and it had even been introduced to the United States before him, so it was his popularity alone that accounts for the honor. The ousted ambassador went on to become President Van Buren's secretary of war before retiring to his South Carolina plantation. The *Poinciana* genus commemorating him is now considered part of the genus *Euphorbia,* but the gorgeously colored Mexican species is still called the poinsettia. In England it is known as the "Mexican flame-leaf."

POISON IVY. "Leaves three, let it be" is an old saying reminding people to beware of unknown plants with three leaves, for they might be poison ivy (*Rhus radicans*). Poison ivy has three leaves and bears small, white, berrylike fruits. One of the few native American plants that is poisonous on contact, poison ivy usually causes an itchy rash.

POKE. Poke or pokeweed (*Phytolacca americana*), also called "inkberry," has highly poisonous, even deadly, roots that cause trouble because they resemble horseradish. It is a handsome plant admired for its blackish-red berries (the seeds are also poisonous) whose young foliage is eaten by some after boiling. Poke played a minor role in American politics that few are familiar with. In the presidential campaign of 1844, supporters of James Polk proclaimed their allegiance by carrying tall stalks from the pokeweed plant through the streets (because *poke* sounded something like *Polk*). Ox drivers who favored Henry Clay covered the horns of their oxen with clay, and the Polk supporters gathered poke berries and stained the horns of their own oxen with these. Polk won, of course, thanks in a small part to poke.

POMEGRANATE. Commonly called "Chinese apples" in America, pomegranates take their name from the Latin for "many-seeded apple." This fruit of the ancients is thick-skinned, red and about the size of an orange. It is divided into numerous cells inside, each containing many seeds encased in a crimson, juicy pulp. When the fruit is eaten raw, it is broken open and red flesh is sucked from the small seeds. Today in Asia, when a newly married couple reaches their new home, pomegranates are broken at the doorway, their crimson-coated seeds signifying both the loss of virginity and an omen that many offspring will come of the union.

A number of other words derive from the pomegranate. The g*renade*, a weapon first used in the late sixteenth century, comes from the French *grenade,* a shortening of the French *pomegranade* for "pomegranate": The weapon was originally filled with grains or "seeds" of powder and thus facetiously named after the many-seeded fruit. The military *grenadier,* originally a soldier who threw grenades, evolved in much the same way from the French *grenade,* as did the drink grenadine, which is made from the fruit. But the garnet stone, its color similar to the flesh of the fruit, was given its name by the Romans, the Latin *granatum* (*Punica granatum* or Punic apple, another name for the pomegranate) becoming *grenat* in Old French and shifting by metathesis to *garnet* in English over the years.

POOR MAN'S WEATHERGLASS. (See *Shepherd's Sundial.*)

POPCORN. Certainly known to the Aztecs, popcorn was so named by American settlers on the frontier in the early nineteenth century. It is a variety of small-eared corn (*Zea mays everta*) whose kernels pop open when subjected to dry heat. Over the years, popcorn has also been called "parching corn," "popped corn," "pot corn," "cup corn," "dry corn" and "buckshot." The great quantities of it sold in movie theaters prompted some early movie house chains to grow thousands of acres of popcorn.

POPLAR. After destroying the monster Kakos in a cavern of Aventine, the legendary hero Hercules took a branch from one of many poplar trees growing there and bound it around his head. When Hercules descended to Hades to return Cerberus, the three-headed watchdog of the infernal regions, the heat there caused a perspiration that blanched the underside of the leaves on the poplar branch, while the smoke of the eternal flames blackened their upper surface. And that is why, according to fable, the leaves of the poplar are dark on one side and white on the other. The poplar takes its name from *populus*, the Latin name for the tree.

POPPY. *Opium* derives from the Greek *opion*, meaning simply "poppy juice" and reflecting the fact that the drug is made from the milky juice of the unripe pods of the opium poppy (*Papaver somniferum*). The poppy and its narcotic properties have been known since prehistoric times, however, and the Egyptians used it medicinally long before the ancient Greeks. There are some 100 other species of poppies besides the opium poppy, many of these beautiful flowers grown in the home garden.

In England, the artificial red flowers sold on Remembrance Day for the benefit of war veterans are called "Flanders poppies." A 1915 poem by John McCrae seems to have been the first to connect this flower with the dead of World War I:

> *In Flanders fields the poppies grow*
> *Between the crosses, row on row*
> *   That mark our place; and in the sky*
> *   The larks, still bravely singing, fly*
> *Scarce heard among the guns below.*
>
> *We are the Dead. Short days ago*
> *We lived, felt Dawn, saw sunset glow,*
> *   Loved and were loved, and now we lie*
> *   In Flanders field . . .*

PORTUGALS. (See *Orange.*)

POSY. Originally a posy was a copy of verses or a poem presented to someone along with a bouquet of flowers. Over time it came to mean a flower alone, or a bouquet of flowers. The word itself reflects its original usage, being a syncopated variation of *posey* or *poetry.*

POTATOES. The white potato is one of the most important vegetables in the world, yet it bears the wrong name. *Potato* derives from the Haitian word *batata* for "sweet potato," which the Spanish found in the West Indies in 1526 and introduced to Europe. *Batata* was corrupted to *patata* in Spanish, then altered to *potato* when first used in England. But then the Spaniards discovered the Peruvian white potato, an unrelated plant, and mistook it for just another variety of the West Indian plant. Ignoring the native name for the white potato, *papas,* they gave it the same name as the earlier tuber, and so it too became known as the *potato* in England. The only distinction between the two unrelated vegetables was that one came to be called the "sweet potato" and the other the "Virginia" or "white potato."

The white potato is called "apple of the earth," *pomme de terre,* in French, and "earth apple," *erdapfel,* in German. It acquired the name "Irish potato" when it was first brought to America in 1719 by a group of Irish Presbyterians who planted it in Londonderry, New Hampshire. The colloquial American name "spud" for it derives from the spadelike tool used in digging potatoes. The humorous "Murphy" derives from the wide consumption of potatoes in Ireland—where there are, of course, many Murphys—at a time when other European countries rarely used the tuber for anything but fodder. Early European distrust of the vegetable may have something to do with the fact that potato foliage is, like tomato leaves, highly poisonous. According to one old story, Sir Walter Raleigh presented potato plants to Queen Elizabeth, and her gardener planted them along the Thames. He then invited the local gentry to a banquet featuring potatoes at every course. But instead of cooking the tubers, an unsuspecting chef cooked the poisonous stems and leaves, and a mass stomachache resulted that set back the cause of potatoes in England for many years. The potato did, of course, recover. The Irish helped it along, as did the botanist André Parmentier, who wore potato blossoms on his coat to publicize it. Parmentier's name is still associated with the vegetable on French menus.

The potato figures in much American slang. An issue or situation that is difficult, unpleasant or risky to deal with is called a "hot potato." This term is apparently an Americanism dating back to the mid-nineteenth century. In the 1920s, a "hot potato" meant a sexually appealing woman, as did "hot patootie" some ten years later. *Potato* itself means the head, a dollar ("This coat cost me 400 potatoes"), and a baseball. A "potato head" is a stupid person, while a "couch potato" is a lazy person and "small potatoes" means something inconsequential.

"Meat and potatoes" means the simple fundamentals. "All that meat and no potatoes" is an exclamation of pleasure and admiration by a man on seeing a woman with an attractive figure, though the term is offensive to many women.

There are many more potato words, including "potato patch" for fruit salad and "potato-trap" for mouth. "Hold your tater" is an Americanism meaning be patient, wait a while, i.e. "Just hold your tater and I'll be right with you". (See *Tomato; Spud.*)

PRAYING MANTIS. The English have been calling *Mantis religiosa* the praying mantis since at least 1706, when this name for the green or brown predatory insect was first recorded. It is also called the "praying locust" because of the position in which it holds its forelegs, as if in prayer. It is a beneficial insect in the garden as it eats many bugs that are harmful to plants.

PRECOCIOUS. Trees and fruits that flowered or ripened early were called precocious by the English in the early seventeenth century. The word derives from the Latin *prae*, "before," and *coquere*, "to cook," which formed *praecoquere*, "to cook beforehand." By the end of the century writers were applying this botanical word to people, especially to children who are especially mature or learned for their ages, who ripen before their time.

PRETTY-BY-NIGHT. One Victorian horticulturist said that pretty-by-night and other flower names beginning with *pretty* were "used only by the vulgar," but folks knew better, and all are still in use, although sometimes little known.

Pretty-by-night is an alias of the common "four-o-clock," also known as "marvel-of-Peru," which lives up to its name when its handsome tubelike flowers open very late in the afternoon. The botanist who first classified the species thought it wonderful, too, for he christened it *Mirabilis jalapa*. It signifies "timidity" in the language of flowers.

"Pretty face" is a showy salmon or salmon-yellow flower streaked with dark purple that is common in Southern California. A lily with slender grasslike leaves, it is known botanically as *Brodiaea ixioides*, the group named for Scottish botanist James Brodie.

"Pretty Nancy" has the folk names "London pride" and "Saint Patrick's cabbage," too. Bearing small white flowers with numerous pink spots, it is often used as a rock garden or edging plant. Pretty Nancy is called *Saxifraga umbrosa* in the textbooks. *Saxifraga* is from the Latin "to break," in allusion to its supposed use as a medicinal remedy for gallstones.

"Pretty Betty," more commonly called "red valerian," goes by the name "Jupiter's beard," "scarlet lightning" and "pretty Betsy" as well. It is officially *Centranthus ruber,* a fragrant red, crimson or white perennial of the Valerianaceae family. The family is named for Roman emperor Valerian. "Pretty Betty" means "affection" in the language of flowers.

PRIEST'S PINTLE. (See *Jack-in-the-pulpit.*)

PRIMROSE. Shakespeare has Ophelia put down her brother Laertes with these words in *Hamlet,* and he seems to have invented the term "primrose path" signifying a "path of pleasure."

> *Do not, as some ungracious pastors do,*
> *Show me the steep and thorny way to heaven,*
> *Whiles, like a puff'd and reckless libertine,*
> *Himself the primrose path of dalliance treads . . .*

Later he used "primrose way" in *Macbeth:* "The primrose way to the everlasting bonfire." The word *primrose* comes from the Latin *prima rose,* "first or earliest rose." The flower is not a rose but a low-growing perennial, also called "the cowslip" (*Primula veris*), with yellow flowers that blooms in the spring. There are some 500 species of *Primula.*

PROPAGANDA. The Latin word *propaganda* was first used by Latin plantsmen to mean "that which should be planted or bound forth" and was applied to the process of grafting shoots. Pope Gregory XVIII organized a *congregatio de propaganda fide,* a "congregation for propagating the Christian faith," using the word in a different way, and over the years this organization's actions caused the word *propaganda* to mean to deliberately spread rumors, lies or information to help or hurt a cause. (See *Graft.*)

PULSE. The word *pulse* in gardening terminology usually means the edible seeds of leguminous plants such as peas, beans and lentils, or these legumes themselves. Sometimes the word is used to characterize any herbaceous plant of the pea family, such as alfalfa, clover and vetch. The harvest festival of the ancient Greeks called the *Pyanepsia* took its name from the cooked pulse that was offered at the festival to the god Apollo as the first fruits of the harvest and eaten by all members of the household.

PUMPKIN. This member of the squash family originated in the Americas, where pumpkins were so ubiquitous among the Pilgrims that some wit wrote the following: "We have pumpkins at morning and pumpkins at noon, / If it were not for pumpkins we would soon be undoon." The pumpkin didn't get its name because it looks "pumped up" into a balloon shape. *Pumpkin* probably comes from the Greek *pepon,* "a kind of melon," literally, "a fruit cooked by the sun." *Pepon* became the Middle French *ponon,* which became the English *pompion,* to which the diminutive suffix *-kin* was finally added. It is just another example of the many English words formed from mispronunciations of foreign words.

Seneca is said to have written a satire on the deification of the Roman emperor Claudius Caesar, which he called *Apocolocyntosis,* coined from the Greek word for pumpkin and meaning "pumpkinification." *Pumpkinification,* suggesting a swollen head the size of a pumpkin and "pumped up," has meant pompous behavior or absurd glorification since at least the mid-nineteenth century, when a British writer called attention to Seneca's satire.

PUTTYROOT. (See *Adam-and-Eve.*)

QUACK GRASS. *Agropyron repens* and the other weedy grasses called "quack grass" are not so named because ducks like them or because they are used by quacks (medical imposters). *Quack grass* derives from the older word *quitchgrass; quitch* is an old form of "quick," and quitchgrass is a very quick grower and insidious spreader into places where it is not wanted. Other names for quack grass include "quatch grass," "twitchgrass," "couch grass," "couch" and "quitch."

QUANDONG TREE. *Quandong* is of interest because it is an Australian Aborigine word that has come intact into English, making it one of our most ancient words. The quandong tree is a sandalwood bearing blue berries the size of cherries whose kernel, or "nut," is edible. It is also called the "native peach" tree.

QUASSIA. The black slave Graman Quassi gives his name to this genus of small trees. Quassi discovered the medicinal value of the bark and heartwood of a group of tropical trees common to the Dutch colony of Suriname in the South American Guianas. Using the drug he extracted to treat his fellow natives, he "came to be almost worshipped by some." When his discovery was communicated to Linnaeus in 1730, the botanist named this genus of trees in Quassi's honor. Quassi's name probably comes from the Ashanti dialect word *Kwasida*. The drug he discovered is known as *Surinam quassi* today, and is effective against intestinal worms, as a tonic and as an insecticide. The drug's chief ingredient is the bitter *quassin*, which is extracted from the nearly white wood in minute quantities.

QUEEN ANNE'S LACE. According to folklore, the beautiful wild carrot (*Daucus carota*) is named for the rather homely Anne of Bohemia, who married England's Richard II in 1382. One story tells of a ward of the queen who chose this herb's delicate flower as a tatting pattern. This little girl came to Anne's attention when she was found innocent of a childish prank and the queen discovered her pattern, which she liked so much that she gave the child permission to name it after her. Another story has it that Queen Anne challenged her ladies in waiting to a contest to see who could make embroidery most similar to the pretty flower: The queen, of course, won. In any case, *Queen Anne's lace* was later transferred to the wild carrot's flower and then to the herb itself.

Still another tale has Queen Anne's lace named for Saint Anne, "Queen of Heaven," the mother of Mary and grandmother of Jesus. Appropriately this Anne is the patron saint of lacemakers. Tradition has it that she and her husband, Joachim, were unable to have children, and only divine intervention enabled her to conceive, which would explain why the plant named after her was long believed to have aphrodisiac properties.

No matter which of these stories is correct, Queen Anne's lace will remain as beautiful as ever. It blooms as an escape on roadsides throughout America and England in late summer and is sometimes cultivated in the garden, as it well deserves to be; in fact, it was first brought to America by Virginia colonists for use in their formal gardens.

QUEEN FRUIT. (See *Durian.*)

QUEEN MARY'S THISTLE. The national flower of Scotland was supposedly named for Mary, Queen of Scots, after attendants presented her a basket of the flowers while she was imprisoned by England's Queen Elizabeth in Fotheringay Castle. Also called the "cotton thistle," *Onopordum acanthium* has a purple top and is covered with little thread-like white hairs.

QUEEN OF THE PRAIRIE. This tall plant of the rose family, *Filipendula rubra,* with branching clusters of pink flowers, was so named by American pioneers in the mid-eighteenth century when they saw the plant growing in meadows and prairies and admired its graceful beauty. *Filipendula* is Latin for "hanging thread," alluding to the root fibers of the plant hanging together by threads.

QUICK FENCE. *Quick*, spelled *cqicu* or *cwic*, originally meant "the presence of life," or "living" in Old English. Therefore, livestock was once called "quickstock," to mean "living stock." "Quicksilver" was so named because it seemed alive and a "quick fence" was a living hedge of plants. A "quick pot of flowers" is another way of saying a living pot of plants or flowers as opposed to a pot of cut flowers.

QUINCE. The word *quince* may come from the Greek *kydonion* ("melon") named for Cydonia in Crete. *Kydonion* became *cydoneum* in Latin, which became *coin* in Old French, then *quoyne* in Middle English; *quince* derived from the plural of the Middle English *quoyne*, which is *quine*. This close relative of the pear, which grows on a small gnarled shrub but has among the most beautiful of fruit blossoms, was dedicated by the Greeks and Romans to Venus or Aphrodite as a symbol of love, happiness and fertility. Still another fruit believed to be the "forbidden fruit" of the Garden of Eden, the quince was guaranteed by some medieval physicians to help women beget sons of marked energy and ability. Mentioned by Keats in one of his poems, it is also the subject of many ancient legends, including a superstition that says it wards off "the influence of the evil eye." The bitter quince is not, of course, eaten raw; it is prepared in preserves, used in sauces and cooked in blends with other fruits. *Cotignac,* an esteemed French preserve, is made from the fruit, and it is also used for a rich wine.

QUISQUALIS. Like *Mahernia,* the name of the plant genus *Quisqualis* is another joke played by the pioneer botanist Linnaeus. *Quisqualis,* the genus containing a few woody vines from Malaya and the Philippines, is today grown in southern Florida for its showy pink or red flowers. When Linnaeus examined the plant, he did not know how to classify it or for whom he could name it. He therefore called the genus *Quisqualis* which in Latin means, literally, "who or what for." *Quisqualis* (kwis-kwal-is) clearly shows that the naming process is not always so serious a matter; it might even be called an anonymous eponymous word, or a word in want of an eponym.

RABAGE. This unfortunate vegetable is quite real but won't be found in any gardening books or seed catalogs. The rabage (*Raphanobrassica*) is a cross between a radish and a cabbage developed by a Soviet geneticist named Alexi Karpenchinko in 1924. What was expected was a plump head of cabbage on an edible round root of radish. Sadly, what developed was a head of scraggly radish leaves and the thin useless roots of a cabbage.

RABBIT-EYE. A blueberry bush native to the southern United States and widely grown there, it is called the "rabbit-eye blueberry" because to some the berries on the tall (up to 20-foot-high) plants resemble rabbit eyes. (See *Blueberry*.)

RABBIT TOBACCO. "Rabbit terbaker," as Uncle Remus called it, is balsam wood, a plant traditionally used as a tobacco substitute by youngsters, despite its bitter taste. It is so named because it grows wild in fields where rabbits run.

RADISH. The easy-to-grow radish (*Raphanus sativus*) takes its scientific name from its Greek name, *raphanes*, "easily reared." *Radish* itself comes ultimately from the Latin *radix*, "root." Greek artisans made small replicas of radishes in gold, while creating images of their other vegetables in lead or silver. The French call the radish by the poetic name *roses d'hiver*, "roses of winter," and they are used in French cookery in hundreds of ways. Ludwig Bemelmans described the Bavarian treatment of them lovingly in his novella *The Blue Danube:*

> *After the wet, scratchy leaves are cut away along with the top of the radish, it is sliced paper thin, but so that the radish remains intact, opened like a fan. It is then salted and left alone until water*

comes oozing out between the slices. When it has wept its last tear, then the radish is ready to be eaten.

RAFFLESIA. The naming of the genus *Rafflesia* after English administrator Sir Thomas Stamford Bingley Raffles (1781–1826) can be interpreted as a compliment or an insult. On the one hand, the species *Rafflesia arnoldi* has the largest single bloom of all—up to six feet in diameter, three-quarters of an inch thick and attaining a weight of 15 pounds. On the other hand, this same bowl-shaped, mottled orange-brown-and-white flower is commonly called "the stinking corpse lily." The plant is a parasite that grows on the roots of vines in its Malaysian habitat and only its bloom is visible aboveground; the rest is a fungus growing beneath it, and its smell of decaying flesh attracts the carrion flies that pollinate it. On balance it seems that Sir Stamford would have been better off if he had had only the world-famous Raffles Hotel in Singapore named for him, but since he discovered the plant genus, he really had no one to blame but himself—he could have kept quiet about it!

Raffles gained no gratitude from the British powers that were, either. An able colonial administrator in the East Indies, he did much to suppress the slave trade. But he was censured for freeing slaves, and after his death his wife had to pay the costs of his mission to found Singapore. The Zoological Society of London was established by Raffles, who served as its first president. He shares his niche in the dictionaries with one other man who did not come out smelling like a rose. Dutch physician J. B. Stapel (d. 1636) is also remembered by a carrion flower: the large flowers of the cactuslike *Stapelia* genus, containing some 100 species, all having a very unpleasant, fetid odor. Native to South Africa, a few of these curiously marked species—variously colored and sometimes marbled or barred—are grown in the greenhouse for their flowers.

Still another fetid plant, said to be the most "evil smelling" of all, is *Amorphophallus titanum,* a rare East Indian herb that has a giant spathe (not a flower) measuring up to four feet across, which has erroneously been called "the largest flower in the world," an honor that belongs to *Rafflesia arnoldi.*

RAGGED ROBIN. The pink or white wildflower *Lychnis flos-cuculi* is known as "ragged robin" because of its dissected petals. In his *Idylls of the King* the English poet Tennyson used the word to mean a pretty girl wearing ragged clothes. Ragged robin is also called the "cuckoo flower." Its genus name *Lychnis* comes from the Greek *lychnos,* "lamp," in reference to the glowing flame-colored flowers.

RAIN TREE. Several trees, including *Tamia caspia* of the Andes, are called "rain trees" or "raining trees" because moisture condenses and collects on their broad leaves. The tropical tree *Samanea saman,* also called the "monkeypod" and cultivated in extreme southern Florida, is so named because its many leaflets fold at the approach of rainy weather.

RAPESEED. The name of seed of rape (*Brassica napus*) of the mustard family derives from the Latin *rapum* for "turnip." It is used to make rape oil, a brownish-yellow oil used chiefly as a lubricant and illuminant, and in the manufacture of rubber substitutes. In 1981 more than 600 Spaniards died in the largest recorded accidental mass poisoning in history from using a commercial cooking oil made with "denatured" industrial oil from rapeseed. Rape is used as a cover crop in the United States. (See *Mustard.*)

RASPBERRY. Known to the Romans as the "Red Berry of Mount Ida" (hence the name of the British species *Rubus idaeus*) for Mount Ida in Greece, the raspberry probably takes its name from the English *rasp,* "to scrape roughly," in reference to the thorned canes bearing the berries. First called the "raspis-berry," it has also been called a "hindberry."

Raspberries have not been cultivated for nearly as long as fruits like apples, peaches and pears. Called a "brambleberry" and considered a nuisance in England, it was not until about 1830 that the delicate, delicious fruit began to be developed in America. The "Fanny Heath" variety is a tribute to a determined pioneer woman who immigrated to North Dakota in 1881. This young bride had been told that she could never grow anything on the barren alkaline soil surrounding her house, but 40 years later her homestead was an Eden of flowers, fruits and vegetables. After her death in 1931, the black raspberry she developed was named in her honor.

A red raspberry variety honoring a famous person is the "Lloyd George," named after British Prime Minister David Lloyd George (1863–1945), who led Britain to victory in World War I and dominated British politics in the first quarter of the twentieth century.

RHODODENDRON. This large genus of shrubs with very large, showy flowers takes its name from the Greek for rose (*rhodo*) and tree (*dendron*). The name was given by the Greeks to the oleander, an unrelated species, but Linnaeus applied it to the shrubs we now know as rhododendrons when classifying them. (See *Azalea; Linnaen system.*)

RHUBARB. Speculation has been rife for years about how the slang term *rhubarb*, "a heated argument," arose from the name of a popular fruit or vegetable. Since the word is often associated with baseball, many writers say it has its origins there. But probably the best explanation was advanced about 50 years ago by a veteran actor familiar with theatrical traditions; apparently actors simulating angry talk in crowd scenes gathered backstage and "intoned the sonorous word 'rhubarb.' " The actor-etymologist, Alexander McQueen, advised that the word produces such an effect "only if two or three work at it," and claimed that this theatrical tradition went back to Shakespearean times, but the slang *rhubarb* for an argument only arose in the late nineteenth century. It therefore came to mean a "rumpus" or a "row" at about the time baseball was fast becoming America's national pastime. It is easy to see how the stage term could have been applied to an argument on the diamond, especially a mass argument that involved both teams, though there is no solid proof of this.

Rhubarb itself has an interesting derivation, taking its name from the Latin *rha barbarum*. The Romans called it this because the plant was native to the river Rha (the Volga), a foreign "barbarian" territory—*rha barbarum*—thus meaning "from the barbarian (foreign) Rha." The first rhubarb planted in America was sent to the great naturalist John Bartram from Siberia in 1770. Americans long called the fruit "pieplant" because it makes such delicious pies, especially when combined with strawberries. It is also called the "go-quick" plant for its laxative quality.

ROAST BEEF PLANT. (See *Stinking Iris*.)

ROOK. Farmers in England called this member of the crow tribe (*Corvus fugilegus*) a *hrooc* as early as the eighth century, probably in imitation of its raucous cry. The bird has long been regarded as a garden pest and was clearly distinguished from the crow, as this old seed-planting rhyme shows: "One for the rook / One for crow / One for the weather / And one to grow." The chess piece called the "rook" has an entirely different origin, deriving from a Persian word whose original sense is unknown. The thieving bird, however, does give us "to rook," or "cheat," which has been used since Shakespeare's time, just as "to gull" has been.

ROSARY. The rope of beads used by Roman Catholics for the repetitions of certain prayers is said to be named a rosary because the first ones were made of rosewood, a hard, reddish, black-streaked wood that often has a roselike odor and comes from several tropical trees, including *Dalbergia nigra* and *Pterocarpus erinaceus,* the African rosewood or *molompi.* Another theory is that it takes its name from the "Mystical Rose," one of the titles of the Virgin Mary, while still another holds that the first rosary beads were beads perfumed with roses given to Saint Dominic by the Virgin Mary. However, the book of prayers called the *rosary* takes its name from the Latin *rosarium,* "rose garden." The prayer book in turn may have given its name to the beads by which prayers are counted. No one is sure which of the four origins is correct.

ROSE. The rose may take its name from the Celtic word *rhod,* "red," in reference to its typical color. There are 100 to 4,000 species of roses, depending on which botanist you believe, not to mention the 8,000 or more rose cultivars. That great teller of tall tales Sir John Mandeville, who wrote of anthills of gold dust and fountains of youth, told the best story about the origin of the rose in his fourteenth-century *Voyage and Travels.* It seems that a beautiful Jewish maiden of Bethlehem rejected the brutish advances of a drunken lout named Hanauel. In revenge Hanauel falsely denounced her as a witch, and she was condemned to burn at the stake. But God answered her prayers and extinguished the flames; the stake itself budded and the fair maiden stood there unharmed under a rose tree of red and white blossoms, "the first on earth since Paradise was lost."

Legends abound about the rose. One says that the white rose was turned red when Eve kissed one in the Garden of Eden; another tells of Cupid's blood shed upon it. Still another story holds that the rose bursts into bloom when a nightingale sings. Edward Phillips in *Sylva Florifera* tells this tale of the birth of the rose:

> *Flora [the Roman goddess of flowers] having found the corpse of a favorite nymph, whose beauty of person was only surpassed by the purity of her heart . . . resolved to raise a plant from her precious remains . . . for which purpose she begged the assistance of Venus and the Graces, as well as of all the deities that preside over gardens, to assist in the transformation of the nymph into a flower, that was to be by them proclaimed queen of all the vegetable beauties. The ceremony was attended by the Zephyrs, who cleared the atmosphere in order that Apollo might bless the new-created progeny by his beams. Bacchus supplied rivers of nectar to nourish it; and Vertumnus [the Roman god of orchards] poured his choicest perfumes over the plant. When the metamorphosis was complete, Pomona [the Roman goddess of fruit] strewed her fruit over the*

young branches, which were then crowned by Flora with a diadem,
that had been purposely prepared by the celestials, to distinguish
this queen of flowers.

Since the beginning of time, it seems, roses have been the flowers of
love, the true flowers of Venus. Cleopatra carpeted a room with red rose
petals so that their scent would rise above Mark Antony as he walked
toward her; Dionysius, the Tyrant of Syracuse, filled his house with
roses for the frequent compulsory orgies he held with the young women
of his city; Nero used millions of the blooms to decorate a hall for a
single banquet, and rose water–saturated pigeons fluttered overhead to
sprinkle the guests with scent. In fact, roses were so popular in ancient
times that they actually became a symbol of the degeneracy of later
Roman emperors, and it took the Church, to which the rose became a
symbol of purity, to rescue it from oblivion during the Dark Ages.
According to one ancient story, a number of noble Romans were suffo-
cated under tons of rose petals dropped on them during one of Emperor
Heliogabalus's orgies. The Romans loved the flower so much that they
imported bargefuls of rose petals and hips from Egypt, where the growing
season was longer. The Romans believed in the flower's powers so fer-
vently that they used rose water in their fountains. Long before this the
Greek physician Galen had used a full pound of rose oil in a facial
cosmetic he invented, and "attar of roses" remains a much-valued cosmetic ingredient to this day.

For centuries the rose has been employed to invoke love in some
rather strange ways. Persian women thought that rose water was a philter
that would bring back straying lovers; one old Chinese love recipe drunk
during the fourth-month rose festivals consisted of prunes, sugar, olives
and rose petals; and colonial ladies made "rose wine" to stimulate their
lovers by marinating rose petals in brandy. Finally we have Napoleon's
empress Josephine, who, when her teeth turned bad, always carried a
rose in her hand with which to cover her mouth when she laughed.

According to legend, the Greek god of silence, Harpocrates, stumbled
upon Venus while she was making love with a handsome youth, and
Cupid, the goddess of love's son, bribed the god of silence to keep quiet
about the affair by giving him the first rose ever created. This story
made the rose the emblem of silence, and since the fifth century B.C., a
rose carved on the ceilings of dining and drawing rooms where European
diplomats gathered enjoined all present to observe secrecy about any
matter discussed *sub rosa* or "under the rose." A similar phrase used
at such gatherings was *sub vino sub rosa est,* "what is said under the
influence of wine is secret," a reminder that things revealed by tongues

made loose with wine weren't to be repeated beyond the walls. The rose was also carved over the Roman Catholic confessional as a symbol of silence, and *sub rosa* became well known in German as *unter der rose,* in French as *sous la rose* and in English as "under the rose" as a term for "strict confidence," "complete secrecy" or "absolute privacy." Incidentally, the ancient legend of Harpocrates was inspired by what the Greeks thought was a picture of the Egyptian god of silence, Horus, seated under a rose with a finger at his lips. Actually, the rose in the picture was a lotus, and the infant god Horus was merely sucking his finger!

What Gertrude Stein really wrote in her poem *Sacred Emily* was "Rose is a rose is a rose is a rose," but her words have been misquoted so often that she might as well have written "a rose is a rose is a rose." In her prose Gertrude Stein had no use for nouns: "things once they are named the name does not go on doing anything to them and so why write in nouns." But in poetry, she felt: "You can love a name and if you love a name that saying that name any number of times only makes you love it more . . ." And poetry is "really loving the name of anything." Which perhaps best explains "Rose is a rose is a rose is a rose." (See *Damask Rose; Dog Rose; York and Lancaster.*)

ROSEMARY. The homely herb rosemary was originally called by the Latin name *ros marinus,* "sea dew," because it was often found on the sea cliffs in southern France. But over the years *ros* sounded more like "rose" to English ears, and *marinus* suggested the common name "Mary." The herb was thus dedicated to the Virgin Mary, and the word *rosemary* was recorded as early as 1440. This flowering shrub has contributed its dried leaves and stems to many recipes, and oils from its leaves and flowers figure in numerous potions and perfumes. Bouquets of rosemary, "emblematical of manly virtues," were once presented to bridegrooms on their wedding mornings, and bridal beds are still bedecked with the flowers in certain European countries to ensure conjugal bliss. Rosemary symbolizes remembrance, and Shakespeare's Ophelia presented a bunch to Hamlet, perhaps to remind him of their meeting on Saint Valentine's day when the melancholy Dane: "Let in the maid, that out a maid / Never departed more."

ROSE OF JERICHO. Native to the deserts of Arabia, the rose of Jericho (*Anastatica hierochuntica*) or "resurrection plant" is when dry a tight ball the size of an orange that is driven across the sands by the winds. It can be kept like this for many years but will often continue to grow, unfolding and revealing small leaves and minute white flowers when exposed to water. It is also called "the rose of the virgin."

ROSE OF SHARON. There are at least 25 species of flowers and shrubs named after the rose, usually because of some physical resemblance. The rose of Sharon is one of them, taking its last name not from any woman named Sharon, but from the Hebrew place-name Sharon. Sharon is the fertile level tract along the coast of Palestine where the flower mentioned in the Bible was said to grow. The identity of the true rose of Sharon is uncertain, and today the name is applied to several plants in America, generally to the showy late shrub *Hibiscus syriacus* (also called "Althea"). Scholars believe the biblical rose of Sharon was a wild tulip.

ROWANBERRY. The European mountain ash, as the rowanberry (*Sorbus aucuparia edulis*) is also called, has an interesting history. It takes the name *rowanberry* from the Danish *rune*, "magic," because it was supposed to have magical powers to ward off evil. The fruit of the rowanberry is used in making preserves and wines.

ROYSTONEA. It isn't often that someone's entire name is taken for a word, but that is just what happened with General Roy Stone, a nineteenth-century American engineer in Puerto Rico who had the Roystonea, or "royal palm," named after him. The genus *Roystonea* is well known and includes six species of palms. Often used as an ornamental to line avenues in tropical America, its beautiful crest dominates every landscape where it grows, and every part from its roots to its crown serves some useful purpose. Some of these feather palm species grow to more than 100 feet high, and the *Roystonea regia* species is widely planted in southern Florida. Florida's Palm Beach, the wealthy resort where 25,000 millionaires are said to reside in season, became a palm-fringed paradise when a cargo of coconuts washed ashore from a shipwreck in 1879, and early residents planted the nuts along the once-desolate beach.

RUBBER TREE. (See *Castilla elastica*.)

RUDBECKIA. A Swedish professor once tried to prove that the site of the Garden of Eden was located in the Land of the Midnight Sun. The professor, Olof Rudbeck (1630–1702), also claimed in his book *Atlantikan* that Sweden had been the locale of Plato's Atlantis. But otherwise he was a fine scientist, discovering the lymphatic system and making various botanical contributions. Linnaeus so admired the Rudbeck family

that he named the North American coneflower after both Professor Rudbeck and his son, the junior Professor Rudbeck, a contemporary of Linnaeus. The *Rudbeckia* genus, of some 25 species, includes the popular
black-eyed susan and golden glow. Plants in the genus are herbs, usually
having yellow rays, and can be annuals or perennials.

RUTABAGA. Commonly called the "Swedish turnip," rutabaga derives
its name from the Swedish dialect *rotabagge* for the plant; this relatively
new vegetable, first recorded in 1620, is extensively grown in Sweden.
Rutabaga is thought to be a hybrid of the turnip and a form of cabbage.
It requires a longer growing season than the turnip and is more nutritious
than its relative.

SAFFRON. Saffron costs about $400 a pound, making it one of the world's most expensive spices. This is primarily because it takes 4,000 blossoms of the autumn crocus (*Crocus sativus*), or 225,000 of its hand-picked stigmas, to make one ounce of saffron. But luckily a little goes a long way, for the spice has been coveted by gourmets and lovers since the Arabs introduced it to Spain in the eighth century A.D. Even before then saffron was used by the Phoenicians to flavor the moon-shaped love cakes dedicated to Astoreth, their goddess of fertility. Today the spice is often called "vegetable gold."

The old expression "he hath slept in a bed of saffron" refers to the supposed exhilarating effects of saffron, meaning "he has a very light heart." As an old poem puts it:

> *With genial joy to warm his soul,*
> *Helen mixed saffron in the bowl.*

(See *Crocus.*)

SAGE. The leaves of sage, a three-foot-high herbaceous evergreen shrub, are still used as a condiment, for stuffings and for a tonic tea. Oils from the entire plant perfume soaps. Sage, a favorite of Marcus Aurelius, has figured in love and youth potions since earliest times: "Why should a man die who has sage growing in his garden?" was a common Roman saying. The flavorsome leaves were a favorite of Charles Dickens, who loved their taste with the roast goose he made famous in *A Christmas Carol.*

SAINFOIN. This perennial herb of the pea family is also called "holy clover" and has long been used as fodder, although it is sometimes planted in flower garden borders. It has among the most unusual of scientific names, *Onobrychis viciifolia;* the genus name *Onobrychis* derives from the Greek for "food for asses," alluding to the plant's use for forage. Sainfoin, sometimes erroneously called "saintfoin," takes its name from the Latin *sānus,* "healthy," plus *foin,* "hay."

SAINT IGNATIUS'S BEAN. The seed or bean of the woody vine *Strychnos ignatti* yields the deadly poison strychnine, which does have curative medical properties as well. All that is known about the bean's namesake is that he is one of seven saints named Ignatius, perhaps the Portuguese-born Jesuit Azevedo (1528–1570), who may have come upon the plant in his travels. *Strychnine* itself is an old Greek name for a kind of nightshade, applied by Linnaeus to the 220 species of this genus because so many of them are poisonous. In the United States only one poisonous *Strychnos* species is found, the *Strychnos nux-vomica* or "strychnine tree" of extreme southern Florida, whose seeds yielded poisons for the arrows of Indians native to the area. A large strychnine tree specimen grows in New York's Brooklyn Botanical Garden.

SAINT PATRICK'S CABBAGE. Though native to Spain, Saint Patrick's cabbage (*Saxifrage umbrosa*) is found on the mountains of west Ireland as well, for which reason it is named for Saint Patrick, Archbishop of Armagh, the Apostle of Ireland. This ornamental with crimson-spotted petals is also known as "London pride." Saint Patrick is responsible for making the shamrock the Irish national emblem. When captured by a pagan ruler while preaching in the country, he is said to have plucked a shamrock and explained that its three leaves were distinct and separate on the plant "just as the Trinity is the union of three distinct persons in One Deity." Shamrock simply means "little clover," deriving from the Irish *seamrog,* the diminutive of *seamar,* "cloves." To "drown the shamrock" means a drinking celebration on Saint Patrick's Day.

SAINTPAULIA. The very popular African violet houseplant species are members of this genus of beautiful tropical African flowers. The genus is not named for a saint, however. It honors the German Baron Walter von Saint Paul, who discovered one of the African violet species.

SALVIA. Some species of Salvia had medicinal properties, causing the Romans to name the genus from the Latin *salver,* to "save" or "heal." The flowers are also known as "sage," which is a corruption of the French word *sauge* for "salvia," and sage tea has long been thought to have healing powers.

SAP. Our word for the sap of a plant comes from the Latin *sapa,* meaning "sap." Sap also came to mean "soft," like the green, unseasoned soft stalks that contain sap, which led to derogatory terms such as "saphead" and "sapskull" for a simpleton or stupid person. These terms were soon shortened to *sap.* By 1815, its first recorded usage, *sap* had succeeded "saphead" for a "cabbagehead" (1622). "Calabash" (1838), "pumpkin head" (1841) and "chump" (1883) are all similar garden-related words for jingle-brained nincompoops.

SARDONE. A sardonic person might be called a dead one, inside or out. The ancient Greeks believed that the sardone (*herba Sardonia*), a poisonous plant growing in Sardinia that gave the island its name, was so deadly that anyone unlucky or foolish enough to eat it would immediately succumb to its effects. Victims were said to literally die laughing, going into convulsions, their final contorted expressions after their death throes resembling bitter, scornful grins. The Greeks called their last bitter appearance of laughter *Sardonios gelos,* "Sardinian laughter," *Sardo* being their name for the island. *Sardonios gelos* became the French *rire sardonique;* this resulted in our expressions "sardonic laughter" and "sardonic humor," laughter or humor characterized by bitter or scornful derision. Whether the folklore is all true or not remains unknown, but there is a plant called the *herba Sardonia,* and its acrid leaves do cause involuntary contortions of the facial nerves when tasted. The contortions resemble a painful or bitter smile. The medical term *risus sardonicus* is still used to describe the peculiar grin seen on the face of a corpse after deaths caused by tetanus and other diseases, an acute spasm of the facial muscles responsible for the bitter "smile."

SARSAPARILLA. True sarsaparilla (*Smilax officinalis*) is related to the asparagus but isn't widely cultivated in the United States. The same legends surround its roots as surround asparagus; Mexican Indians, for example, have long used the roots of the vine in a concoction they believe cures impotence. In 1939 it was discovered that the sarsaparilla root contains large amounts of testosterone, and today much of the male sex hormone manufactured commercially comes from the plant. (See *Asparagus.*)

SASS. The word *sass* is still used to refer to stewed fruit or fresh vegetables in sections of the United States, as is "garden sass." The word, first recorded around 1760, originally meant garden vegetables: "Short sass" was potatoes, onions or turnips; "long sass" was carrots, parsnips and other vegetables. *Sass,* which is probably an American alteration of "sauce," didn't acquire its more common meaning of "backtalk" until about the middle of the nineteenth century. This meaning possibly has something to do with the "freshness" of both long and short sass.

SASSAFRASS. Folklore holds that the genus of small plants called *Saxifrage,* from the Latin *saxum,* "rock," and *frangere,* "to break," is so named because the plant was used by the ancients as a medicine to break up kidney stones. However, it probably got that name because the plants grow naturally in the clefts of rocks and could be imagined to have broken them. A plant that was named for its use against kidney stones is sassafras. The Romans used a concoction made of the bark of the sassafras tree (*Sassafras albidum*) to break up stones in the bladder, which is why its name means "stonebreaker," from the Latin for this word. Sassafras tea, used as a stimulant and diuretic, is also made from the tree's bark, and sassafras oil, used in flavoring, perfume and medicine, is made from its roots.

SCABIOSA. Not a very nice name for a very pretty flower, *scabiosa* derives from the Latin word *scabies,* "itch." But the plant doesn't cause itching. It was highly valued by the ancients as a cure for certain skin diseases. Scabiosas make good garden plants, and several species of them are grown in the United States.

SCALLION. Crusaders returning from the Holy Land probably introduced the word *scallion* to Europe. These small onions were raised in the Palestinian seaport of Ascalon, now just ancient ruins, and had been named *Ascalonia caepa,* "Ascalonion onion," by the Romans. This was shortened to *scalonia* in the common speech of the Romans and passed into English as *scalyon,* which finally became *scallion.* (See *Onion.*)

SCHIZOCARP. The "wings" or "helicopters" on maple trees that spin like pinwheels when you toss them into the wind, and which you may have attached to your nose when you were a kid, are technically called schizocarps. *Schizo* means "split," and the scientific definition for a schizocarp is "a dry dehiscent fruit that at maturity splits into two or more one-seeded carpels." "Wings," or "helicopters," is better.

SCOOTBERRY. The "scoots" was slang for diarrhea in nineteenth-century New Hampshire, and since the sweetish red berries of *Streptopus roseus* always acted as a physic on the youngsters who eagerly ate them, they were called scootberries. The plant's purplish-pink, bell-shaped flowers grow on a short, twisted stalk from the axils of the leaves, giving it its other popular name, "twisted stalk." Also called "liverberry," it is native to eastern North America, preferring to grow in damp, shady places.

SCUPPERNONG. *Scuppernong* is the popular name for the muscadine grape (*Vitis rotundifolia*). Grown in the southern United States, it has large sweet fruit often used to make scuppernong wine. The name derives from the Scuppernong river and lake in Tyrell County, North Carolina, where the grape was discovered in the eighteenth century.

SEASON. *Season* derives ultimately from the Latin word *sation* meaning "time of sowing," or "seed-time." The word was long used just for the time of the year when seed was sown. The division of the year into four separate seasons dates only to around the twelfth century.

The season of the year all gardeners look forward to takes its name from the sense of the noun *spring* meaning a "rising" or "springing into existence" of plants and flowers. In popular use, spring in the United States comprises part of March, April, May and part of June, while in England it includes February, March and April. The romantic Romans named April after the flower buds that open in that month, basing their *Aprilis* on the Latin *aperia*, meaning "open."

The seasons of the year used to be called "spring tyme, Somer, faule [fall] of the leafes, and winter." But by the late seventeenth century "faule of the leaves" was replaced by the abbreviated *fall*, which it has been ever since. *Autumn*, on the other hand, isn't a native word for the season; it derives from the Latin *autumnus*.

Climate is another word that has its origins in a foreign language. The ancient Greeks thought that the earth sloped toward the North Pole from the equator and for this reason named any particular part or region of the earth *klima*, from their verb *klinein*, "to slope." Since they also believed that the earth's slope accounted for the varied weather in these different regions, they called the weather of a specific region its *clima*, which evolved into the English *climate*.

SEQUOIA. The largest and tallest living things on earth, the giant sequoias of California and Oregon are named for the exalted Indian leader Sequoyah, who invented the Cherokee syllabary, which not only made a whole people literate practically overnight but formed the basis for many Indian languages. Sequoyah (also Sequoya, or Sikwayi) was born about 1770, the son of a white trader named Nathaniel Gist; his mother was related to the great king Oconostota. Though he used the name

George Guess, Sequoyah had few contacts with whites, working as a silversmith and trader in Georgia's Cherokee country until a hunting accident left him lame. With more time on his hands, Sequoyah turned his attention to the "talking leaves" or written pages of the white man and set out to discover this secret for his own people. Over a period of 12 years, withstanding ridicule by family and friends, he listened to the speech of those around him, finally completing a table of characters representing all 86 sounds in the Cherokee spoken language.

Sequoyah's system was adopted by the Cherokee council in 1821; one story claims that his little daughter won over the council chiefs by reading aloud a message that they had secretly instructed her father to write down. Thousands of Indians would learn to read and write thanks to Sequoyah's "catching a wild animal and taming it." He joined the Arkansas Cherokee the following year, and in 1828 moved with them to Oklahoma after helping to negotiate in Washington, D. C., for more extensive lands. For the rest of his life he devoted himself to his alphabet and the study of common elements in Indian language, translating parts of the Bible into Cherokee and starting a weekly newspaper. Sequoyah was also instrumental in avoiding bloodshed and forming the Cherokee Nation when in 1839 the federal government heartlessly drove other Cherokee to Oklahoma from their ancestral homes in Alabama and Tennessee. He is believed to have died somewhere in Mexico around 1843 while searching for a lost band of Cherokee who were rumored to have moved there at about the time of his birth. It is said that he and his party of horsemen did ultimately find their lost brothers and taught them to read and write.

Sequoyah, legendary in his own time among Indians and whites, is one of a few men to invent an entire alphabet adopted by a people. In 1847, not long after Sequoyah's death, the Hungarian botanist Stephan Endlicher gave the name *Sequoia sempervirens* to the redwood tree, and it is generally assumed, though not definitely known, that he had the great Cherokee leader in mind. There are three types of sequoias, all members of the pine family. The redwood species mentioned, native to the coast of California and a few miles into Oregon, is probably the tallest tree currently standing in the world; one sequoia growing in California's Redwood National Park stands 373 feet tall. (The tallest recorded tree of all time is probably an Australian eucalyptus that measured 470 feet before it fell in 1885.)

Another sequoia type is *Sequoia gigantea*, which grows on the western slopes of California's Sierra Nevada. These are generally called giant sequoias or "big trees," not redwoods. They are not as tall as their relatives but are the largest plants on earth. Greatest among them, at

274.9 feet tall, is the General Sherman sequoia in California's Sequoia National Park. This largest of all living things is popularly named for Union Civil War General William Tecumseh Sherman (1820–1891). It would take at least 17 adults with outstretched arms to encircle this tree, which contains enough timber to make 5 billion matches. From its beginnings as a minuscule seed nearly 40 centuries ago, the massive General Sherman increased in weight more than 125,000 millionfold and in combined height and girth dwarfs any other plant. The General Sherman, 3,000 years old, is also one of the oldest of living things, but a bristlecone pine in California's Inyo National Forest holds the age record: "Methuselah" has endured for more than 4,600 years on the windswept slopes of the White Mountains—since 2600 B.C.

The third sequoia type is the "dawn redwood" or "living fossil," *Metasequoia glyptostroboides.* Discovered growing in China in 1946, these trees are reputedly the ancestors of all sequoias, and their fossil remains date back 30 to 50 million years. The dawn redwood is now grown in the United States and has thus far reached heights of up to 35 feet; although it closely resembles other redwoods it is more similar to the cypress of the southern United States. Incidentally, it is little known that some sequoias have been grown successfully in the East; one grown in Rochester, New York, reached a height of more than 50 feet. Adrian Le Corbeaum's *The Forest Giant,* translated by T. E. Lawrence, "Lawrence of Arabia," is a beautifully written appreciation of the giant sequoia.

SERVICEBERRY. Another name for the "juncberry" (*Amelanchier species*). "The blueberry of the northern plains" was dubbed the serviceberry as far back as the eighteenth century, and the name has a touching story behind it. Since its white blossoms appeared almost as soon as the ground thawed in spring, American pioneer families that had kept a body through the winter to bury in workable ground used these first flowers to cover the grave.

SHADDOCK. The ancestor of the grapefruit, the shaddock, or pomelo, reached Europe in the middle of the twelfth century from the Malay archipelago. It was called the "Adam's apple" at first and didn't receive its common name until Captain Shaddock, a seventeenth-century English voyager, brought its seed from the East Indies to Barbados, where it was grown extensively. The grapefruit (*Citrus paradisi*) is neither a mutation of the thicker-skinned shaddock (*Citrus grandis*) nor a cross between the shaddock and sweet orange. It was developed in the West Indies and was given its name because it often grows in clusters like grapes. To further complicate matters, the shaddock is sometimes called the "forbidden fruit," and the grapefruit is called the *pomelo* in different parts of the world. The pink grapefruit was developed in Florida, as was the seedless variety.

SHAMROCK. (See *Saint Patrick's Cabbage*.)

SHEPHERD'S SUNDIAL. Shepherds used to tell time by the scarlet pimpernel (*Anagallis arvensis*), which opens a bit after 7:00 A.M., closes at a little past 2:00 P.M., and never opens at all if bad weather is imminent. Its genus name is from a Greek word meaning "delightful," though it is not a delight to one garden writer who classifies the low prostrate annual herb with tiny, red bell-shaped flowers as one of the 50 worst garden weeds. "Poor man's weatherglass" is another name for it.

SHOOFLY PLANT. There is only one garden species of the *Nicandra* genus, which is named after Nicander of Colophon, a Greek physician, poet and botanist of the second century A.D. And this annual species, *Nicandra physalodes,* seems to have but one distinction: It is a repellant to the white fly if grown next to other plants troubled by this pest. It is also called "Apple-of-Peru," because it is plentiful in that country.

SHORTIA. Shortia is definitely a "low-growing" genus of evergreen herbs, comprising only two species, but that is not the reason for its name. The genus honors Dr. Charles W. Short (1794–1863), a Kentucky botanist. Native to the mountains of the Carolinas and Japan, the flowers are well adapted for use in rock gardens. The American species is sometimes advertised as "Oconee bells" and the Japanese as "Nippon bells." The plants have beautiful white bell- or heart-shaped flowers, solitary and nodding on long stalks. They are more often called shortia, or "coltsfoot," than by their "bell" names.

SIMPLES. *Simples* is an old word for medicinal herbs. In days past, the market gardeners of Battersea in England used to grow simples, and London apothecaries went to the town to select or cut the herbs they wanted. The similarity of the word *simpleton* and the *simples* of this common practice led to the use of "you must go to Battersea to get your simples cut" as a reproof to a simpleton or someone who made a very foolish observation.

SKUNK CABBAGE. The much-maligned marshland skunk cabbage (*Symplocarpus foetidus*) bears little relation or resemblance to the cabbage (*Brassica capitata*). The plant takes its name, an Americanism first recorded in 1751, from its fetid smell and its leaves' supposed resemblance to cabbage leaves. Actually the skunk cabbage's large, nearly round leaves are far more handsome and its sheathlike spathe is beautifully colored. But the plant's foul smell has caused it to be called "polecat weed" as well as skunk cabbage. Other names for it are "tickleweed" and "dock." Cheap, poor liquor used to be called "skunk cabbage brandy."

SLUG. The slug is possibly the most disgusting thing one will encounter in the garden. It is hard to find anything good to say about the creature, which is technically a snaillike terrestrial gastropod with no shell that feeds on leafy garden crops. Interestingly, the slug takes its name from the Scandanavian *sluggje,* a heavy, slow person. In fact, in English the word *slug* first meant a fat person before it was applied to the garden pest. Like the shark and the shrimp, the slug is named for a person sharing its characteristics, not the other way around, as is usual. (See *Snail.*)

SMALLAGE. (See *Celery.*)

SNAIL. Since at least 1592 a "snail's pace" has meant "exceedingly slow," but until recently no one knew just how exceedingly slow that was. Recent studies have shown that garden snails travel at about two feet an hour, or one mile every three months or so.

In the expression "to draw in one's horns," *horns* refers to the horns of the snail, because the garden pest draws in its horns and remains in its shell when threatened with danger, or when weather conditions aren't favorable. The snail's actions do suggest someone who draws in his horns, that is, draws away from a situation and takes no action while reconsidering the matter. The expression is first recorded in the early 1300s and clearly indicates that the garden snail is its source. (See *Slug.*)

SNATH. Another unusual garden word whose use will make you look knowledgeable—or archaic. A snath is the handle of a scythe. "Do you carry scythe snaths?" you can ask your much-impressed garden supply store owner. (See *Berm.*)

SOAPBERRY. The scientific name (*Sapindus*) for this tree explains the berry's use: *Sapindus* is a combination of the Latin for "soap" (*sapo*) and "Indus" (Indian). American Indians used the berries for soap. The pulp of soapberries contains saponin, so they lather up easily and were valued as shampoo, although the soap made from them does damage some materials. Two species are of horticultural importance. *Sapindus marginatus* is a deciduous tree up to 30 feet tall with yellow, egg-shaped fruit about one inch long that grows only in the southern United States. *Sapindus saponaria*, an evergreen, also grows up to 30 feet, but is only hardy in southernmost Florida. Both trees can be propagated by seed and do best in dry, sandy soil. Saponin, the lather-producing agent in soapberries, can be poisonous if taken internally; in fact, American Indians caught fish by stupefying them with bits of the fruit thrown into pools.

SOLOMON'S SEAL. As the root stalk of the flowering plant called Solomon's seal (*Polygonatum multiflorum*) decays, it becomes marked with scars bearing some resemblance to official seals. This may be the reason it was called Solomon's seal. More likely it takes its name from its root's medicinal value in closing or sealing wounds. It was a medicinal seal so good people might have reasoned that wise King Solomon must have prescribed its use. Its other names include "conjuer john" and "Big John the Conqueror."

SOYBEAN. The ancient Chinese made a sauce called *shiyu* (*shi*, "salted food" + *yu*, "oil") from this bean, which they apparently named after the sauce; *shi-yu* became *shoyu* and then *shoy* in Japanese, which ultimately became *soy* and *soybean* ("soy" + "bean") in English. The Japanese valued soy sauce so highly that it was part of the salary of Japanese imperial court officers in the fifth century. The versatile high-protein soybean can be used like other beans, or to make sauce, milk, curd and cheese or as a cooking oil. When they germinate in the dark for a week, the beans yield the crisp sprouts used in Chinese cooking.

SPANISH MOSS. The familiar Spanish or long moss (*Tillandsia us-neoides*), which drapes live oaks, cypresses and other trees from Virginia southward, is not a moss but an epiphytic (tree-perching) nonparasitic plant that takes its own nourishment from the air and does not kill any supporting plant, as many believe. Contrary to what the great Linnaeus thought, it does best in moist locations. The Swedish botanist was so sure the plant disliked moisture that he named the genus after his countryman Elias Tillands, a physician and botanist traveler who so feared water that he once walked 1,000 miles out of his way to avoid crossing the narrow Gulf of Bothnia.

SPILLING THE BEANS. (See *Beans*.)

SPINACH. Popeye did so much for this vegetable with the young set that spinach growers in one Texas town erected a large statue to him. Many kids, however, still share the sentiments of the girl in Carl Rose's famous *New Yorker* cartoon who refused her alleged broccoli with the words, "I say it's spinach, and I say the hell with it." Some authorities claim *spinach* derives from the Latin *hispanicus olus,* "the Spanish herb." The word does come to us from Spain, but probably not directly. Apparently the Persian and Arabian *isfanakh* became the Old Spanish *espinaca,* which eventually changed into the Middle French *espinach,* which resulted in our word *spinach.* At any rate, the Arabs did introduce the vegetable into Spain, and then it spread to the rest of Europe. Dr. Johnson, for one, enjoyed it, according to Boswell.

Napoleon did almost as much for spinach's fame as Popeye by decorating the golden epaulettes of his colonels with what looked like gold spinach leaves and were thus referred to as *spinach*—a term that lingers to this day. The phrase "gammon and spinach," meaning "nonsense," or "humbug," is not as familiar today as it was in Dickens's time, when he wrote in *David Copperfield,* "What a world of gammon and spinnage it is, though, ain't it!" The phrase, most likely an elaboration of the slang word *gammon,* which meant "nonsense" or "ridiculous story," is probably patterned on the older phrase "gammon and patter," the language of London underworld thieves. The nonsense part of it was possibly reinforced by the old nursery rhyme "A Frog He Would A-Wooing Go" (1600), which was heard by millions: "With a rowley powley gammon and spinach / Heigh ho! says Anthony Rowley."

E. B. White wrote the caption that became the catchphrase "I say it's spinach, and I say the hell with it" for the Carl Rose cartoon that appeared in the December 8, 1928, issue of *The New Yorker.* It shows a spoiled little girl who rejects her indulgent mother's offer of broccoli with words that have come to mean, "When I'm indulging my prejudices I don't want to be confused with facts." The phrase's abbreviated form, *spinach,* means "baloney," "malarkey," "bull," etc. In 1991 President George Bush joined the ranks of broccoliphobes when he told the press that he hates the stuff. President Clinton has gone on record that he likes it.

SPRUCE. During the reign of England's Henry VIII, courtiers affected the dress of Prussian noblemen, those hautest of the haute who wore such fashionable attire as broad-brimmed hats with bright feathers, silver chains around their necks, satin cloaks and red velvet doublets. Anything from Prussia had been called "Pruce" during the Middle Ages, but by the sixteenth century an *s* had somehow been added to the word, and courtiers who dressed as elegantly as Prussian noblemen were said to be appareled in "spruce fashion." *Spruce* soon described a smart, neat or dapper appearance, reflected in the phrase "to spruce up." The neat, trim form of the spruce tree may have suggested its name, too, but it more likely derives from the belief that the spruce was first grown in Prussia.

Spruce gum was the first American chewing gum. All types of *Picea* produce an abundance of resin, this genus name for the spruce deriving from the Latin word for "pitch." Here in America a number of cultivated spruce species—as well as other native trees like the sweet gum and juniper—have been valued from colonial days for their chewy resins. But the black or bog spruce (*Picea mariana*) and the red spruce (*Picea rubens*) are the principal producers of resin gum. The Indians introduced us to chewing gum from these trees and they, in turn, may have emulated a bear or another animal "gumming up" on spruce resin in prehistoric times. Hunters say that bears customarily "gum up" before they hibernate by swallowing quantities of spruce gum as large as a man's fist. Chewing gum is today mainly made from synthetics and from chicle, the thick creamy latex of the sapodilla tree (*Archas sapota*), native to Central America. The Mayans chewed chicle, wrapping it in banana plant leaves for an edible package.

SPUD. *Spud* is a Scottish term that dates back at least to the nineteenth century when a spud was a raw potato, and a roasted spud was a "mickey," cooked skin and all in the cinders. The word derives from the sharp spade called a "spud" used to dig potatoes. This early use of spud is of unknown origin, possibly deriving from the Middle English *spuddle*, a kind of knife. *Spud* definitely is not an acronym for the *S*ociety for the *P*revention of *U*nwholesome *D*iets! (See *Potato*.)

SQUASH. *Asquutasquash*, meaning "that which is eaten raw," was the Narraganset Indian word for a kind of melon. It is no wonder that early colonists pronounced the word *squash*, using only the last syllable. Later, they somehow transferred the word *squash* to what we now know as squash—a vegetable that is not eaten raw but does resemble a melon in that it grows on a vine and is sometimes round.

STAPELIA. (See *Rafflesia*.)

STARLING. This bird, whose name is akin to the Old English *stearn*, for "tern," was brought across the Atlantic in 1890 and released in Central Park by literary enthusiasts seeking to introduce to America all the birds mentioned in Shakespeare. It has since become a garden pest, reminding some gardeners of the Englishman who said in 1886, "Few people are aware of how good the starling is to eat." The starling (*Sturnus vulgaris*) constitutes more of the 100 billion birds in the world than any other species, and has long been noted for its ability to speak and whistle.

STINKING CLOVER. The rank-smelling plant *Cleome serrulata*, of the caper family, is called "stinking clover," but is better known as the "Rocky Mountain beeplant" after the many bees that are attracted to its showy, dense clusters of pink or white flowers. (See *Clover*.)

STINKING CORPSE LILY. (See *Rafflesia*.)

STINKING IRIS. The bruised evergreen foliage of the "stinking iris" (*Iris foetidissima*), also called "stinking gladium," makes up for its unpleasant smell by its medicinal uses. In fact, some gardeners must have *liked* its smell, for it went by the common name "roast beef plant" in days past. (See *Iris*.)

STINKWEED. (See *The Tree of Heaven*.)

STRAWBERRY. Several theories have been proposed about the origin of the word *strawberry*, but none is convincing. Some say the straw mulch often used by gardeners in its cultivation inspired the name, others claim the dried berries were once strung on straw for decorations; still others say the long strawlike runners of the mother plant (strawlike when dry) gave the fruit its name. The word was used as early as A.D. 100 in England and isn't derived from any other language. It may be that the "straw" in *strawberry* is a corruption of the word *strew*. Certainly the mother plant strews or scatters new plants all over a patch when it propagates itself by sending out runners.

There has always been mystery surrounding strawberries. The early Greeks, in fact, had a taboo against eating them because of their bloodlike red color, and pregnant women in the Middle Ages avoided them because they believed their children would be born with "strawberry marks" (small, slightly raised birthmarks resembling strawberries) if they did.

"Strawberry friend" is a term common in the Ozarks. It is used to describe a freeloader or a sponger from town or from a big city, who visits only during the strawberry season; that is, when strawberries are plentiful, when times are good.

STRING BEANS. First recorded in 1759, *string beans* is an American-ism for "green beans," and refers to the stringlike fibers along their sutures. When Burpee & Co. Seedsmen developed the Beautiful Burpee, "the stringless string bean" in 1894, the term *string bean* began to take a backseat to "green bean." It is still often heard, however, along with other synonyms like "snap beans" (named for the sound the pods make when broken), "wax beans" (yellow varieties), "kidney beans" and *haricot*. "String bean," for a very thin, tall person, has been American slang for at least a century.

SUNFLOWER. Sunflowers are so named because they resemble the full sun, not because they follow the direction of the sun during the day. *Helianthus* actually turns in every direction daily whether the sun is out or not. Sunflowers are cultivated for their seeds, which are eaten roasted and used to make cooking oil. Gardeners often enter local garden contests to see who can grow the tallest sunflower plant and the largest sunflower bloom. The world record for a sunflower plant is 25 feet, 5½ inches; the world record for a sunflower bloom is 32¼ inches in diameter.

SWISS CHARD. Swiss chard is a variety of beet that is cultivated for its leaves and stalks. It apparently takes its name from the French *chardon*, "thistle," a word closely related to the Latin word for thistle. Swiss chard, sometimes called "silverbeet," has been grown for thousands of years and is mentioned by Theophrastus, the Greek "Father of Botany." (See *Beet*.)

SYNGREEN. (See *Houseleek*.)

SYRINGA. In days past, the stems of this plant were used in making pipes. Because the stems resembled hollow reeds the attractive, fragrant, ornamental bush was named from the Greek *syringos*, "reed." The syringa (*Philadelphus coronarius*) is also called the "mock-orange." Linnaus named the genus *Philadelphus* after King Ptolemy Philadelphus, who ruled Egypt in the third century B.C.

TANGERINE. This fruit is called the "kid-glove orange" because its loose skin can be peeled off as easily as a soft kid glove can be peeled off the hands. But it is far better known as the tangerine after the seaport Tangier in Morocco, where the small deep-orange fruit was extensively cultivated and first called the "tangerine orange." Tangerines, however, belong to the mandarin group of oranges, which were first cultivated in southeast Asia.

TANSY. Common as a roadside weed, the very strong-scented, yellow–flowered tansy (*Tanacetum vulgare*) takes its name ultimately from the Greek *athanasia*, meaning "immortality," because it is a long-lasting flower. Another popular name for the flower is "bitter button."

TEA. British slang for a cup of tea is "cuppa char." *Char* is a corruption of *cha*, which means tea in England, deriving from the Mandarin *ch'a* for the same. *Tea* comes to us from the Chinese Amoy dialect *t'e*. Tea bags weren't invented until the turn of the century, when an American tea wholesaler named Sullivan began mailing prospective customers one-cup samples of his tea contained in little silk bags. The idea didn't catch on because the cloth changed the flavor of the tea, but during World War II chemists developed a tasteless paper tea bag that became extremely popular and accounts for most of the tea sold in America today.

When an Irishman says he'll have "a spot of tay" he's talking more English than the English. *Tay* is not "an ignorant Irish pronunciation of tea." The Portuguese introduced the drink we now know as tea into Europe as *cha* and that was the first English name it went by. But as far back as 1650 Englishmen were using the name the Dutch got from the Malayans for tea, *te*. This was pronounced "tay" in English long before it was pronounced "tea" and was often spelled "tay" to indicate this pronunciation, which was common up until the end of the eighteenth century. In his "Rape of the Lock," for example, Pope spells the word *tea* three times, but rhymes it with "obey," "stay" and "away." The scientific name of the tea plant, *Thea sinensis,* sometimes grown in the United States, is the Latinized version of the Chinese name for tea.

"All the tea in China" would be 369,000 tons or so, according to the 1977 *Food and Agricultural Organization of the United Nations Yearbook,* and I can find no updating of these crop statistics. It may be an Americanism, but this expression denoting a great sum probably is of British origin and more than a century old. No one has been able to authoritatively pin it down.

TEASEL. There are scores of tiny hooks on the dried seed pods of the teasel plant (*Dipsacus fullonum*). These hooked seed pods have long been grown for use in mills to raise or tease up the nap on woolen cloth. From this practice we get the hairdressing expression "teasing," as well as the "teasing" that irritates somebody, just as drawing a teasel pod across someone's skin would do.

THISTLE. The thistle became the heraldic emblem of Scotland in the eighth century or earlier in commemoration of the role it played in an attack by the Danes on Stirling Castle. Barefooted Dane scouts stepped on thistles during that night attack, alarming the Scots and enabling them to defeat the raiders. All thistles are members of the Compositae, one of the largest families of plants in the world, including among other relatives such fine garden flowers as marigolds, asters, cosmos, dahlias and chrysanthemums. But thistles are generally thought of as prickly weeds of little value. Abraham Lincoln's lowest estimate of a man was to call him a thistle. The word dates back in English to at least A.D. 752, and its origins are unknown.

THYME. We pronounce the "th" in thyme as *t* because it passed into English from French with that pronunciation at an early date. The word *thyme* ultimately comes from the Greek *thuo,* "perfume," in reference to the herb's sweet smell.

TICK. Ticks, which spread Lyme disease, are insects gardeners should try to avoid. Though only pinhead-size in most cases, they attach themselves to the skin, gorging themselves on blood until they swell to twice their size or larger. This led to the expression "full as a tick" to describe someone who has had much too much to drink.

TIGER LILY. This ubiquitous flower, often found on roadsides and in woods in the northeastern United States, originated in Japan or China. It takes its name from its orange and black colors. According to a Korean legend, *Lilium tigrinum* was named when a magician-hermit turned his pet tiger into a flower he could keep in his garden. After the magician died, the tiger lily left the garden and journeyed all over the world searching for his friend, which is why the flower is so widespread.

There is no reason why tiger lilies should talk more than other flowers, except that Lewis Carroll made them so inclined in *Through the Looking-Glass.* The tiger lilies there tell Alice that they talk all the time "when there's anybody worth talking to." They also offer a tip to gardeners who'd like to hear their flowers talk. "In most gardens," they explain, when Alice wants to know why she's never heard flowers talk in other gardens, "they make the beds too soft—so that the flowers are always asleep."

TILLANDSIA. (See *Spanish Moss.*)

TIMOTHY GRASS. *Timothy* is another, more popular name for "herd's grass." Both designations refer to meadow cattail grass, *Phleum pratense*, which is native to Eurasia and widely cultivated in the United States for hay. The species was probably brought to America by early settlers. Then in about 1770, John Herd supposedly found the perennial grass with its spiked or panicled head growing wild near his New Hampshire farm, and the grass received his name when he began cultivating it shortly thereafter. Timothy Hanson or Hanso gave his prename to the same grass when he quit his New York farm in 1720 and moved to Maryland, or possibly Carolina, introducing *Phleum pratense* seed there. "Timothy's seed" became "timothy grass" when it grew and was finally shortened to "timothy." *Phleum pratense* is America's leading dry-grass crop.

TOBACCO. The common name for the tobacco plant is the result of a mistake and seems to have first been recorded in Christopher Columbus's journal for November 6, 1492: "My messengers reported that after a march of about twelve miles they had discovered a village with about 1000 inhabitants. The natives had received them ceremoniously, and had lodged them in the most beautiful houses. They encountered many men and women carrying some sort of cylinder in which sweetly smelling herbs were glowing. The people sucked the other end of the cylinder and, as it were, drank in the smoke. Natives said they called these cylinders tabacos." Clearly then, the Carib word *tabaco* meant the reed pipes in which the natives smoked the dried leaves, but over the years *tabaco,* the ancestor of our *tobacco,* came to designate the leaves themselves and then the tobacco plant.

TOMATO. Those "affected" people who pronounce *tomato* "toe-mahtoe" are historically correct. The plant was first called *tomate* in Spain when introduced there from the New World as the Mayan *xtomatl* in the early sixteenth century, and it was pronounced with three syllables. The *o,* incidentally, has no place at all in *tomato;* it's there because mideighteenth-century Englishmen erroneously believed that it should have this common Spanish ending. *Lycopersicon esculentum* has also been called the "wolf apple," the "wolf peach" and the "love apple." The first two designations arose because most Americans thought that tomatoes were poisonous and didn't eat them until about 1830: The tomato *vine* is, in fact, poisonous, as the plant is a member of the deadly nightshade family.

If any one man liberated *Lycopersicon esculentum* it was Colonel Robert Gibbon Johnson, an eccentric gentleman of Salem, New Jersey. In 1808, after a trip abroad, Johnson introduced the tomato to the farmers of Salem, and each year thereafter offered a prize for the largest locally grown fruit. But the Colonel was a forceful individualist and wanted his introduction to be regarded as more than an ornamental bush. On September 26, 1820 (some say 1830), he announced that he would appear on the Salem courthouse steps and eat *not one but a whole basket of "wolf peaches"*!

Public reaction in Salem was immediate. Declared Johnson's physician, Dr. James Van Meeter:

> *The foolish colonel will foam and froth at the mouth and double over with appendicitis. All that oxalic acid! One dose and you're dead. Johnson suffers from high blood pressure, too. That deadly juice will aggravate the condition. If the Wolf Peach is too ripe and warmed by the sun, he'll be exposing himself to brain fever. Should he survive, by some unlikely chance, I must remind that the skin of the Solanum-Lycopersicum [as it was then called] will stick to the lining of his stomach and cause cancer.*

Van Meeter was there, black bag in hand, along with 2,000 other curious people from miles around, to watch Colonel Johnson commit certain suicide. Johnson, an imposing figure dressed in his usual black suit and tricornered hat, ascended the courthouse steps at high noon as the local fireman's band played a dirgelike tune. Selecting a tomato from his basket, he held it aloft and launched into his spiel:

> *The time will come when this luscious, golden apple, rich in nutritive value, a delight to the eye, a joy to the palate, whether fried, baked, broiled or eaten raw, will form the foundation of a great garden industry, and will be recognized, eaten and enjoyed as an edible food. . . . And to help speed that enlightened day, to help dispel the tall tales, the fantastic fables that you have been hearing about the thing, to show you that it is not poisonous, that it will not strike you dead, I am going to eat one right now!*

Colonel Johnson bit into the tomato, and his juicy bite could be heard through the silence. He bit again and again and again—at least one spectator screaming and fainting with each succeeding chomp. The crowd was amazed to see the courageous Colonel still on his feet as he devoured tomato after tomato. He soon converted most onlookers, but not until the entire basket was empty did Dr. Van Meeter slink away and the band strike up a victory march and the crowd begin to chant a cheer that eventually led to Johnson's election as mayor when Salem was first incorporated as a township.

We should note that Colonel Johnson's words, as well as those of Dr. Van Meeter, may be apocryphal in part, but this is the way they come down to us in history through secondary accounts. An effort to get at primary sources was thwarted when I learned that a fire in the local newspaper office had destroyed all records of the period; however, several scholarly books on the Garden State endorse the Johnson yarn in essence, and the prestigious Massachusetts Horticultural Society magazine *Horticulture* (August 1966), among others, firmly supports the Salem, New Jersey, saga. It seems almost certain then that Colonel Johnson's bite was heard around the country, if not the world. His efforts at least turned the tide for the tomato (though he was not, of course, the first American to eat the fruit), and it was appearing regularly in markets by 1835, when it was served at Delmonico's. But prejudices still lingered. As late as 1860 the popular *Godey's Lady's Book* warned its readers that tomatoes "should always be cooked for three hours before eating," and word detective Dr. Charles Funk noted in his *Horsefeathers* that at the turn of the century in rural Ohio his mother was averse to eating what was then known "only as the love apple and believed to possess aphrodisiac properties, and was therefore feared by virtuous maidens."

The myth still persists that tomatoes make the blood acid; and a

"health food" brochure printed as recently as 1970 warns: "Many vegetables are actually toxic and consuming them will pollute the body and
taint the brain. Tomatoes are a bigger threat to the health of this country
than any other vegetable because they are related to such poisonous
plants like [*sic*] nightshade, belladona [*sic*] and tobacco." Considering
that we've been so ignorant and prejudiced about an innocuous fruit for
almost 400 years, we're fortunate that we've advanced as far as we have
in other areas.

Up until the latter part of the nineteenth century tomatoes were usually
lobed in form. Few people realize that one variety changed our prefer-
ence. As L. H. Bailey recalled in *How Plants Get Their Names* (1933):

> *The lobulate tomato fruit . . . is now seldom seen in the United
> States, the larger or more uniform "smooth" fruit being preferred;
> but this flat creased tomato was frequent when I began work on
> tomatoes now well on fifty years ago; I still see it commonly in the
> tropics. It was not until Waring [a U.S. seedsman] introduced the
> Trophy [variety] in 1870 that the modern race of North American
> tomatoes began rapidly to displace all others.*

The author remembers writing an article about tomatoes for a national
magazine about ten years ago and receiving a 14-page masterpiece of
vituperation from a reader accusing him of trying to poison the world.
(See *Love Apple*.)

TOPIARY. Topiary is the clipping and training of plants like yew and
arborvitae into fantastic shapes such as peacocks, elephants, foxes, birds
and grotesque geometrical figures. The word itself comes to us from the
Latin word *topia*, akin to "artificial landscape." The Romans were expert at the art or craft, as were the English in Tudor times, and topiary
is still far more common in England than in America. Alexander Pope
denounced topiary, inventing a mock garden catalog description of:
"Adam and Eve in Yew. Adam a little shattered by the fall of the tree
of knowledge in the great storm: Eve and the Serpent very flourishing
. . . Divers eminent modern poets, in bays, somewhat blighted, to be
disposed of, a pennyworth." But topiary can be used effectively. Examples often cited are the topiary at the Alhambra in Granada and Italian
gardens at Florence and Rome.

TOUCH-ME-NOT. The very popular *impatiens* (from the Latin for "im-
patience") is called "touch-me-not" from the words Christ said to Mary
Magdalene after his resurrection (John 20:17). Both terms are appropriate

because seed often bursts impatiently from the pods when the plant is touched. The impatiens is called "busy Lizzie" because it blooms so prolifically through the season. Still another name for the plant is "snapweed."

TREE. In his *Origins,* etymologist Eric Partridge traces the adjective *true* to the Old English *treow,* which means both "loyalty" and "tree." A true person is thus "as firm and straight as a tree."

Trees figure in many other words and phrases. The "Tree of Knowledge of Good and Evil" is an unidentified tree in the Garden of Eden (Gen. 2:17, 3:6 24) bearing the forbidden fruit that Adam and Eve tasted. The "Tree of Life" is another name for this tree (Gen. 2:9, 3:22), while "the tree is known by its fruit" is an old biblical proverb (Matt. 12:33) meaning "one is judged by actions not by words."

An expression common to several languages, "a tree must be bent while it's young" means essentially "you can't teach an old dog new tricks." The Scottish version is "throw the wand while it is green."

A "Gregorian tree" is a synonym for the gallows. Obsolete in speech, though not in literature, since the early nineteenth century, the expression derives from the names of two hangmen, Gregory Brandon, royal executioner in the time of England's James I, who was succeeded by his son Richard, often called "Young Gregory."

In the United States poplars and other trees, called "trees of liberty," were planted as symbols of growing freedom during the Revolutionary War. The custom was adopted by other countries, notably France during the French Revolution.

First recorded in the early 1900s but probably older, "go climb a sour apple tree" means "go to blazes, go to hell." It is an Americanism that is still occasionally heard in its shortened form "go climb a tree." To hang someone from a sour apple tree was to show the ultimate contempt for him, hence the Union Civil War lyric "We'll hang Jeff Davis [president of the Confederacy] from a sour apple tree."

"Tree Day" is the exact translation of Arbor Day, *arbor* being the Latin word for "tree." Arbor Day was first celebrated in 1872, when Nebraskan J. Sterling Morton and his supporters persuaded their state to set aside April 10th for tree planting, to compensate for all the trees Americans had destroyed over the years in clearing the land for settlements. More than a million trees were planted on just the first Arbor Day alone and today the holiday is celebrated in every state. (See *Adam's Apple Tree.*)

TREE OF HEAVEN. Though never named in Betty Smith's novel *A*

Tree Grows in Brooklyn nor the movies made from it, the tree in the book is *Ailanthus altissima,* also called the "tree of heaven." No other tree withstands smoke and city conditions so well, and the ailanthus seeds easily everywhere, often growing out of cracks in deserted sidewalks. Only female trees should be planted, however, as the odor of the male flower is noxious to many, which is why the ailanthus, a native of China, is also called the "stink tree" or "stinkweed." The tree was brought to France by a missionary in 1751 and reached America 39 years later.

TREE OF SADNESS. This pretty name describes the small Indian tree *Nyctanthes arbortristis* of the verbena family. It has very fragrant white and orange flowers that bloom at night. Also called the "sad tree," it apparently suggested sadness to the unknown person who named it more than a century ago.

TREMBLING POPLAR. The "trembling" or "quaking poplar," also known as the "aspen" is said to have trembling leaves because it began shaking in shame and horror when Christ's cross was made from its wood. *Populus tremula* and its quaking related species have long, compressed, twisted leafstalks that cause the leaves to tremble in even the slightest wind. *Aspen* is an old English name for the tree. (See *Poplar.*)

TRUFFLE. The "diamonds of gastronomy," as black truffles are called, and the "pearls of the kitchen," white truffles, are the world's most expensive food (save for a few rare spices), selling in 1991 for more than $2,000 a pound. The underground fungi probably take their name from the Osco-Umbrian *tūfer,* which is a variation of the Latin *tuber,* "truffle." According to this explanation *tūfer* changed to the Vulgar Latin *tufera,* which became by metathesis (the transposing of letters) the Old Provençal *trufa,* which was the basis for the French *truffe* and the English *truffle.* So far, so good—black truffles, after all, are more plentiful in Italy's Umbria region than anywhere in the world. But why the *l* in truffle? Some authorities believe that it's there because the English *truffle* derives directly from the Swiss *trufla,* not from the French *truffe.* The Swiss word, they claim, comes from the French *truffe,* with the *l* added from another French word, *trufle,* which means "mockery" or "cheating," alluding to the hard-to-find fungi's habit of hiding underground. In any event, there was inevitably confusion between the French *truffe* and *trufle,* and it is easy to believe that people accidentally combined the two words, given the truffle's evasive qualities.

It's interesting to note that the eponymous hero of Molière's famous play *Tartuffe* was named for the Italian word for truffles. Tartuffe appears to have been drawn from the character of a bawdy French abbot of the period, and Molière is thought to have used *tartuffe* to symbolize the sensuous satisfaction displayed by certain religious brethren when contemplating truffles. It is said that the name came in a flash to the playwright "on seeing the sudden animation that lighted on the faces of certain monks when they heard that a seller of truffles awaited their orders." People have always been excited by truffles, so much so that they have gone to the trouble of training many animals with keen senses of smell to sniff them out under the earth—pigs, dogs, goats, ducks and even bear cubs among them.

No other food has been so eulogized. The "pearl of banquets" has been apostrophized by poets like Pope—"Thy truffles, Périgord!" Porphyrus called truffles "children of the gods"; they were "daughters of the earth conceived by the sun" to Cicero, and *"la pomme feerique"* (the fairylike apple) to George Sand. "Who says truffle," wrote Brillat-Savarin of the reputed aphrodisiac, "pronounces a grand word charged with toothsome and amorous memories for the skirted sex, and in the bearded sex with memories amorous and toothsome." Perhaps the truffle's aphrodisiac reputation can be explained by the old French proverb, "If a man is rich enough to eat truffles, his loves will be plenty." But aside from this cynical saying, little can be found in any language derogatory of the truffle. About the only such expression is the French slang word *truffle*, which means a "peasant" or "boor," in reference to the peasants of the Périgord and elsewhere who dig for truffles. Truffles are found by gatherers throughout America, though they are inferior varieties and no dogs or pigs are employed to sniff them out. There have been recent successful efforts to farm truffles in Spain.

TUBEROSE. This plant is no relation to the rose and, in fact, was first pronounced in three syllables, "tu-ber-ose." However, people so often mistakenly associated the flower with the rose that its name came to be pronounced in two syllables, "tube rose." The tuberose is the only cultivated species of the genus *Polianthus* and has many fragrant waxy-white flowers that are used in making perfume.

TULIP. Of all the foolish investment schemes the world has known, the eighteenth-century tulipomania was certainly one of the most reckless. Starting in Holland, the mania for the purchase of tulip bulbs spread throughout Europe and rose to its height from 1634 to 1637, when investors purchased bulbs for more than $10,000 each and people lost fortunes on speculations in unusual bulbs that often came to nothing. The tulip takes its name from a Latinized version of an Arabic word for "turban," in allusion to the shape of the flower. Tulips were first grown in Turkey and brought with the Turks to Europe when they invaded the Continent. They have since become one of the most popular flowers in the world, with thousands of varieties available. (See *Mulberry*.)

TURMERIC. The powdered root of the East Indian turmeric plant is the chief ingredient in a flavorful curry dish. This led the French to name it *terre merite*, roughly "worthy of the earth," which gives us its English name, *turmeric*. The plant is botanically called *Curcuma domestica*.

TURNERA APHRODISIACA. As its name implies, this Mexican and African plant, commonly known as "damiana" and scientifically named by Linnaeus in honor of William Turner, author of the *New Herball* (1551), has been widely used as an aphrodisiac. Distributed throughout tropical America, the plant is believed to be effective in treating impotence and is supposed to have a tonic effect on the genitals and nervous system. Long ago, the Aztecs used the leaves of damiana to make an aphrodisiac tea. A commercial liqueur made from damiana, called "Liquor for Lovers," can be purchased in the United States. The plant's scientific name is sometimes given as *Turnera diffusa*.

UGLI FRUIT. *Ugli* here is simply a spelling variation of *ugly* and is used to describe a large sweet variety of tangelo with rough, wrinkled yellowish skin that originated in Jamaica. A tangelo is a cross between a tangerine and grapefruit. (See *Grape; Tangerine.*)

UPAS TREE. According to fable, a foul vapor rises from the Javanese Upas tree (*Antiaris toxicaria*) and "not a tree, nor blade of grass is to be found in the valley or surrounding mountains near it, not a beast or bird, reptile or living thing lives in the vicinity." A Dutch physician noted in 1783 that "on one occasion 1600 refugees encamped within fourteen miles of one and all but 300 died within two months." Such legends inspired the use of the word *upas* for a corrupting or evil influence. Legends aside, the milky juice of the upas contains a virulent poison that is used for tipping arrows and the word *upas* itself is Javanese for "dart poison."

URGINEA. Ben Urgin, the name of an Arabian tribe in Algeria, gives its name to the genus *Urginea,* comprising about 75 species belonging to the lily family and native to the Mediterranean, the East Indies and South Africa. The bulbs of *Urginea maritima,* the only species found in the Mediterranean, are known in medicine as squills. Generally gathered for their drug properties, they are used in Sicily for making whiskey. These bulbs often weigh up to four pounds and yield a fluid once considered valuable as an expectorant, as a diuretic and for its digitalislike action on the heart. The first specimen of *Urginea* was found in the territory of the Ben Urgin tribe and named by the German botanist Steinheil.

VALERIAN. The small fragrant white and lavender flowers of valerian (*Valeriana officinalis*) were common in the Roman province of Valeria, for which the plant may have been named (most sources say it was named for the Roman emperor Valerian). At one time a drug called "Valerian" made from its root was used as a nerve sedative and antispasmodic.

VANILLA. Vanilla was thought to be wickedly aphrodisiac in Elizabethan England because the pod of the plant resembled the vagina. In fact, the word *vanilla* comes from the Spanish for "little vagina." Queen Elizabeth I used vanilla to flavor her marzipan, making it a favorite flavoring for candy ever since, and Thomas Jefferson was the first to introduce it as a flavoring in America. Today, however, natural vanilla is in short supply and we generally use a synthetic; there isn't enough natural vanilla in the world to flavor the vanilla ice cream made in America alone. Needless to say, natural vanilla is much more flavorsome than the synthetic product. (See *Avocado*.)

VEGETABLE. Vegetables have usually been highly prized; the word *vegetable* derives from the Latin *vegetabilis*, which means "animating" or "life-giving." The Greeks venerated vegetables, making small gold and silver replicas of the most prized ones. The Roman Fabii, who took their name from the *faba*, or "bean"; the Piso clan, who derived theirs from the *pisa* or "pea"; the Lentuli, who named themselves after the *lente*, or "lentil"; and the great house of Cicero, which took its name from the *cicer*, or "chickpea" are only a few of many noble Roman families whose patronymics honored widely hailed vegetables.

   Veggies, a "cute" word for vegetables, apparently became popular in the early 1960s, as it is first recorded in 1966. Obviously a shortening and rearrangement of the word *vegetables,* it is used by young and old alike.

Vegetarianism is a relatively recent word, used in 1895 by a British health magazine to describe the eating habits of a Chinese sect and modeled after the word *unitarianism.* Eating only vegetables may or may not be the thing for you, though it certainly was the thing for Pythagoras, Aristotle, Epicurus, Diogenes, Cicero, Plato, Socrates, Buddha, Montaigne, Wesley, Pope, Wagner, Swedenborg, Shelley, Tolstoy, Shaw, Gandhi, Mussolini, Hitler, and many other famous, infamous and obscure people. The word *fruitarian* was coined at about the same time (1885) to describe people who eat only fruit, but it is rarely used anymore.

VEGETABLE GOLD. (See *Saffron.*)

THE VEGETABLE LAMB. In medieval times the Far Eastern fern *Dicksonia barometz* was thought to be a hybrid animal and vegetable, mainly because of its woolly rootstalk. The down of the plant is used in India to staunch wounds. It is called the "Tartarian" or "Scythian lamb," as well as the vegetable lamb.

VENUS'S-FLYTRAP. The popular novelty plant is said to have been discovered by the governor of North Carolina, Arthur Dobbs, in 1760 and named "Fly Trap Sensitive." One of the few plants that wreak revenge on insects, the Venus's-flytrap was officially named *Dionaea muscipula* by English naturalist John Ellis in 1770. This translates as "Aphrodite's mousetrap" (*Dionaea* is a synonym for Aphrodite, the Greek goddess of beauty and sensual love). However, shortly afterward Ellis also coined the common name "Venus's-flytrap" for the plant (Venus is the Roman version of Aphrodite or Dionaea). Mousetrap or flytrap is understandable, but why was the vegetable animal eater named after Venus or Aphrodite when it is not particularly beautiful? Though neither etymological nor entymological reference books make such mention of it, John Ellis clearly referred to the similarity of the plant's leaves to the human vagina when he named it for the goddess of love.

Venus's-flytrap, a perennial native only to North and South Carolina, though widely grown indoors by gardeners, operates in a unique manner. On each of its leaves the blade consists of two hinged lobes that are fringed with six sensitive hairs, three on each side. Sap glands on the leaf surface attract insects, but when an insect lands and touches one of the hairs, the hair triggers a mechanism that snaps the leaf halves shut over it. Like flypaper, the sticky sap on the leaf surface catches the insect until the trap closes in ten seconds or so and crushes it. In eight to fourteen days the insect is eaten, except for its indigestible skeleton, which is spit out by the plant. (See *Avocado*.)

VENUS'S-LOOKING GLASS. Their strikingly beautiful purple flowers are responsible for all species of the bluebell family (Specularia), especially the bellflower or campanula, "Venus's-looking glass," being named for Venus, the Roman goddess of beauty. Other plants named after Venus include "Venus's basin bath," the wild teasel; "Venus's-comb," the shepherd's needle; "Venus's-golden apple" (*Atlantia monophylla*); "Venus's-hair," the maidenhair; "Venus's-lover"; "Venus's-pear"; "Venus's pride," Blue *Houstonia;* and "Venus's-slipper," the lady slipper. Because its calyx is shaped like a human navel, the white annual flower *Omphalodes linifolia,* native to Southern Europe, takes the unusual name "Venus's navelwort." (See *Venus's-Flytrap*.)

VIOLET. The word *violet* derives from the classical Latin name for this flower, *viola*. There are blue, white, reddish-purple, lilac, yellow and gold violets. In 1324, a golden violet was offered as a prize for the best poem written in the Provençal language:

> *And in that golden vase was set*
> *The prize—the golden violet.*

Napoleon Bonaparte, the Little Corporal, who stood barely 5'2", was nicknamed "Corporal Violet" by his followers after he was banished to Elba and boasted that he would "return with the violets." His followers used the question "Do you like violets?" to identify one another. Napoleon did indeed return to France on March 20, 1815, when the violets were at the height of their bloom.

VITEX. Vitex are ornamental shrubs often planted to attract bees. They take their name from the Latin *vieo,* "to bind with twigs," in reference to the flexible nature of their twigs. *Vitex agnus-castus* is called the "chaste tree" because the Romans considered it an antiaphrodisiac that calmed the body. Athenian maidens who wished to remain chaste often strewed their couches with its leaves.

VOLUNTEER. A volunteer plant is any plant that grows without being seeded, planted or cultivated by a person; it is one that springs up spontaneously. The expression goes back at least to the turn of the century.

WALLFLOWER. The prosaic explanation for our word describing a girl who sits to the side at a dance or party because she is shy or without a partner is simply that it originated with some poor girl who sat against the wall during a party. But the romantic story is nicer. This holds that such girls are named after the common wallflower of Europe (*Cheiranthus cheiri*), a sweet-scented, yellow spring flower that grows wild on walls and cliffs. Indeed, the English poet Robert Herrick (1591–1674) claimed that the flower itself is named after such a girl, his delightful derivation telling of a fair damsel who was long kept from her lover and finally tried to escape to him:

> *Up she got upon a wall*
> *'Tempting down to slide withal;*
> *But the silken twist untied,*
> *So she fell, and, bruised, she died.*
> *Love in pity of the deed,*
> *And her loving luckless speed*
> *Turned her to this plant we call*
> *Now the "Flower of the wall."*

WALNUT. England's native Celts were called *wealhs*, "foreigners"— by the invading Saxons of all people—and driven off into the western hills. *Wealhs* became *Welsh*, but the original name remains in *walnut*, an ancient word that derives from the Anglo-Saxon *wealhhnutu*, "the foreign or Welsh nut."

WARS OF THE ROSES. (See *York and Lancaster*.)

WATERCRESS. Both watercress and land cress are herbs of the mustard group. Cress takes its name from the German *kresse*, for the salad green; this word may derive from an older German word that meant "to creep or crawl" and described the plant's way of growing.

WATERMELON. Originating in Africa, watermelon has been cultivated for thousands of years, but seems to have been so named only since 1605. There were many old names for the melon, including names in Arabic and Sanskrit. The watermelon is an important water source in many arid regions but considered a fruit dessert in most places. Mark Twain considered it "chief of the world's luxuries. . . . When one has tasted it, he knows what angels eat."

WEED. "What is a weed? A plant whose virtues have not yet been discovered," Ralph Waldo Emerson wrote in *Fortune of the Republic* (1878). But James Russell Lowell seems to have expressed the same sentiment 30 years earlier in *A Fable for Critics* (1848): "A weed is no more than a flower in disguise." Later, Ella Wheeler Wilcox wrote in her poem "The Weed" (1872): "A weed is but an unloved flower." In any case, these sentiments are the ancestors of our current expression "a weed is just an uncultivated plant." Poet Mildred Howells spoke less admiringly of weeds in her poem "The Difficult Seed" (1910):

> *And so it criticized each flower*
> *This supercilious seed*
> *Until it woke one summer hour,*
> *And found itself a weed.*

While a weed is really only an uncultivated plant, weeds are generally regarded as unwanted pervasive plants to be rooted out from gardens. The word *weed,* recorded in one form or another since the ninth century, comes from the Old English *wiod,* a variant of an early Saxon term for "wild." Nevertheless, plants regarded as weeds change from century to century. The tomato was considered a pernicious weed in cornfields until the Mayans began cultivating it. Similarly, rye and oats were once known as weeds in wheat fields. Today, experts regard the world's worst land weeds as purple nutsedge, Bermuda grass, barnyard grass, jungle rice, goose grass, Johnson grass, Guinea grass, Cogan grass and lantana.

Some weeds aren't plants but simply clothing of any kind, deriving from the Anglo-Saxon word *waede,* "garment." "Widow's weeds" are mourning garments, the black often worn by widows. The expression contributes the only use of the word *weeds* for clothing remaining in English, but *weeds* was used by Spenser, Shakespeare and many other writers to mean everyday clothing of both men and women.

WEIGELA. The long-popular *Weigela* genus of the honeysuckle family, containing some 12 species, is named for German physician C. E. Weigel (1748–1831). Weigela, sometimes spelled *weigelia,* is often grouped with the *Diervilla* genus, the bush honeysuckle, but its bushes have larger, much showier flowers than the latter. *Diervilla* is named for a Dr. Diervilla, a French surgeon in Canada. Native to Asia, the weigela bush is easily cultivated in America and Europe. Its funnel-shaped flowers are usually rose-pink but vary in color from white to dark crimson.

WHORTLEBERRY. The word *whortleberry* originated as the dialect form of *hurtleberry* in southwestern England. *Hurtleberry,* however, remains a mystery etymologically speaking, though there have been attempts to link the *hurt* in the word to the fact that the blue berry could resemble a small black-and-blue mark or "hurt" on a person's body. Both words refer to the berry *Vaccinium myrtillus* of the blueberry family, and our word *huckleberry* probably derives from *hurtleberry,* which makes Mark Twain's famous character, perhaps aptly, "Hurt" Finn.

WILD OATS. The wild oat (*Avena fatua*) is a common tall plant that looks like its relative the cereal plant oat, but is really a pernicious weed that infests the planting fields and gardens of Europe and is difficult to eradicate. About all wild oats or "oat grass" have ever been used for is making hygrometers, instruments that measure the humidity in the air—the plant's long, twisted awn or beard readily absorbs moisture. The wild oat's uselessness has been known since ancient times, and for almost as long as we have had the expression "to sow wild oats," meaning to conduct oneself foolishly, "to sow weed-seed instead of good grain." The expression has been traced back to the Roman comic Plautus in 194 B.C. and was probably common before his time. It is usually used to refer to a young man who fritters his time away in fruitless dissipation, or to describe the prolific sexual activities of a young man, and is almost always said indulgently. The expression is sometimes used in the singular to describe a prudish young man who "sows his one wild oat." In the sixteenth and seventeenth centuries dissolute or wild young men were called "wild oats."

Someone "feeling his oats" or "full of oats" is in high spirits, full of energy, so full of himself that he may even be showing off a bit. The allusion is to lively horses fed on oats, and the expression is American, first recorded in 1843 by Canadian Thomas Haliburton, the humorist whose character Sam Slick gave us "cry over spilt milk" and many other expressions. Men, women and children can "feel their oats," but only young men are said to "sow their wild oats."

WILD RICE. The seed of an aquatic grass rather than a true rice, wild rice was grown and eaten by American Indians. The words were first recorded in 1778. Wild rice was earlier called "water oats" and "water rice" and has also been known as "Indian rice" and *Meneninee*, after a Chippewa subtribe that grew it. (See *Carolina Rice; Piedmont Rice.*)

WILLOW. The willow is a lovely tree with a lovely name full of *l*'s and *w*'s. As Ivor Brown wrote in *A Word in Your Ear* (1945): "The willow has ever been as much the poet's joy as a symbol of mourning and melancholy. It both weeps and bewitches. 'Sing, willow, willow, willow.' Always it sings . . . so lovely is the tree, in all its forms, not least *Salix babylonica,* the weeping willow." To wax prosaic, a few species of the *Salix* genus yield the drug salicin, used in making aspirin.

"Wearing the willow" means to be in mourning, especially for a wife or sweetheart, the weeping willow from earliest times having been a symbol of sorrow. In the Book of Psalms the Jews in captivity are said to hang their harps on willow branches as a sign of mourning. Shakespeare's famous song in *Othello* has the refrain "Sing Willow, willow, willow":

> *The fresh streams ran by her, and murmur'd her moans;*
> *Sing willow, willow, willow*
> *Her salt tears fell from her and softened the stones;*
> *Sing willow, willow, willow.*

"To wear the green willow" means to be sad or disappointed in love.

WINGS. (See *Schizocarp.*)

WISTERIA. An error made by Thomas Nuttall, curator of Harvard's Botanical Garden, led to the accepted misspelling of this beautiful flowering plant: *Wisteria* is the common spelling today even though *wistaria* is correct. "Wisteria . . ." Nuttall wrote in his *The Genera of North American Plants II* (1818), "In memory of Caspar Wistar, M.D., late professor of Anatomy in the University of Pennsylvania." Nuttall, who named the plant after Wistar, had meant to write *Wistaria,* but his slip of pen was perpetuated by later writers and *wisteria* has become accepted. All attempts to remedy the situation have failed, even Joshua Logan's play *The Wistaria Trees,* in which the author purposely spelled the word with two *a*'s. Philadelphia Quaker Caspar Wistar taught "anatomy, midwifery, and surgery" at what was then the College of Pennsylvania. The son of a noted colonial glassmaker, Dr. Wistar wrote

America's first anatomy textbook and succeeded Thomas Jefferson as head of the American Philosophical Society. His home became the Sunday afternoon meeting place of many notable Philadelphians. The good doctor was only 57 when he died in 1818, the same year in which Nuttall honored him but spelled his name wrong.

The *Wisteria* genus includes seven species native to Japan, China and eastern North America. A climbing woody vine of the pea family, the plant blooms profusely in the late spring, its flowers hanging in clusters up to three feet long and either lilac-purple, violet, violet-blue, white or pink in color. Old gnarled wisteria often reach to the tops of the houses and are a sight to behold when flowering. If you are ever in the vicinity of Sierra Madre, California, in the late springtime, go out of your way to see the giant Chinese wisteria near the Los Angeles State and County Arboretum. During its five-week blooming period this giant Chinese species becomes a vast field filled with more than 1½ million blossoms. Planted in 1892 and the largest flowering plant in the world, it covers almost an acre and weighs more than 252 tons.

WITCH HAZEL. Witch hazel solution is extracted from the leaves and bark of the witch hazel shrub. This plant, in turn, might take its first name from the fact that its branches were often used for divining or dousing rods used to locate water by witches and others claiming supernatural powers. The *Oxford English Dictionary,* however, believes that the *witch* comes from the Anglo-Saxon *wych,* meaning "a tree with pliant branches." Witch hazel (*Hamamelis*) are not true hazel trees. They are also called "winter bloom" because they bloom from October to April when their twigs are bare. The "cuckold hazel," also called the "beaked hazel," is a true hazel of the genus *Corylus,* and takes its name not because wives betrayed their husbands under it but because of its long, hornlike fruits, which someone centuries ago compared to a cuckold's horns.

WOLF PEACH. "Wolf peach" was a common name for the tomato in the early nineteenth century, when the fruit was thought to be poisonous. In fact, the tomato's genus name, *Lycopersicon,* is Greek for "wolf peach." (See *Tomato.*)

WOLF'S BANE. This species of poisonous aconite, *Aconitum lycoctonum,* may have been called wolf's bane because meat soaked in its juices is poisonous to wolves. But it could have arisen through an involved etymological error, as explained by a nineteenth-century writer:

*Bane is a common term for poisonous plants, and some early bota-
nist translated it into the Greek* kuamos, *meaning bean. The plant
has a pale yellow flower and was thus called the* white-bane *to
distinguish it from the blue aconite. The Greek for white is* leukos,
hence leukos-kuamos; *but* lukos *is the Greek for wolf, and by mistake got changed to* lukos-kuamos *(wolf-bean). Botanists, seeing the
absurdity of calling an aconite a bean, restored the original word*
bane *but retained the corrupt word* lukos *(a wolf) and hence we
get the name* wolf's *bane for white aconite.*

(See *Aconite.*)

WOODBINE. Woodbine is a honeysuckle (*Lonicera pericylmenum*) that
was often planted on graves in years past. An 1870 song written as a
tribute to those who died in the Civil War went: "Then go where the
woodbine twineth / When spring is bright and fair, / And to the soldier's
resting place / Some little tribute bear." From this song by Septimus
Winner the expression "gone where the woodbine twineth" came to
describe someone who had died, or even someone who had gone someplace from where he or she would never return.

WORM. The worm so essential in aerating garden soil had a grand
name to begin with. *Worm* derives from the latin *vermis,* which first
meant "dragon" or "serpent." In time, however, it came to include the
"lowly" garden worm as well. Today worms are raised on "worm
farms" and sold to gardeners to help them aerate the soil and their
compost piles.

WORMWOOD. Since there is nothing wormy about it, why is this herb
so named? The best theory is that the *worm* in the word is from the
Teutonic *wer,* "man," and the *wood* from *mod,* the Teutonic for "courage." By this account the word was originally *wermod,* meaning "man's
courage," in reference to the herb's supposed aphrodisiac and healing
properties. Or it may be that since the plant was used as a remedy for
worms in the body and *wermod* sounded like *worm,* people began to call
it wormwood. Another contributing factor might be the legend that the
plant sprang up in the slithery path of the serpent that left the Garden
of Eden. *Artemisia absinthium,* the classical wormwood, is an ingredient
of absinthe, the so-called aphrodisiac that has probably killed more people than it has sexually inspired. Tarragon is also one of the wormwoods.

XERISCAPING. This new word coined from the Greek *xeros,* "dry," and "land*scaping,*" describes water-sensible gardening, such as using plants that need little water, practicing mulching and adding organic matter to the soil, among other practices. The Xeriscaping movement began a few years ago in Denver, Colorado, but it has been practiced for ages by good gardeners who never knew its name. Xeriscape or drought-resistant plants would fill a book and include the Russian olive tree, Bar Harbor juniper, honey locust trees, goldenrod, lavender, mulberries, Queen Anne's lace, Russian sage, mullein, sedum, thyme, yarrow and yucca.

XIPE. (See *Garden Gods.*)

XYST. A xyst (pronounced *zist*) is a garden walk planted with trees, or a covered portico in a garden used as a promenade. Both were common in Roman villas and take their name from the Latin *xystus,* "garden terrace."

YAM. The word *yam* can be traced back to the Senegal *nyami*, "to eat," and was introduced to America in the South, via the Gullah dialect *njam*, meaning "to eat," in 1676. However, the word had come into European use from the same source long before this date. (See *Dioscorea*.)

YARROW. A plant with whitish flowers, yarrow has often been used as a medicine and love tonic. According to one old superstition, the drinking of such potions insured "seven years love for wedded couples." Strictly speaking, *Achillea millefolium* is an herb, named for the legendary Achilles, who is supposed to have used one species to heal his wounds. It is sometimes called "Old Man's Pepper," to which family it does not belong, although it may make old men peppery. American folklore gives us the following advice concerning the plant: "Pick a sprig of yarrow, put the stem up your nose and say: *Yarrow, yarrow, if he loves me and I love he, / A drop of blood I'd wish to see.* If blood appears, it shows that you are loved." Yarrow is called the "carpenter's herb" in France, because it was once widely used there to heal cuts made by carpenter's tools.

YELLOW ROSE OF TEXAS. The yellow rose of Texas, which is part of that state's folklore and even has a famous song written about it, actually originated in the 1830s on a farm in New York City near the present-day Pennsylvania Station. There a lawyer named George Harrison found it as a seedling growing among other roses on his property and began cultivating it. Settlers soon took the yellow rose west with them, and legend has it that Texans finally claimed it as their own when Mexican General Santa Anna, the villain of the Alamo, "was distracted by a beautiful woman with yellow roses in her hair." We have this nice story on the authority of Stephen Scanniello, rosarian of the Crawford

Rose Garden in the New York Botanical Gardens, who told it to garden columnist Anne Raver of the *New York Times* (6/19/92). (See *Blushing Thigh of the Aroused Nymph.*)

YGGDRASIL. In Scandanavian mythology the yggdrasil is the world tree, an evergreen ash tree whose roots and branches bind together heaven, hell and earth. Sitting in this fabulous tree from which honey flows are an eagle, a squirrel and four stags; at its base is a fountain of wonders. Its name is pronounced "ig-dra-sill."

YORK AND LANCASTER. In 1551 the red and white variety of the damask rose (*Rosa damascena versicolor*) was popularly named "York and Lancaster" to memorialize the English Wars of the Roses between the houses of York and Lancaster. This 30-year struggle for the throne of England began in 1455; the house of York adopted a white rose for its emblem and the house of Lancaster chose a red rose. The war ended only when the two houses were united through marriage.

YOUNGBERRY. The youngberry is generally considered to be a hybrid variety of dewberry, which, in turn, is simply an early ripening, prostrate form of blackberry. The large, dark-purple, sweet fruit has the high aroma and flavor of the loganberry and native blackberry. The youngberry was developed by Louisiana horticulturist B. M. Young about 1900 by crossing a Southern dewberry and trailing blackberry, or several varieties of blackberries. Its long, trailing canes are generally trained on wires. Popular in the home garden, the berry is extensively planted in the American Southwest, South, Pacific Northwest and California.

YUCCA. (See *Adam's Needle.*)

ZALUZIANSKYA. Polish physician Adam Zaluziansky von Zaluzian probably didn't expect that his long tongue-twister name would be given to anything, yet it became the scientific designation for not one but two plant genera. *Zaluzianskya* (often spelled with an *ie* ending) is the beautifully fragrant, night-blooming phlox, the genus embracing about 40 South African species. While all such nocturnal flowers may bloom in daytime, on overcast days or toward evening, their finest flowering and greatest fragrance come long after sunset. The Prague doctor, who published an important herbal, *Methodus Herbariae* (1602), has his last name honored by the genus *Zaluzania,* comprising about seven species of small shrubs with white or yellow flowers that are mainly grown in greenhouses outside their native Mexico. Strangely enough, despite their cumbersome scientific designations, neither genus seems to be known by any popular common name.

ZINNIA. The Zinnia species *elegans* is called "youth and old age," and anyone who has seen how profusely the annual flower blooms and how quickly it succumbs to the first frost will appreciate the folk name. The same applies to all species of the *Zinnia* genus, which Linnaeus named for Johann Gottfried Zinn, whose life was as bright and brief as his namesake's. Zinn, a German botanist and physician who was a professor of medicine at Gottingen, died in 1759 when barely 32 years old. In 1753 he had published what is said to be the first book of the anatomy of the eye. One old story says that he discovered the flower named after him while on a plant-collecting expedition in Mexico; bandits who captured him with all his botanical specimens let him go because they considered any man who had only flowers as his possessions to be a fool, and it was bad luck to harm fools.

There are about 15 species of Zinnia, which is the state flower of Indiana. Most modern tall forms, with flowers in many colors, come from the Mexican *Zinnia elegans* introduced in 1866, which grows to heights of about three feet. One explanation for the "youth and old age" nickname of *elegans* may be the stiff hairs on the stem of the coarse plant itself, in contrast to the soft flowers; another may be the plant's tendency to develop powdery mildew disease when poorly cultivated. The first frost analogy is nicest.

ZOYSIA GRASS. Zoysia grass is commonly planted today, especially for play areas and for lawns in the Deep South. The popular grass, generally planted by bits of rootstock called "zoysia plugs," is named for Australian botanist Karl von Zois. There are only four species of the creeping grass. Zoysia takes a lot of wear and tear, forming a dense, tough turf, but has one major drawback: It turns a haylike color in the late fall and is among the slowest of grasses to green up again in the spring. Some zealous zoysia lawn keepers give nature a tender, loving hand by painting their grass with green latex and other preparations in the off-seasons—yet another reason why anyone reincarnated in this part of the world wouldn't do badly if he or she came back as a lawn. (See *Lawn.*)

ZYZZYVA. Often destructive to plants, the zyzzyva (pronounced "ziz-ih-vuh") weevil is a leaf-hopping insect of tropical America that provides one of the best examples of onomatopoeia at work in the creation of words. Although most dictionaries give its origin as "obscure," if they give it at all, the word probably derives from the Spanish *ziz zas!*, which is "echoic of the impact of a blow," the reference being, of course, to the noise made by these cicadalike insects.

APPENDIX

Floral Vocabulary

I've seen many lists relating the language or meaning of flowers, but none so painstakingly complete and historically accurate as this very old one from a rare little (2 × 4) book called *Drops from Flora's Cup* written by Miss Mary M. Griffin in 1845. I can find no biography of Miss Griffin, a Boston lady, but here is her list, in her own words, to help perpetuate her name.

Acacia, Yellow	Concealed love
Acacia, Rose	Elegance
Acalea	Temperance
Acanthus	The Arts
Aconite-leaved crowfoot	Lustre
Agnus Castus	Coldness without love
Agrimony	Thankfulness
Althea Frutex	Consumed by love
Almond	Hope
Aloe	Bitterness
Alyssum, Sweet	Worth beyond beauty
Amaranth	Immortality
Amaranth, globe	Unchangeable
Amaryllis	Beautiful, but timid
Ambrosia	Returned affection
Anemone	Frailty
Angelica	Inspiration
Angrec	Royalty
Apocynum	Falsehood
Apple-Blossom	Fame speaks him good & great
Arum	Ferocity and deceit
Ash	Grandeur
Aspen tree	Sensibility

Asphodel	My regrets follow you
Aster	Beauty in retirement
Auricula, Scarlet	Pride
Bachelor's button	Hope in Misery
Balm	Social intercourse
Balsam	Impatience
Barberry	Sourness
Basil	Hatred
Bay leaf	I change but in dying
Bay Wreath	The reward of merit
Beech	Prosperity
Betony	Surprise
Bindweed	Humility
Birch	Gracefulness
Black Poplar	Courage
Black Thorn	Difficulty
Blue Bell	Constancy
Borage	Bluntness
Box	Stoicism
Broom	Neatness
Buck Bean	Calm Repose
Burdock	Importunity
Buttercup	Ingratitude
Calla	Feminine Modesty
Calycanthus	Benevolence
Candy Tuft	Indifference
Canterbury blue bell	Gratitude
Cardinal's Flower	Distinction
Carnation	Disdain
Catchfly	Artifice
Cedar Tree	Strength
Chamomile	Energy in adversity
Cherry Blossom	Spiritual beauty
Chestnut	Render me justice
China Aster	Variety
China Pink	Aversion
Chrysanthemum	Cheerfulness
Clematis	Mental beauty
Coltsfoot	Maternal care
Columbine	Folly
Coreopsis	Ever cheerful
Coriander	Concealed worth

Cowslip	Native grace
Crocus	Youthful gladness
Crown Imperial	Majesty
Cypress	Mourning
Daffodil	Delusive hope
Dahlia	Dignity and elegance
Daisy	Innocence
Dandelion	Oracle
Dew Plant	Serenade
Dogwood	Durability
Dragon Plant	Snare
Eglantine	Poetry
Elder	Compassion
Elm	Dignity
Enchanter's Nightshade	Fascination
Evergreen	Poverty
Everlasting	Unceasing remembrance
Fennel	Strength
Fern	Symmetry
Fir	Time
Flax	Acknowledged kindness
Flowering reed	Confidence in Heaven
Flower-me-not	True love
Foxglove	I am ambitious for your sake
Fuchsia	Confiding love
Geranium, Ivy	Bridal flower
Geranium, Lemon	A tranquil mind
Geranium, Nutmeg	I shall meet you
Geranium, Oak	True friendship
Geranium, Rose	Preference
Geranium, Scarlet	Consolation
Geranium, Silver-leaved	Recall
Gilly Flower	Lasting beauty
Glory Flower	Glorious beauty
Golden Rod	Encouragement
Grape, Wild	Charity
Grass	Utility
Harebell	Grief
Hawthorn	Hope
Hazel	Reconciliation
Heath	Solitude
Heart's-Ease or Pansy	Think of me

Heliotrope	Devotion
Hellebore	Calamity
Holly	Domestic happiness
Hollyhock	Fruitfulness
Honesty or Satin Flower	Honesty
Honeysuckle	Bonds of love
Hops	Injustice
Horn Bean	Ornament
Horse Chestnut	Luxuriancy
House Leek	Vivacity
Houstonia	Content
Hyacinth	Game. Play
Hydrangea	Heartlessness
Ice Plant	Your looks freeze me
Iceland Moss	Health
Iris	A message for you
Ivy	Friendship
Jasmine, White	Amiability
Jasmine, Yellow	Elegant gracefulness
Jonquil	Desire
Judas Tree	Unbelief
Juniper	Protection
Kennedia	Mental excellence
King-Cup	I wish I was rich
Laburnum	Pensive beauty
Lady's Slipper	Capricious Beauty
Larch	Boldness
Larkspur	Fickleness
Laurel	Glory
Laurustinus	I die if neglected
Lavender	Acknowledgment
Lemon-Blossom	Discretion
Lettuce	Cold hearted
Lilac	First emotions of love
Lily of the Valley	Return of Happiness
Lily, White	Purity and Modesty
Linden Tree	Matrimony
Lobelia	Malevolence
Locust	Affection beyond the grave
London Pride	Frivolty
Lotus	Estranged love
Love-in-a-mist	Perplexity

Love-in-a-puzzle	Embarrassment
Love-lies-a-bleeding	Hopeless, not heartless
Lucern	Life
Lupine	Sorrow, dejection
Madwort, Rock	Tranquility
Magnolia	Love of nature
Maize	Plenty
Mallow	Sweet disposition
Mandrake	Rarity
Maple	Reserve
Marigold	Inquietude
Marvel of Peru	Timidity
Meadow Saffron	My best days are past
Meadow Sweet	Uselessness
Mercury	Goodness
Mezereon	Desire to please
Mignonette	Excellence and loveliness
Mimosa	Sensitiveness
Mint	Virtue
Mistletoe	I surmount all obstacles
Moonwort	Forgetfulness
Moss, Tuft of	Maternal love
Motherwort	Secret love
Mouse Ear	Forget-me-not
Mulberry Tree	Wisdom
Mushroom	Suspicion
Myrtle	Love in absence
Narcissus	Egotism
Nasturtium	Patriotism
Nettle	Slander
Night-blooming Cereus	Transient beauty
Nightshade	Dark thoughts
Nosegay	Gallantry
Oak	Hospitality
Oleander	Music
Olive Branch	Peace
Orange Flower	Chastity
Orange Tree	Generosity
Orchis	A Belle
Osier	Frankness
Ox-Eye	Obstacle
Palm	Victory

Pansy, or Heart's Ease	Think of me
Parsley	Entertainment
Passion Flower	Religious Superstition
Pea, Everlasting	Wilt thou go with me
Pea, Sweet	Departure
Peach Blossom	I am your captive
Pennyroyal	Flee away
Peony	Ostentation
Periwinkle	Sweet remembrances
Peruvian Heliotrope	Infatuation
Phlox	We are united
Pimpernel	Assignation
Pine	Pity
Pineapple	You are perfect
Pink	Purity of affection
Plane Tree	Genius
Plum Tree	Keep your promises
Polyanthus	Confidence
Pomegranate	Foolishness
Poppy	Consolation of sleep
Prickly Pear	Satire
Primrose	Early youth
Primrose, Evening	I am more constant than thou
Privet	Prohibition
Pyrus Japonie	Fairies' Fire
Petunia	Thou art less proud than they deem thee
Quamoclet	Busybody
Queen's Rocket	Queen of Coquettes
Ragged Robin	Dandy
Ranunculus	You are radiant with charms
Red bay	Love's memory
Red Mulberry	Wisdom
Rose	Beauty
Rose, Austrian	Very lovely
Rose, Bridal	Happy love
Rose, Bergundy	Simplicity and beauty
Rose, Damask	Bashful love
Rose, Monthly	Beauty ever new
Rose, Moss	Pleasure without alloy
Rose, Multiflora	Grace
Rose, Musk	Capricious beauty

Rose, White	Silent sadness
Rose, Yellow	Infidelity
Rose Bud	A young girl
Rosemary	Remembrance
Rush	Docility
Rue	Purification
Saffron	Excess is dangerous
Sage	Domestic virtues
Saint John's Wort	Animosity
Scabious	Unfortunate attachment
Scarlet Ipomoea	Attachment
Sensitive Plant	Sensitiveness
Serpentine Cactus	Horror
Snap Dragon	Presumption
Snow-Ball	Thoughts of Heaven
Snowdrop	Consolation
Southern Wood	Jesting
Spider Wort	Transient happiness
Star of Bethlehem	The light of our path
Strawberry	Perfect excellence
Striped Pink	Refusal
Sumac	Splendor
Sun-Flower	False riches
Sweet Brier	Poetry
Sweet Flag	Fitness
Sweet Sultan	Felicity
Sweet-scented Tussilage	Justice shall be done you
Sweet William	A smile
Syringa	Memory
Tamarisk	Crime
Tansy	Resistance
Teasel	Misanthropy
Thistle	I will never forget thee
Thorn Apple	Deceitful charms
Thyme	Activity
Tremella	Resistance
Trumpet Flower	Separation
Tulip	Declaration of love
Valerian	Accommodating disposition
Venus's Looking-glass	Flattery
Venus's Fly-trap	Deceit
Verbena	Sensibility

Vine	Intoxication
Violet, Blue	Modesty
Violet, White	Candor
Violet, Yellow	Rural happiness
Virgin's Bower	Filial love
Wall Flower	Fidelity in misfortune
Water Lily	Ardor
Wax Plant	Susceptibility
Wheat	Riches
Willow, Weeping	Purity of heart
Winter cherry	Deception
Witch Hazel	A spell
Wood Sorrel	Joy
Woodbine	Fraternal love
Wormwood	Absence
Yarrow	Thou alone can'st cure
Yew	Sorrow
Zinnia	Absence

BIBLIOGRAPHY

There is no room here for all the many books, essays and articles I have consulted for this work. Over the years my notebooks have been filled with stories, poems and quotations from works as diverse as Pliny's *Natural History,* Virgil's *Georgics,* Herodotus's *Histories,* the King James and other versions of the Bible, *Culpeper's Herbal* (1653), Linnaeus's *Species Plantarum* (1753) and *Systeme Naturae* (1758), all of Shakespeare's works and a vast number of novels, poems, memoirs and collected letters, including those of Thomas Jefferson, who once wrote a friend that he would rather be "a common dirt gardener" than President. I am not being invidious by not including any deserving book in this bountiful listing, just forgetful, and I apologize to anyone I may have offended. Many of these more than one hundred books should be in every gardener's library, and the same can be said of many others not mentioned here but referred to in the text.

Adams, James T. *Dictionary of American History.* 7 vols. New York: Charles Scribner's Sons, 1940.

American Heritage Dictionary of the English Language. New York: American Heritage Publishing Co., 1969 and 1992 editions.

Aresty, Ester. *The Delectable Past.* New York: Simon & Schuster, 1964.

Asimov, Isaac. *Biographical Encyclopedia of Science and Technology.* New York: Doubleday & Company, 1964.

———. *Words From The Myths.* Boston: Houghton Mifflin, 1961.

Bailey, Liberty Hyde. *Cyclopedia of American Horticulture.* New York: 1900–02.

———. *Hortus Third.* New York: Macmillan Publishing Company, 1976.

———. *How Plants Get Their Names.* New York: Dover Publications, 1963.

Bartlett, John R. *Dictionary of Americanisms.* Boston: Little, Brown & Company, 1877.

Bartlett, John, ed. *Familiar Quotations.* 13th edition. Boston: Little, Brown & Company, 1955.

Bates, Marston. *Gluttons and Libertines.* New York: Random House, 1967.

Berrey, Lester V. and Melvin Van Den Bark. *The American Thesaurus of Slang.* New York: Thomas Y. Crowell Company, 1962.

Bloomfield, Leonard. *Language.* New York: Henry Holt & Co., 1933.

Blumberg, Dorothy Rose. *Whose What?* New York: Holt, Rinehart and Winston, 1969.

Bodmer, Frederick. *The Loom of Language.* New York: W. W. Norton & Company, 1944.

Bombaugh, C. C. *Oddities and Curiousities of Words and Language.* Edited by Martin Gardner. New York: Dover Publications, 1961.

Brewer, E. Cobham. *A Dictionary of Phrase and Fable.* New York: Harper & Row, 1964.

————. *A Dictionary of Miracles.* Philadelphia: J. B. Lippincott Co., 1934.

————. *The Historic Note Book.* Philadelphia: J. B. Lippincott Co., 1891.

Bridgewater, William and Elizabeth J. Sherwood. *The Columbia Encyclopedia.* New York: Columbia University Press, 1950.

Brown, Ivor. *A Word In Your Ear.* New York: E. P. Dutton & Co., 1963.

————. *I Give You My Word.* New York: E. P. Dutton & Co., 1964.

————. *Just Another Word.* New York: E. P. Dutton & Co., 1964.

————. *Say The Word.* New York: E. P. Dutton & Co., 1964.

————. *Words In Our Time.* London: Jonathan Cape, 1958.

Bulfinch, Thomas. *Bulfinch's Mythology.* New York: Random House Modern Library, 1948.

Cambridge Modern History. 13 vols. Cambridge: Cambridge University Press, 1902-12.

Chambers, Robert. *The Book of Days.* Philadelphia: J. B. Lippincott Co., 1899.

Ciardi, John. *A Browser's Dictionary.* New York: Harper & Row, 1980.

————. *Good Words To You.* New York: Harper & Row, 1987.

Clairborne, Robert. *Loose Cannons and Red Herrings.* New York: W. W. Norton & Co., 1988.

Coombes, Allen. *Dictionary of Plant Names.* Portland: Timber Press Co., 1985.

Dictionary of American Biography. 20 vols. New York: Charles Scribner's Sons, 1928–37. Supplement One, 1944; Supplement Two, 1958.

Dictionary of American Regional English, Federick C. Cassidy, Chief Editor, volumes, 1, 2. Cambridge, Mass.: Belknap Press, 1985 & 1991.

Edwards, Gillian. *Uncumber and Pantaloon.* New York: E. P. Dutton & Co., 1969.

Encyclopedia Britannica, 1957 edition.

Ernst, Margaret S. *More About Words.* New York: Alfred A. Knopf, 1964.

Evans, Bergen. *Comfortable Words.* New York: Random House, 1962.

Farmer, John S. and W. E. Henley. *Slang and Its Analogues.* 7 vols., New Hyde Park, N.Y.: University Press, 1966.

Flexner, Stuart Berg. *I Hear America Talking.* New York: Van Nostrand, 1976.

———. *Listening to America.* New York: Simon and Schuster, 1982.

Frazer, Sir James. *The Golden Bough.* 3rd. edition. London: The Macmillan Company, 1951.

Funk, Charles Earle. *A Hog On Ice.* New York: Harper & Row, 1985.

———. *Heavens to Betsy! And Other Curious Sayings.* New York: Harper & Brothers, 1955.

———. *Thereby Hangs a Tale.* New York: Harper & Row, 1950.

——— and Charles Earle Funk, Jr. *Horsefeathers and Other Curious Words.* New York: Harper & Brothers, 1958.

Funk, Wilfred. *Word Origins and Their Romantic Stories.* New York: Funk & Wagnalls, 1950.

Garrison, Webb. *What's In A Word?* New York: Abingdon Press, 1965.

———. *Why You Say It.* New York: Abingdon Press, 1955.

Gerad, John. *The Herball or Generall Historie of Plants* (1597). New York: Dover Publications, 1963.

Gledhill, D. *The Names of Plants.* New York: Cambridge University Press, 1989.

Goldberg, Isaac. *The Wonder of Words.* New York: Frederick Ungar Publishing Co., 1957.

Guinness Book of Records, Donald McFarlan, ed. New York: Bantam Books, 1992.

Hargrove, Basil. *Origins and Meanings of Popular Phrases and Names.* Philadelphia: J. B. Lippincott Co., 1925.

Harvey, Sir Paul. *The Oxford Companion to Classical Literature.* Oxford: Clarendon Press, 1955.

Healey, B. J. *A Gardener's Guide To Plant Names.* New York: Charles Scribner's Sons, 1972.

Holt, Alfred H. *Phrase and Word Origins.* New York: Dover Publications, 1961.

Hunt, Cecil. *Word Origins, The Romance of Language.* New York: Philosophical Library, 1949.

Lehner, Ernst and Johanna Ernst. *Folkways and Odysseys of Food and Medicinal Plants.* New York: Tudor Publishing Co., 1962.

Lyons, Albert. *Plant Names.* Detroit: Nelson, Bater & Company, 1907.

Mathews, Mitford M., ed. *Dictionary of Americanisms.* Chicago: University of Chicago Press, 1951.

Mencken, H. L. *The American Language.* 3 vols. New York: Alfred A. Knopf, 1936–48.

Morris, William and Mary Morris. *Dictionary of Word and Phrase Origins.* 3 vols. New York: Harper & Row, 1962.

Nicholson, George, ed. *The Illustrated Dictionary of Gardening.* 4 vols. Mass., U.S.A., N.p., n.d. (ca. 1890).

Onions, C. T. *The Oxford Dictionary of English Etymology.* London: Oxford University Press, 1966.

Oxford Dictionary of Quotations. London: Oxford University Press, 1954.

Oxford English Dictionary and Supplements. Oxford: Claredon Press, 1990.

Oxford Latin Dictionary. Oxford: Clarendon Press, 1982.

Partridge, Eric. *A Dictionary of Slang and Unconventional English.* New York: The Macmillan Company, 1961.

———. *Origins.* London: Routledge and Kegan Paul, 1958.

———. *A Dictionary of Catch Phrases.* Stein and Day, 1977.

Pei, Mario. *All About Language.* Philadelphia: J. B. Lippincott Co., 1954.

Pyles, Thomas. *Words and Ways of American English.* New York: Random House, 1952.

Radford, Edwin and M. A. M. Radford, eds. *Encyclopedia of Superstitions.* New York: Philosophical Library, 1945.

———. *Unusual Words and How They Came About.* New York: Philosophical Library, 1946.

Random House Dictionary of the English Language. New York: Random House, 1987.

The Royal Horticultural Society Dictionary of Gardening. London: The Royal Horticultural Society, 1969.

Shipley, Joseph T. *Dictionary of Word Origins.* New York: Littlefield, Adams & Company, 1967.

Skeat, Walter W. *An Etymological Dictionary of the English Language.* Rev. ed. London: Oxford University Press, 1963.

Smith, A. W. *A Gardener's Book of Plant Names.* New York: Harper & Row, 1963.

Sperling, Susan Kelz. *Tenderfeet and Ladyfingers*. New York: Viking Press, 1981.

Stearn, William. *Botanical Latin*. London: David and Charles, 1973.

Stevenson, Burton, ed. *Home Book of Quotations*. Rev. Ed. New York: Dodd, Mead & Co., 1947.

―――. *The Home Book of Proverbs, Maxims, and Familiar Phrases*. New York: The Macmillan Company, 1948.

Steward, George R. *American Place Names*. New York: Oxford University Press, 1971.

Taylor, Isaac. *Words and Places*. London: Dent, 1911.

Taylor, Norman, ed. *Taylor's Encyclopedia of Gardening*. Boston: Houghton Mifflin Company, 1961.

Urdang, Laurence. *A Fine Kettle of Fish*. Detroit: Visible Ink Press, 1991.

Wason, Betty. *Cooks, Gluttons and Gourmets*. New York: Doubleday & Company, 1962.

Webster's New Twentieth Century Dictionary. Unabridged. 2nd ed. New York: World Publishing Company, 1966.

Webster's Word Histories. New York: Merriam-Webster, 1989.

Weekley, Ernest. *Concise Etymological Dictionary of Modern English*. New York: E. P. Dutton & Co., 1924.

―――. *The Romance of Words*. New York: Dover Publications, 1961.

Wentworth, Harold and Stuart Berg Flexner. *Dictionary of American Slang*. New York: Thomas Y. Crowell Company, 1960.

Woodwarad, Marcus. *Leaves From Gerad's Herball*. New York: Dover Publications, 1963.

Zimmer, G. F. *Dictionary of Botanical Terms*. London, 1965.

Index

223